THE COMPLETE
CANADIAN HOME BUSINESS GUIDE TO TAXES

EVELYN JACKS

For those who begin again.

McGraw-Hill Ryerson Limited
Toronto, Montréal, New York, Auckland, Bogotá
Caracas, Lisbon, London, Madrid, Mexico, Milan
New Delhi, San Juan, Singapore, Sydney, Tokyo

McGraw-Hill
Ryerson Limited

A Subsidiary of The McGraw·Hill Companies

The Complete Canadian Home Business Guide to Taxes

Copyright © 1997 by Evelyn Jacks. All rights reserved. No part of this publication may be reproduced or transmitted in any form or by any means, or stored in a database or retrieval system, without the prior written permission of McGraw-Hill Ryerson Limited, a subsidiary of The McGraw-Hill Companies.

McGraw-Hill Ryerson Limited
300 Water Street
Whitby, Ontario L1N 9B6

3 4 5 6 7 8 9 0 W 6 5 4 3 2 1 0 9 8

Care has been taken to trace ownership of copyright material contained in this text. However, the publishers welcome any information that will enable them to rectify any reference or credit in subsequent editions.

Canadian Cataloguing in Publication Data
Jacks, Evelyn
    The Complete Canadian home business guide to taxes

Includes index.
ISBN 0-07-552815-0

1. Home-based businesses — Taxation — Canada — Popular works.   2. Tax planning — Canada — Popular works.
I. Title.

HJ4662.A3J32 1996   343.7105'26   C96-931307-1

Publisher: Joan Homewood
Editor: Erin Moore
Production Coordinator: Sharon Hudson
Cover Design: Lisa Hastings
Interior Design/Composition: Bookman Typesetting Co.
Editorial Services: Drew McCarthy

NOTICE TO READERS

CONTENTS

TABLES

CHAPTER ONE

Your New Relationship with Revenue Canada

In order to win, you must expect to win.
—Dan Fouts

TAKING THE ENTREPRENEURIAL LEAP

So you're in business for yourself! Congratulations. Your home is your office and your office is your home. You have convenience, drive, energy, and support. You're ready to take flight!

... starting a new business can be a lot like jumping off the side of a cliff ...

Starting a new business can be a lot like jumping off the side of a cliff . . . if you're not adequately prepared, the forces of gravity will ensure a short-lived experience.

But if you have anticipated the consequences of your actions, and equipped yourself properly, you may be in for the experience of a lifetime . . . in fact, you may even soar to unprecedented heights, before coming down for a smooth, planned landing.

What possesses people to take the "entrepreneurial leap" and go into business for themselves?

Ask a few new business owners, and they might say:

"I lost my job and decided I wanted to be in control of my own future."

"I wanted to put the fruits of my labours into my own pocket."

"I was frustrated by the endless meetings, the politics and the bureaucracy . . . I wanted to make my ideas happen."

"After contributing to my employer's bottom line for 15 years, I wanted to be in charge of how much I was earning — and, of all that equity I was creating."

1

In short, entrepreneurs are people who are ready to invest in themselves; to take control of their own lives, take responsibility for their own actions, risk their time and money on a vision or dream that leads them to financial independence. They are people who are willing to work 18 hours a day, 7 days a week. They are leaders. They have the discipline to see a project through from beginning to end. They are resourceful. They are problem-solvers. They have energy and persistence. They usually have good support systems in family and friends . . . and if they don't, they soon learn that networking skills are mandatory for survival.

While successful entrepreneurs are goal-oriented, to some degree they will act on intuition. And, as visionaries, they know that desire will become intention, intention will give rise to an action plan and the follow-through of this plan will lead to accomplishment.

Recognizing these personal traits in ourselves is most important, from a tax point of view. Especially if you run your business from home, you may be called upon to explain why you deserve to write off your mortgage interest expenses or the cost of your expensive car repairs. Most importantly, you must explain why it takes you 15 hours a day over many weeks to make your income flow, . . . and you will be explaining this to a tax auditor, an employee of Revenue Canada, whose job it is to make a judgement call about whether or not to allow your claims for tax deductions.

. . . when it comes to maximizing your after-tax dollars, knowledge is power . . .

In short, when it comes to maximizing your after-tax dollars, knowledge is power.

YOUR NEW PARTNER — REVENUE CANADA

As a home-based proprietor, you join the ranks of a tax-filing minority. While self-employment is growing in Canada, there are relatively few of us (about 1.2 million)* compared to all tax filers in Canada (about 20 million). As a group, we report about $21.3 billion in income. This compares to $314 billion in income being reported from employment sources.

The self-employed, however, have a much greater likelihood of facing a tax audit than other Canadian taxpayers, especially if they run an unincorporated home-based business. (*See* "Why All the New Auditors at Revenue Canada?" later in this chapter.) While employees have tax deducted from their earnings at source before they ever see it, Revenue Canada must count on you to self-assess the amount of tax you owe on your income and *remit it to them* at the end of the year. So, there's a question of trust . . . and the start of a new relationship between you and your silent partner . . . Revenue Canada.

---

*Based on most recent statistics available from Revenue Canada at the time of writing.

It is also important to recognize, that while business owners can be highly effective, visionary, and hard-working people, many are not blessed with an aptitude for keeping any type of formal records. It's not necessarily that they don't want to or can't — it's more that they are so busy running their businesses that, well, organizing their personal records is left until the very last minute. This can cost you dearly over the long run, mainly in overpaid taxes. You must make a concerted effort to keep accurate books and records, because, in fact, you are obliged to do so, by law . . . even if the only way to do this is to hire a bookkeeper.

Moreover, the tax affairs of a home-based business owner can fall into many "grey areas". That is, depending upon circumstances, an expenditure may be deductible, not deductible or partially deductible. While the tax deductions allowed to any employee are specified in the Income Tax Act and rigid in their application, the taxable income of a self-employed person can be reduced by a host of expenditures that are not specifically outlined in the Act. (For more on this, *see* "What to Expect in a Tax Audit," later in this chapter.)

Business or Hobby? — Keep a Diary

The expenses of your home-based business must be incurred for the purposes of earning income in a business that has "a reasonable expectation of profit". This means that your activities must be more than a hobby run out of your basement — there must be evidence of a viable commercial activity. This is why it is as important to keep a detailed daily log of your business activities, as it is to keep the actual receipts, logs and documents you will need to justify the figures on your tax return.

While you may think an expense is easily justifiable, given your management style or the type of business you own, Revenue Canada might disagree, citing that there is no reasonable expectation of profit. Or, Revenue Canada could take the position that given the amount of time you spend on pursuing profits from the commercial activity, as compared to your "day job," the expenditures are unreasonable. It's good to know about this when you start your business, because you will likely then make a point of keeping your "Business Diary".

This Business Diary, which lists the activities you undertake, why you are undertaking them, and how they have increased the expectation of profit from your business, can be the key to winning a tax audit, when the test becomes one of "reasonableness".

UNDERSTANDING THE TAX AUDITOR

The Revenue Canada auditor who is assigned to your file must ensure that you have followed the law in preparing your income tax return. Because Revenue

Canada must rely on your own declaration of income and expenses under our self-assessment system, the only way to check the integrity of your return is to audit your returns periodically.

Let us look at this task from the auditor's viewpoint for a moment. This person is a salaried employee whose remuneration depends on on-the-job performance, skill, experience, education and the ability to follow the instructions of the employer.

While there are certainly common trends among different industry groups that allow the auditor to compare your business venture with similar ones in your region and/or across the country, it may not be apparent, from your records, why you must use your car 95% of the time for business, or why you are justified in paying your wife $5 an hour more than a stranger would be paid for doing the same work.

He or she may not understand that to make the earnings from your business happen, you may have to work many hours a day for many months, to make the first sale. You may have to reinvest your revenues into income-producing assets before you can draw any money out for yourself. You may have to spend several hundreds of dollars networking before you connect with that one contact that can make your business take off and grow.

. . . you have to help the tax auditor understand your business . . .

Therefore, you have to help the tax auditor understand your business, the reasons why your expenditures are reasonable and incurred to earn income, from a venture that has, over the long run, a reasonable expectation of profit. In fact, *the onus of proof is on you.* If you signed your tax return, you have taken responsibility for what was reported in it. This is so even if you had someone else do the return for you.

It's a Whole New Relationship

So, as a new business owner you need to know this: The status of your relationship with Revenue Canada is now completely different from that of an employee or even an investor, both of whom usually receive T-Slips to report their income. Despite your best negotiating skills, Revenue Canada can and will disallow your claims for deductions, based on their opinion that what you have claimed is not "reasonable" under the circumstances, or that, from what they can tell, your business has no profit motive. To defend yourself, you have to be able to tell the story of your business activities well.

Also, please be aware that Revenue Canada has the power to reassess your return for the current tax year and up to two years back. Just because your return was accepted as filed initially, does not necessarily mean your troubles are over. It is common for Revenue Canada to request additional information after the initial filing rush has subsided, — or later, as a part of a special audit initiative. (*See* "Why All the New Auditors at Revenue Canada?" later in this chapter.)

This means that you could be required to unearth documents from at least a couple of years back, when the audit call comes. The more accurate and organized your records, the easier it will be to remember what activities you undertook and how they contributed to the profit potential of your business. It is always much easier to argue reasonableness when you have the records that help you remember why you took the actions you did.

And, just to put your mind at ease, auditors can and do understand the uniqueness of your situation when presented with the facts.

WHY ALL THE NEW AUDITORS AT REVENUE CANADA?

Have you ever wondered just how much money the tax department makes? The statistics are interesting, especially for the most recently available years 1993-94.

TABLE 1-1
TAX DOLLARS (1993-94)

Total Federal Taxes	$ 59,631,277,000
Total Provincial Taxes	$ 26,292,113,000
Total All Taxes Collected	$ 85,923,390,000
Total Income*	$353,000,000,000
Total Canadian Taxpayers	19,829,240
Average Canadian Income*	$ 18,580
Average Tax Bill	$ 4,333
Average Effective Tax Rate	23%

*From Employment, Business, Investments

On closer look, one finds that the tax structure in Canada is really quite progressive and, as reported by The Fraser Institute (July 1996 edition of *Fraser Forum*), "very competent at extracting money from those at the higher end of the income scale". In fact, the top 10% of income earners in Canada, whose income represents 25% of total Canadian income, pay almost 31% of all taxes in Canada at a tax rate of almost 60%. See Table 1-2, below.

Example

A family of four: Parents and two children under the age of 18.

Average Cash Income in Canada	*$57,666*
Total Taxes paid to Federal, Provincial & Municipalities	*$28,773*
Tax Rate	*49%*

TABLE 1-2
DISTRIBUTION OF INCOME AND TAXES ACROSS GROUPS REPRESENTING 10% OF FAMILIES IN EACH OF 10 INCOME CATEGORIES

Income Category	1	2	3	4	5	6	7	8	9	10
% of total income in Canada	1.7	3.8	5.2	6.5	7.8	9.3	11.1	13.3	16.3	25
% of total tax paid in Canada by all taxpayers	.6	1.8	3.3	5	6.9	8.9	11.1	13.9	17.8	30.8
% of income paid in taxes (average tax rates)	16.5	22.6	30.8	37.9	42.7	46.3	48.4	51.0	52.9	59.8

The Fraser Forum, July 1996

The Underground Economy

So while the basic functions within our tax system seem to have the desired effect — to take more of the taxable income earned by upper middle and higher income families in Canada — there is, unfortunately, a compliance problem . . . the "Underground Economy".

Since launching its "Underground Economy Initiative" in November 1993, the tax department has assessed more than $1.1 billion in additional taxes. According to Revenue Canada, tax losses seeping through the Underground Economy are enormous. This is a serious concern for everyone. Why? When some taxpayers cheat on their taxes, honest taxpayers can be forced out of business. Here's how:

▶ *. . . the tax department has assessed more than $1.1 billion in additional taxes . . .*

Case Study #1

MAX AND JUDY ENCOUNTER UNFAIR COMPETITION

Max, a home-based Internet consultant and his partner Judy, have quoted against their competitor, SFC (Sly Fox Communications), on numerous occasions. Each time, they listened to their prospective clients' wishes, identified a professional strategy and then presented a quotation that they felt was competitive, and, at the same time, allowed them an adequate after-tax profit. Each time, SFC's quote came in under Max and Judy's. The prospective clients chose SFC, even though the SFC quote was based on the proviso that the clients had to pay cash.

SFC's quotes were always lower because they were based on before-tax dollars. Because SFC was not reporting income to the tax department, they quoted half of what Max and Judy did. The honest taxpayers, Max and Judy, always included their projected tax obligation (calculated at a marginal rate of 50%) as part of their price. Max and Judy could not compete with their dishonest competitor.

According to Revenue Canada, tax compliance initiatives are necessary to protect honest taxpayers like Max and Judy. Without these initiatives, the integrity of the tax system as a whole is at stake. To strengthen the impact of the audit process, Revenue Canada has implemented a variety of new measures over the past several years.

It has established special audit teams to focus on areas of high non-compliance. This includes jewelry sales, the hospitality industry, the car repair industry, and most notably, the construction and home renovations businesses. Recently a joint initiative was implemented between Revenue Canada and Canada's major construction company associations and unions, to introduce a voluntary system of tax reporting of payments made to subcontractors whose principal business is construction.

Paying a "Fair Share"

In the March 6, 1996 Federal Budget, further measures were introduced to strengthen the fight against the Underground Economy.

1. A Technical Committee on Business Taxation was established.

    Its mandate is to report to Canadians ways in which our business tax system can contribute more to job creation and economic growth. Simplification of the tax system will be considered in order to make compliance and administration easier for businesses. In particular, it will be the Committee's task to ensure that all businesses share in the cost of providing government services by paying their fair share of the tax burden.

2. More resources will be devoted specifically to audit Unincorporated Businesses and Self-Employed Individuals.

. . . Revenue Canada expects to reap large returns . . .

    Revenue Canada expects to reap large returns over the cost of hiring approximately 800 new tax auditors — $25 million in the fiscal year 1996-97; $60 million in the year 1997-98 and $100 million by the year 1998-99.

Taking a Careful Look

For Revenue Canada, the unincorporated small business audit obviously has been a lucrative target market. When we look at the statistics, it's easy to see why. Approximately 32% of all tax returns filed in Canada are not taxable*:

Total number of taxable returns	13,569,050
Total number of non-taxable returns	6,260,190
Total returns	19,829,240

*Based on 1993–94 tax years.

This could be because of part-time earnings, credit-only filers or the use of income tax reducing provisions that eliminate taxes. Since most employees and investors are not eligible to use these provisions, certain groups can be easily identified for audit purposes because they claim specialized deductions that require post-assessment verification. For example:

1. Investors who claim interest and other carrying charges on Line 221 ("Interest and Other Investment Income");

2. Employees who claim employment expenses on Line 229 ("Other Employment Expenses") or Child Care Expenses (Line 214);

3. Those who claim RRSP deductions, moving or alimony deductions; and

4. Those who claim deductions from self-employment.

Add to this, the fact that there's no shortage of moonlighting in Canada. Many Canadians report both employment *and* self-employment income. Just look at the tax filing patterns of these who report (at least some) self-employment income.

Characteristics of Tax-Filers Reporting Self-Employment Income

TABLE 1-3
CHARACTERISTICS OF TAX-FILERS REPORTING SELF-EMPLOYMENT INCOME

(Based on 1993-94 tax years)

Employment	Number of Returns	11.3 million
	Income	$314 billion
	Reported	**$509 million in Business Losses**
Proprietors	Number of Returns	734,310
	Net Business Income	$7.2 billion
	Reported	159,990 or 22% of returns reported employment income of $1.9 billion; **315,060 or 43% of returns were not taxable**
Professionals	Number of Returns	215,440
	Net Profits	$12.2 billion
	Reported	44,030 or 20% reported employment income of $640 million; **38,180 or 18% were not taxable.**
Farming	Number of Returns	239,750
	Income	$1.9 billion
	Reported	65,220 returns or 27% reporting employment income of $860,809; **80,750 or 34% were not taxable**

With 43% of those proprietors reporting business income showing non-taxable returns, and over $500 million in business losses being claimed by moonlighters, an audit-direction is clear: There's money in checking the returns of unincorporated small business.

... there's money in checking the returns of unincorporated small business ...

There also appears to be a perception by those who make the tax laws, that the tax system is too generous for small business owners. This has recently been confirmed in budget changes proposed in Quebec for those who run home-based businesses there, only one-half the normal deductions for home-office expenses will be allowed for 1996 forward. This may be a sign of tax increases to come from the federal government as well.

So those are some of the reasons why, historically speaking, the unincorporated business is the subject of more intense audit scrutiny.

WHAT TO EXPECT IN A TAX AUDIT

If you were to look up the definition of "fear" in *The Concise Oxford Dictionary*, you would see it defined as "the painful emotion caused by impending danger or evil, state of alarm, dread or anxiety." Notice, it does not say "what happens when Revenue Canada audits you!"

While a tax audit can certainly cause some alarm, dread or anxiety, fear is certainly not necessary if you are prepared for the inevitable. A tax audit is usually a random selection of taxpayers with specific types of income or deductions, so the best way to prepare for the day when your return is chosen, is to file an audit-proof tax return every year. (For tips on tax audit strategies, *see* "Ten Secrets to Satisfying the Tax Auditor," later in this chapter.)

Even though you may never have been audited before, chances are you will be, if you've recently started your own small business. As previously discussed in this chapter ("Why All The New Auditors at Revenue Canada?"), this is because Revenue Canada plans to increase the size of its audit staff over the three year-period ending in 1998, specifically for the purposes of checking your books. Revenue Canada's Underground Economy Initiative has been so successful in tax recovery, that it is being extended to collect a projected $200 million in additional taxes over this three-year period. So consider yourself warned.

The Taxpayers' Rights and Duties

It is important for you to know that all Canadians have the right and duty to arrange their affairs under the framework of the law so as to pay only the correct amount of tax — no more and no less.

Revenue Canada's Mandate for Audits

Revenue Canada, on the other hand, is mandated to assess the tax returns you file, collect the monies you owe and refund any overpayments or send out refundable tax credits, in a timely manner. To do this task, the Verification, Enforcement and Compliance Division has several enforcement activities:

- Basic Tax Files Audit
- Business Files Audit
- Large File Audits
- Special Investigations
- Office Examination
- Tax Avoidance/Tax Incentives
- International and Non-Resident Audits

Revenue Canada also administers the Employment Insurance Act (EI — formerly the Unemployment Insurance Act, UI) and the Canada Pension Plan (CPP). It is responsible for deciding which employment income is insurable or pensionable, and collecting the contributions made by employers and employees for these statutory source deductions. Eligibility for CPP and EI, however, is set by the Department of Human Resources Development.

Know the Consequences

The tax audit process and your responsibilities as a taxpayer begin as soon as you have signed and submitted your tax return. You should, therefore, be fully aware of the consequences of your reporting activities.

SIGNING YOUR RETURN

. . . understand the significance of that signature . . .

Before you sign your personal income tax return, you must understand the significance of that signature. It means that you know and understand the calculation of your taxes and the amounts payable to Revenue Canada and that you consider the return to be true and correct . . . even if you have had someone else prepare it for you. Willful blindness or ignorance simply will not cut it with Revenue Canada. If you signed, but didn't know what you were signing, and it turns out to be grossly negligent or fraudulent in Revenue Canada's opinion, you will pay the penalties.

RECORD RETENTION

Under Section 230 of the Income Tax Act, any person who carries on a business in Canada and anyone who is required to pay or collect taxes, must keep books and records at their place of business or residence, in Canada, in such a format or order to enable the assessment and payment of taxes. If you are a lousy bookkeeper, Revenue Canada has the power to require you to keep proper books. These books must be kept for a period of at least six years from the end of the tax year.

Example

> *Marie's fiscal year end is December 31, 1996. She must keep her books and records for that year for at least six years: to December 31, 2002.*

Marie could request permission for earlier disposal of these books and records, using "Form T137" — "Request for Destruction of Books and Records". (*See* Appendix 1.)

VOLUNTARY COMPLIANCE

At all times, you can choose to notify Revenue Canada to make adjustments to your tax return, if you know there was an error made in the way you filed it. This includes the understatement of income or overstatement of expenses. If you request the adjustment for correction before Revenue Canada notifies you, you can avoid gross negligence penalties, or tax evasion fines, because you can show this was an honest error, corrected as soon as you became aware of it, and therefore not wilfully fraudulent. The key is to let them know before they let you know.

You can file for an adjustment to your return by filing "Form T1ADJ"–"Adjustment Request," (*See* Appendix 2.) and including any new or supporting information to back up your request. Please note that receipts for business income and expenses generally do not need to be filed with the original tax return, but should be attached to adjustment requests.

WHEN THE AUDITOR CALLS

You'll know that you've been selected for audit when you receive a letter from Revenue Canada in the mail. Usually, this letter will look something like this:

Sample Audit Letter (Exhibit 1-1)

January 4, 1997

Your name and address

Dear Sir/Madam:

Re: Tax Years 1994 and 1995

The tax returns you have filed for the years noted above have been selected for review.

Please provide the following information:

1. Receipts to verify income and expenses claimed on your business statement
2. Automobile distance logs for each year
3. Official receipts for RRSP contributions claimed
4. Receipts for carrying charges claimed
5. Receipts for donations to registered charities

(A detailed description of what is requested for each of the above usually follows).

Please respond to this request within 30 days. Failure to respond will result in a reassessment of the above-mentioned claims. Please call the undersigned if there are any questions.

At this point you would normally take one of two steps: (1) If you have the information at hand, take the information you have down to the auditor (in person or by mail) and wait for acceptance or rejection of your claim; or (2) if you need some additional time to put the information together, request an extension. Then take the information to the auditor on time. Always keep a photocopy of anything you send in to Revenue Canada.

. . . keep a photocopy of anything you send in to Revenue Canada . . .

The beauty of audit-proofing your return before you sign it and send it in to Revenue Canada is this: now when you are being asked to provide records from two to three years ago, there is no extra stress or expense, or for that matter fear, because you know you have already met your obligations under the Income Tax Act. No problem.

However, it's when you have made a decision a couple of years ago to pay the least amount of taxes possible, based on undocumented expenditures, or worse, inflated expenses or understated income, that we have a completely different problem when Revenue Canada requests more information. Now you must again choose one of two paths: (1) you either deal with Revenue Canada yourself; or (2) you hire some help to get yourself through this. Either way, the results can be expensive.

Hire a Professional or Face the Auditor Alone?

Taxpayers often wonder at what point in your relationship with Revenue Canada would it be wise to get some help. Let's have a look at some guidelines.

DO-IT-YOURSELF AUDITS

This is an option for taxpayers who are absolutely certain they have filed their returns using all the tax deductions and credits they are entitled to, and are emotionally able to deal with their auditor on a professional basis. If you know that you can meet Revenue Canada's requests fully, there is likely little reason to seek professional help, unless there are some "grey areas" to negotiate.

THIRD PARTY ASSISTANCE

If you suspect that your return was not filed correctly to begin with, and some adjustments may need to be made which could rule the entire process in your favor, you may wish to enlist the help of a tax professional. This is especially important if you are absolutely panicking because you know you are completely disorganized, don't have an auto log, can't find your tax files, feel you are being unfairly singled out, get hot flushes every time you see Revenue Canada's letterhead on an envelope, and have cold sweats at night thinking about this audit. **Get some professional help immediately.**

WHAT A PROFESSIONAL CAN DO FOR YOU

First, it is important for you to be aware that the fees a professional accountant or lawyer charges you to defend an income tax assessment, reassessment or appeal are tax deductible on your personal return. That will give you some financial relief when you file next year's return.

Second, the tax professional is an independent third party who can deal with Revenue Canada on an unemotional level. If you think you will loose your cool, cry or wail, it's likely best for someone else to handle the audit for you. While most Revenue Canada auditors are sympathetic to the emotional challenges their presence may cause you, neither yelling nor tears will sway their decisions. It's compliance they are after.

. . . a sharp tax professional will look at the whole picture . . .

That's not to say a tax auditor is always right. Quite often, in fact, their audit requests focus on only certain aspects of your affairs. A sharp tax professional will look at the whole picture to maximize your tax advantage, and will ensure that you haven't missed filing for an allowable tax provision in the past. Consider this example (the names, circumstances, and numbers are fictitious as are all such cases in this book).

Case Study #2

MARK AND JENNA HIRE A TAX PROFESSIONAL

Mark and Jenna, an honest, hard-working married couple with four teenagers, owned a multi-suite rental property. The rental income transactions fell under review by Revenue Canada. Mark had a nervous condition that became progressively worse as their tax audit intensified. The auditor was requesting receipts for specific tax deductions, some of which Mark and Jenna could not find. The couple knew that such expenses would be automatically disallowed.

No automobile expense log had been kept by either Mark or Jenna. Their auto claims of 80% were estimated at the time they filed their return, and it looked like the auditor was going to arbitrarily drop this claim to 20% of expenses. This would be very expensive.

As the interest clock ticked on, there was another serious problem with the way these returns had originally been filed: all the expenses that Mark and Jenna paid to upgrade old sinks, washers, dryers and other replacements for the property had been written off in full as maintenance and repairs. But, the Revenue Canada auditor considered these items to be capital in nature, and added them to Class 8, which normally calls for a Capital Cost Allowance deduction of only 20% of the actual costs; half this amount in the year of acquisition. (*See* Chapter Five.) This meant that 90% of these expenses were specifically disallowed.

The result? A tax reassessment notice arrived in the mail, with a bill of over $15,000 payable within 30 days. It was at this point that Mark had his breakdown, and Jenna sought professional help to deal with the tax problem.

Fortunately, there was a happy ending to this sad story. Mark completely recovered and the tax professional, through some extensive digging, found that Mark and Jenna's original accountant had not scheduled all the equipment and furniture in the building at the time it was acquired. A percentage of over $40,000 in furniture and fixtures costs could be used to offset the proposed increases in tax suggested by the auditor. In addition, although Mark and Jenna bought the building together, only Mark reported the original transaction. This was changed on the prior filed returns to split income and expenses between the two of them, resulting in taxation of income at two lower marginal tax rates. Finally, many of the original costs of acquisition of the building were not added to the cost base, again increasing the deductions claimable.

In the end, the couple owed one-tenth of the original reassessment to Revenue Canada . . . a much more manageable scene. In addition, Revenue Canada agreed to waive interest and penalties on the outstanding amount from the time of Mark's medical challenge. This was because the tax professional pleaded for consideration of hardship under Revenue Canada's Fairness Package. (*See* "When the Audit's Over," later in this chapter.)

In short, a tax audit will not necessarily push you into the poor house. But, the truth is, the organized, informed and honest tax filer pays less over the long run — in time, money, and stress factors.

Summary

In summary, here is what you can expect at the audit interview:

1. The auditor will request to see several categories of receipts and documents to verify the amounts claimed on the originally filed tax return.

2. The auditor will request to see auto logs, appointment logs, home-office details or other information to verify discretionary claims.

3. The auditor will ask you to explain why certain claims made are reasonable under the circumstances.

4. The auditor will propose to allow or disallow all or part of your claims.

5. A letter will be forwarded to you with these proposals for change, to which you will have time to agree or disagree and present additional information.

6. The return will be reassessed, with any balance due payable, usually in 30 days (20 days before interest is charged.)

7. You have appeal possibilities should you disagree with the Reassessment (*See* "When the Audit's Over," later in this chapter.)

TEN SECRETS TO SATISFYING THE TAX AUDITOR

It can be done. You can win at the tax filing game, if you know the rules. So, if you are facing a tax audit now, or sometime in the future, here are ten secrets to satisfying Revenue Canada's requests for information in a tax audit . . . and keep from losing sleep.

1. Hire an Impartial Third Party

Take the emotion out of the process . . . hire a tax professional who will put distance between you and the auditor. This person can communicate not only the results of your documentation search, but also why the amounts were reasonable and incurred to earn income.

Someone once said that the relationship a taxpayer has with Revenue Canada is not unlike that of two teams in a football game . . . but because Revenue Canada also acts as the referee, it can pay to hire a quarterback who also knows the rules and how to use them to your best advantage.

2. Establish Errors or Omissions in Prior Year's Returns

One of the first things to do before you file any tax return is to establish whether there were any errors or omissions in filing previous tax returns. This way, carry-over provisions, such as undepreciated capital cost balances, or loss carry-overs can be utilized from year to year. However, particularly during a tax audit, take another look. It may be possible to offset any tax liability from the audit with previously missed tax provisions. You can usually go all the way back to 1985 to recover tax credits and deductions that would normally have been allowed to you. Ask your tax professional about this.

3. Establish Flaws in the Auditor's Position

The auditor can make errors, omissions or adjustments in the audit process that are not necessarily in your favor. That includes the application of depreciation provisions, terminal losses and loss carry-overs, Allowable Business Investment Losses, interest deductibility provisions and others. You can make claims for these amounts if they are missed by the auditor. Remember, you are only obliged to pay the correct amount of tax. Under our current tax system there are often several ways to mathematically calculate your return accurately — you are looking to claim all the tax provisions that legally reduce, to a minimum, the taxes that you and your family owe.

4. Establish Strengths and Weaknesses in Your Position

Sometimes it pays to open your audit interview with an admission of your weak links. Tell your auditor flat out the items for which you could not find backup documentation. Then use any discretionary provisions at your disposal to offset the lost deductions: such as unused home-office expenses of prior years, previously unclaimed business loss carry-overs, and so on. (*See* "Financing Your Business with Start-up Losses," in Chapter Two.)

5. Establish a Response Time

Depending on how close to the audit deadline you contact your tax professional, it is usually a good idea to request an extension of time to prepare your documentation. It is not unusual for Revenue Canada to grant additional time to you or your professional to put the information together. Once the extension has been granted, make sure you meet the deadline, or keep the auditor closely informed of any required changes to the time line. This is most important.

6. Meticulously Organize Your Presentation

Make sure all your receipts and documentation are in a precise and orderly fashion before you see the tax auditor. All categories of expenses, for example, should be supported with adding machine tapes that show a circled total matched to the specific line number on the business statement. (*See* Appendix 4.) This will give your auditor confidence in your bookkeeping system.

Have at hand a chronological diary of significant income-producing events in the business, unreceipted expenses such as telephone calls, coin parking or coin car washes, and of course that difficult-to-keep-up auto log.

Also have at hand, information about carry-forward provisions you would like to invoke, if not previously applied.

7. Establish Your Audit Negotiation Strategy

As mentioned earlier, it is important to know your concessions, as well as your aces. Back up all positions you take with references to the Income Tax Act, Revenue Canada's tax guides, interpretation bulletins and other publications. Be aware that verbal advice previously given to you over the counter or telephone at Revenue Canada is not binding.

8. Knowledge Is Power

Be prepared to help the auditor apply discretionary tax provisions to your best benefit. Study all the tax applications of the provisions being questioned. Look up recent court cases to see how similar situations have faired in front of a judge. Know the tax changes that have occurred in each year of the audit, and each subsequent year since. This will assist both you and the auditor to make the right decisions from a tax planning perspective. Remember, the auditor is looking very specifically at the numbers claimed in two, maybe three tax years. You, or your professional must watch out for the best tax applications on your returns, over the long run.

9. Never Bluff or Bluster

Let your tax professional do the talking. If you've hired a barking dog, don't wag the tail. Hopefully your professional will know better than to bluff any answer. If more information is required for verification, request that this be put in writing and request additional time to comply.

10. Put the Emphasis on Listening

As explained above, should the auditor request any additional information outside of the original written request, you can ask that these new requests be put in writing. In that way, everyone stays focused on what is missing, and no new cans of worms are opened. It is your goal to satisfy the auditor's requests for information completely, and to listen well, but *not to volunteer* any information that's irrelevant to the issues at hand. You can be held liable if the volunteered information turns out to be incorrect. *(See* "When the Audit's Over," later in this chapter.)

... a tax audit need not be acrimonious, stressful or burdensome ...

Finally, a tax audit need not be acrimonious, stressful or burdensome. Remember, the person whose job it is to examine your books and records is working to maintain integrity in the tax system for the majority of taxpayers who are honest, file their returns on time, and fully support all facts and figures claimed.

It is in certain "grey areas" of interpretation that the outcome of the audit process can be tricky. However, there are ways to overcome negative interpretation positions.

WHAT'S BEING DISPUTED?

Despite the millions of dollars that annually go into the creation of tax law, tax policy, tax guides and a host of informational services by both the Department of Finance and Revenue Canada, the courts are still full of tax-related challenges. These disputes come from both taxpayers and the Minister alike. So what's being disputed?

Common Problem Areas

A look at some of the many court cases heard over the last year or so, indicate some common problem areas.

NO EXPECTATION OF PROFIT

This problem appears over and over again . . . the taxpayer claims operational losses from a business against other income earned during the year, and Revenue Canada disallows them, citing "no reasonable expectation of profit". In one case, for example, the taxpayer was a dedicated horseman who attempted to deduct farming losses against other income; but his appeal was dismissed, as it was found that his activities were carried on for the love of the sport rather than any serious prospect of financial gain in the future. In short, the courts agreed with the Minister that the activities were in the nature of a hobby, not a commercial business.

DEFINITION OF INCOME

Different income sources are subject to different tax treatment. (*See* "How Income Is Taxed in Canada" and "More than One Tax Calculation," in Chapter Two.) For this reason, income classification is often challenged. Especially when real estate transactions are involved, taxpayers tend to classify profits on sale as a "capital gain" subject to income inclusion at only 75%. Revenue Canada, however, has often been successful in having this reclassified as "income" — which means that profits must be included in income on the return in full. Even a one-time transaction can be classified as "an adventure or concern in the nature of trade" if one of the parties had real estate experience or knowledge or a "quick flip" indicates a trading motive. (*See* "Taxation of Investors and Traders," in Chapter Seven.)

CHILD SUPPORT PAYMENTS*

An area where the law appears to be followed to the letter by the courts, is in the deductibility of child support. Again and again one reads about situations where claims were dismissed because the written separation agreement was not signed by both parties, the payments were made to the child instead of the custodial parent, and so forth. In a recent case, a taxpayer's deductions were disallowed because they were not made "pursuant" to a court order. In another, an ex-spouse was permitted to stay in a residence paid for by the taxpayer, on a rent-free basis because the amounts paid by the taxpayer for the residence were given a periodic equivalent value in the separation agreement. The wording of the law, and its application, is significant.

REASSESSMENTS DUE TO FILING NEGLIGENCE

. . . Revenue Canada has a secret weapon . . .

Revenue Canada has a secret weapon in assessing the taxes of someone who has no records: the net worth assessment. A net worth assessment is Revenue Canada's own estimate of how much money you must have made, what your expenses must have been, and so on, given your lifestyle.

---

*New rules are being introduced on May 1, 1997 to render child support payments under new agreements, not taxable.

In an interesting case involving a golf pro, the Minister imposed net worth assessments to increase taxable income, due to the sketchy records of the taxpayer himself. There were no tapes from cash registers of his sales and the pro had made the classic error of combining his personal and business finances in one bank account. While his reassessed tax bill proved hefty, he was granted some mercy, and because of his co-operation throughout the audit, he was able to avoid gross negligence penalties. Whew!

FAMILY TRANSACTIONS

Revenue Canada is very fussy about personal-use allocation, which will be discussed in more detail in later chapters. It is very important that any expense that is used partially for business and partially for personal use, be prorated on the return. This extends to business travel, as well.

In a recent case, a taxpayer who was an executive of an insurance company, was requested to accompany a group of successful brokers on an international vacation. The Minister assumed that the business portion of the trip was to be 38% for the taxpayer and 25% for his spouse, and that the balance of the value be added to income as a taxable benefit. The taxpayer appealed to the Federal Court of Appeal and won. The court agreed that the principal purpose of the trip was business, that the spouse attended the same meetings as her husband and devoted her time to the entertainment of the other brokers and their wives. It was ruled that any personal enjoyment during the trip was incidental to the primary purpose. Nice one!

And so one can see that proper documentation, and the collection of the facts concerning a taxpayer's activities are the two key criteria in winning challenges surrounding the interpretation of the Income Tax Act.

Negotiating Those Grey Areas in Your Favor

Here are ten basic guidelines to follow . . . when negotiating those grey areas.

1. KNOW WHAT'S INCOME . . . WHAT'S NOT . . . AND KEEP THEM SEPARATE

Business income is income from any undertaking in which there is an expectation of profit sometime in the future. Specifically, the Income Tax Act defines a taxpayer's income from a business or property as his or her "profit" from that business or property.

Profit from your home-based business is calculated according to generally accepted accounting principles, as set out by the Canadian Institute of Chartered Accountants in their *CICA Handbook*. A profit will result when business income exceeds allowable deductions. A loss will result when deductions exceed business income.

Income is usually the receipt of money, but it can be the receipt of anything that has a commercial value — shares, grain, construction materials, services, and so on. That's why "barter" transactions are considered to be taxable, at their "fair market value". If you trade in goods and services, report such items as income (or expenses where applicable), supported by a receipt or invoice.

. . . never give a tax auditor a reason to check anything but your required tax records . . .

Finally, never give a tax auditor a reason to check anything but your required tax records . . . don't mix personal and business funds. Make sure you can verify the income you report with cash register tapes, sales records and a separate bank statement.

2. SHOW THAT THE EXPENSE IS DIRECTLY ATTRIBUTABLE TO BUSINESS INCOME

An outlay or expense of the business may only be deducted if it was incurred for the purpose of gaining or producing income from the business or property. Therefore, you must always be prepared to match the expenses you claim on the tax return with an income-producing activity.

To do this, keep a journal of activities of the business including day books, appointment logs, credit card documentation or any other notes that can help you trace your expenditures to the eventual income they helped to create. This tracking of present day activities will help you prepare more accurate financial statements.

3. SHOW THAT THERE IS A REASONABLE EXPECTATION OF PROFIT IN THE FUTURE

When a start-up business reports losses for several years, especially if the proprietor has income from other sources, such as a full-time job, Revenue Canada is more likely to question whether there is a reasonable expectation of profit.

To prove that there is, you must be prepared to project the results of your activities into the future. Present your auditor with cash-flow projections, budgets, letters of intent, contacts, or any other activities that can substantiate the potential for income.

You must also be prepared to show that the time you have spent in running the business and the investments you have made in the assets of the business, relate to the potential for earnings in the future. Even though you have a full-time job, it is possible you are spending an equal number of hours each week on your business. Be sure you can prove this, if you show an operating loss on your tax return.

4. HAVE A SYSTEM FOR MEETING DOCUMENTATION REQUIREMENTS

Instead of dropping a box of receipts in his or her lap, impress your tax auditor by passing this test: have every receipt for expenses claimed on your return, filed in envelopes with the Line Number and Total from the statement marked on the front. Inside will be the individual chits. Your auditor will only need to look through a couple of them to see that you have done your homework well.

People have tried many methods, some more effective than others, but whatever works for you, use it to keep all receipts and invoices faithfully. Some keep an accordion file, others a series of envelopes marked in categories of expenses, still others three-hole punch and insert documents into a binder. What's important to know is that each receipt can save you approximately 27% to 50% depending on your tax bracket (*See* "How Income Is Taxed in Canada," in Chapter Two.) That's a big return on the time invested in filing.

5. KNOW THE DIFFERENCE BETWEEN EMPLOYEES AND INDEPENDENT CONTRACTORS

As an employer or potential employer, it is important for you to distinguish between an independent contractor and an employee who is in a master-servant relationship with you. (*See* "How Income Is Taxed in Canada," in Chapter Two.) An independent contractor will not receive a "T4 Slip," will pay his or her own Canada Pension Plan Premiums and remit his or her own taxes. An employee, on the other hand, is available to the employer at the place of employment for a set time, and a set remuneration to perform the required duties. In this latter case, the employer must remit source deductions to Revenue Canada, usually monthly, and prepare "T4 Slips".

A misinterpretation of the structure of the contract or the duties can lead to penalties and interest charges if the independent contract is judged to be an employee by Revenue Canada.

6. PRESERVE YOUR ACCESS TO THE FAIRNESS PACKAGE

Because of the increased potential for audit and reassessment faced by the self-employed, it is most important to file on time (June 15 for all unincorporated small business owners and their spouses). Sometimes, people don't bother to file on time, because they think they have a tax refund coming back. (Go figure!) Should you lose your tax audit and have your return reassessed sometime in the future, the result could be a balance due on your return. If this happens, the late filing penalty will be invoked, together with interest charges, all the way back to the original filing due date.

Also, the character who is chronically late in filing may compromise any relief for hardship that Revenue Canada's Fairness Committee may have been able to extend. (*See* "When the Audit's Over," later in this chapter.)

7. VERIFY YOUR HOME-OFFICE CLAIMS WITHOUT A VISIT FROM THE AUDITOR

Writing off a portion of the costs of your home can be a lucrative deduction for home-based businesses. (*See* "Write Off Your Home-Office Expenses," in Chapter Four.) However, short of having the auditor come out to see the space, the only way to verify the size and use of the space is to forward to the auditor, a sketch drawn to scale of both the business space and its relationship to the rest of the home. Do this drawing the first time you claim home-office expenses, in order to determine what portion of the home expenses to claim for business use, and make sure you file this drawing with your tax files.

8. KNOW YOUR ATTRIBUTION RULES

Income splitting — the transfer of income from a higher income earner to a lower earner in the family to reduce or avoid tax — is specifically prohibited under the Income Tax Act. Revenue Canada considers that you are not "dealing at arm's length" with your spouse, or your minor children, or other "related persons".

Income on property that is transferred to spouses or minor children must be taxed in the hands of the transferor. But there are legal exceptions to this rule. For example, minor children may report the capital gains from investments transferred to them by their parents. Spouses and children may be paid a salary or other remuneration for work done in their parent's business.

For these reasons it is very important to establish employment contracts with family members. Pay them what you would pay a stranger to do the same work. Make sure that the work is actually done by the relative. If you can show this, Revenue Canada cannot reverse your deductions for such payments to family members. (*See* "Tax Obligations for Human Resources," in Chapter Six.)

9. MAKE SURE YOU HAVE AN AUTO LOG

If you have claimed automobile expenses, be prepared to give your auditor a distance log that shows how much driving you do for business purposes. Even if you haven't regularly kept one in the past, even a record of current business driving trends could be acceptable, in the absence of anything else. Most taxpayers, however, can go back to their appointment or day books and retrace their steps quite accurately for the auditor. While this is not as sure as a log that is keep throughout the year, often it is better than nothing . . . and so well worth the effort.

10. CO-OPERATE IN A NON-HOSTILE MANNER

Like our friend the golf pro, you may minimize your grief with the right attitude. Set the tone for audit negotiations with mutual respect. This can really pay off when negotiating your position in the grey areas.

WHEN THE AUDIT'S OVER

Once you have come through the audit process, it may be that Revenue Canada owes you some money. This happens quite often, particularly in cases where people have missed filing prior years' returns and can take advantage of refundable tax credits.

However, if you do owe money, and you are in agreement that there are no further provisions to be applied in your favor, sooner or later the time comes to pay your bill.

Paying the Piper

If you did in fact file late, Revenue Canada will generally add a late filing penalty to your return, back to the original due date. This is 5% of the taxes due. In addition, there is a penalty of 1% per month for a maximum of 12 months. Finally, interest is charged at the prescribed rate, compounded on a daily basis. The prescribed rate is the average interest rate paid on 90-day Treasury Bills plus 4 percentage points, as of July 1995. This can get very expensive. The costs are higher if you are a chronic non-filer.

By the way, the filing due date for unincorporated businesses was recently changed. It's now June 15. This means that the 1996 income tax return, for example, must be filed by June 15, 1997, and so on. This applies for both the proprietor and his or her spouse. But, if you owe any money to Revenue Canada when you do file, interest will be charged back to the normal due date for everyone else — April 30.

. . . if you know you can't pay, don't procrastinate . . .

If you know you can't pay, don't procrastinate. Make arrangements with the Collections Department at Revenue Canada to pay your bill over time. If there was a hardship beyond your control, that caused you to file your returns late, incomplete, or not at all, you may be able to have penalties and interest waived under the "Fairness Provisions".

The Fairness Provisions

Special measures took effect on December 17, 1991, applying to 1985 and subsequent tax years. Penalties and interest on a tax assessment or reassessment can now be waived if they result from consequences beyond the control of the taxpayer.

It may also be possible to waive or cancel penalties and interest if a previously uncollectible amount of taxes becomes collectible. In such cases, or where a payment arrangement is hampered because interest charges absorb most of the tax liabilities, you can make a formal appeal to the Fairness Committee at Revenue Canada.

To make a claim under these provisions, write a letter to the Fairness Committee, at your local Tax Services Office, or have your tax professional do so on your behalf. In your letter, explain why you wish the penalties and interest to be waived under the special provisions of The Fairness Package and include all documentation in support of your position. Then propose a payment plan for the tax liability itself. It is necessary that this plan accompany the request for waiving penalties and interest, as the Fairness Committee cannot waive taxes owing.

. . . the Fairness Committee will take your prior tax filing habits into account . . .

The Fairness Committee will take your prior tax filing habits into account in making their assessment of your request. Therefore, if you have been a model citizen in the past, it can work in your favor when you come cap-in-hand to Revenue Canada asking for forgiveness.

If You Want to Appeal

If you are dissatisfied with the outcome of your tax reassessment, you may take several appeal routes. In tax years 1993-94 approximately $2.7 billion of taxes payable were in dispute, according to Revenue Canada. Appeals activities account for 2.5% of Revenue Canada's total program expenditures and 2.7% of total full-time equivalents or full-time positions. Of total planned expenditures for appeals activities, 94.3% relate to personnel and 5.7% to operating and minor capital expenditures.

It is interesting to note that the estimates for the appeals process for 1995-96 are $1.8 million, or 3% lower, than for the previous year. Apparently, the Fairness Package has had a lot to do with this. Approximately 4,900 objections involving the Fairness Provisions were solved in 1995-96. This a good trend, as the simpler objections tend to be dealt with here.

For more complicated matters, according to Revenue Canada's statistics, the average number of working days to resolution has recently increased to 175 days from 153 days. Revenue Canada is estimating that of the 55,000

Exhibit 1-2
A Sample Letter to the Fairness Committee

Date of Letter:

To: The Fairness Committee
     Revenue Canada Taxation
     Your Local Tax Service Office
     City, Province, Postal Code

Re: (Taxpayer's Name, Social Insurance Number and Tax Year in Question)

Regarding the above-mentioned taxpayer, we wish to make the following appeal to the 1994 Notice of Reassessment, to have Revenue Canada waive penalties and interest assessed due to (*late filing, failure to file, or failure to pay*).

The reasons for the delinquency were the following:
(*Outline reasons, emphasizing the facts concerning one or more of the following circumstances:*)
* natural or man-made disaster,
* civil disturbance or postal strike,
* serious accident or illness,
* serious emotional or mental distress caused by family events (*e.g.,* death),
* processing delays at Revenue Canada that result in the taxpayer not being informed of amounts owing,
* errors in public documents issued by Revenue Canada, incorrect advice from Revenue Canada about a taxpayer's matters including the payment of instalments, or
* errors in processing by Revenue Canada.

(*Or, if previously unpaid amounts of tax have now become payable by the client, state this in the letter.*)

Prior to these circumstances, which caused severe hardship to the taxpayer, he/she had a flawless filing record. (*Expand on this by indicating occasions when the taxpayer voluntarily complied to correct errors in filing; emphasize the fact that the taxpayer has never filed late before; or has never missed filing a tax return,etc.*)

The taxpayer also wishes to propose the following payment schedule for the outstanding taxes. (*Outline here the repayment schedule the taxpayer can afford, or indicate that the full payment will be made as soon as the Committee can approve the waiving of penalties and interest.*)

We would like to thank the Committee for considering this request. Kindly contact the undersigned, should you need any clarifications, or have any questions.

Yours truly,

objections and appeals they are expecting in the 1995-96 year, they will complete all of them and in addition, finish off 10,000 or so left over from the year before. This will leave unfinished files of about 34,000 in inventory to hold over to the next year.

Summary

So to sum up, here are your appeal rights.

FILE A NOTICE OF OBJECTION

For appeals of a current year assessment on a tax return that was filed on time, you may forward a Notice of Objection to Revenue Canada within one year of the filing due date or within 90 days of the mailing of the Notice of Assessment, whichever is later.

If you are a late filer, that is, you are filing your 1993 return in 1997; you may file a Notice of Objection within 90 days of the Notice of Assessment only. (Another reason why it pays to file on time.)

The Notice of Objection is filed with the Chief of Appeals at your local Tax Services Office. The file is given to an Appeals Officer who will give you another opportunity to explain why your return should be assessed as originally filed. This is an impartial review. Over 90% of all tax disputes are settled here. Of the 65,000 objections estimated to be filed in the year 1995-96, 96% of them are not expected to be appealed to a higher court.

In fact, one might think that it's odd that so many people choose to take their lumps at this point, rather than to appeal further. However, higher appeals are expensive, and your chances of winning are slimmer.

APPEAL TO THE TAX COURT OF CANADA

If you are dissatisfied with your appeal at the Tax Services Office, you may initiate an appeal (within 90 days of Revenue Canada's response to the Notice of Objection), to the Tax Court of Canada. This travelling court will hear disputes using one of two types of procedure.

1. The Informal Procedure

The Informal Procedure is employed in cases where the tax in dispute is $12,000 or less, or losses in dispute are $24,000 or less. If the dispute involves interest charges, this informal procedure may be chosen regardless of the amounts in dispute.

2. The General Procedure

The General Procedure is employed in cases where the taxes or losses in dispute exceed $12,000 and $24,000 respectively. Here, the case decisions are precedent-setting and if you lose, you must pay the full amount in dispute or furnish acceptable security for the debt, before you go further in the appeals process.

It is interesting to note from recent statistics that Revenue Canada wins about 75% of these cases, so the odds are not in your favor. In 1993-94, for example, of the total actual judgements (1257), 916 or 73% of them were found to be in the Minister's favor; only 336 in the full favor of the taxpayer, and in 651 cases, taxpayers won a partial reprieve.

APPEAL TO THE HIGHER COURTS

Legal counsel is necessary to appeal further to the Federal Court of Appeal or the highest court, the Supreme Court of Canada. It is estimated that approximately 3,500 appeals will be heard in Canada's tax courts in 1995-96 with just under 3,000 going to the Tax Court, 435 going to the Federal Court, Trial Division and 82 to the Federal Court of Appeal. The Supreme Court of Canada has heard an average of two cases a year in the years 1993 to 1995.

DON'T END UP ON THE WRONG SIDE OF THE LAW

Before we leave this discussion of your rights to fairness and appeal, it is important to know the consequences if you end up on the wrong side of the law.

If you write an NSF cheque to Revenue Canada, for example, you will be fined $10. If you fail to file a tax return on time, the first time you'll be fined 5% of taxes owing plus 1% per month for a maximum of 12 months, plus interest.

If you are late filing again within a three-year period that late filing penalty jumps to 10% of the unpaid taxes and 2% per month for a maximum of 20 months.

If you close a blind eye to your tax affairs and plead ignorance, but, in Revenue Canada's view you should have known better, you can be assessed a gross negligence penalty of 50% of the unpaid taxes in addition to the other penalties mentioned above. The onus of proof is on you to show you were not grossly negligent.

Finally, there is one instance when the onus of proof is on Revenue Canada. This is when there is fraud or wilful failure to keep books and records. Revenue Canada must prove that you wilfully and on purpose understated income or overstated deductions in order to minimize tax.

In the case of the former, wilful failure to keep books or to file, there is a minimum fine of $1,000 and a maximum of $25,000, and /or prison of up to one year.

For tax evasion, convictions carry a minimum fine of 50% of the taxes payable to a maximum of 200%, and/or prison of up to two years. And for volunteering false information, a new penalty will be imposed, according to new provisions in the June 20, 1996 Technical Notes from the Department of Finance (Income Tax Act, Section 163(2)), if such statements are wilfully false or grossly negligent.

So now you know.

CHAPTER TWO

A Crash Course: How a Small Business is Taxed in Canada

It is better to be defeated on principle than to win on lies.
— Arthur Calwell

CREATING WEALTH WITH PROFIT AND EQUITY

The profitable small business can create wealth in more than one way. Most entrepreneurs are prepared to work hard to generate revenues; but one should also look forward to increasing the saleable goodwill that may accumulate in the enterprise itself. Let's have a look at the role that saleable goodwill might play in a small business.

Case Study #3

MARNIE'S FOOTCARE EQUITY

Marnie, a retired registered nurse, started a home-based business last year. Her specialty is footcare. Four days a week, Marnie makes house calls to her patients who have special needs for footcare, but who are not mobile enough to visit a clinic or hospital. She charges a consulting fee for her services.

Over the past year, Marnie has seen her business grow from a handful of clients to over 300 people she visits regularly. Her revenue flow has increased from 10 visits a week at $25 per visit ($250) to 40 visits a week, for a weekly revenue of $1,000.

Her ongoing operating expenses include the use of her car, the use of her home office to make appointments, do books and keep client files, and recently, the hiring of her son, James, to field calls on her behalf and do her bookkeeping entries. She pays him $15 an hour to do this work.

At the end of the year, come tax time, Marnie realized that she had earned over $50,000 from her home-based business. After expenses, her taxable income was $35,000, and Marnie found herself owing a large sum of money to Revenue Canada.

This is a common good news story. A profitable home-based business! Marnie is on the threshold of creating wealth for herself and her family in two ways:

1. through the revenues generated by the business operations, and

2. through the goodwill that is being built up in her client list.

The idea that a small business may be creating something over and above revenue, is an important concept to discuss before we move on to the tax reporting details of your income, expenses and asset acquisitions. The equity you build in your home-based business can be sold or transferred to someone sometime in the future . . . quite possibly on a tax-free basis . . . and this is a goal you should strive towards.

. . . equity you build in your . . . business can be sold or transferred . . . possibly on a tax-free basis . . .

Marnie, for example, found that after several years, her home-based business had expanded dramatically. She now has trained a part-time assistant to perform ongoing patient care; her son works for her as a full-time administrative assistant. Her revenues have grown to $80,000 a year and she finds herself at a fork in the road.

Recently, a fellow nurse offered to buy her business for $100,000. This is a very tempting offer, given Marnie's age of 56 . . . and a wonderful acknowledgment of the many hours she has spent nurturing and building her business enterprise.

However, over the past several months, together with her son, Marnie has developed a franchising proposal for her footcare services, which has the potential to bring in another $250,000 in revenues over the next two years. Still working out of her home, Marnie is considering incorporating her business to take advantage of the lower corporate tax rates available to her. She also wishes to use her $500,000 Capital Gains Exemption on her Small Business Corporation, should another offer to sell come her way after the franchise company is set up.

This story highlights a focus you should remember as you work in your home-based business: While the revenues your business generates is your lifeline to survival . . . the equity you build is the icing on the cake. Always ask yourself: Is it possible for me to build reasonable equity as well as ongoing profits?

HOW INCOME IS TAXED IN CANADA

Most home-based businesses begin as sole-proprietorships. These are unincorporated small businesses whose tax-filing obligations include little more than filing a "Business Income and Expense Statement" with the personal income tax return no later than June 15 of the year following the current calendar year.

Revenue Canada provides a special form called a "Statement of Business Activities" (*See* Appendix 4, which shows four variations of business income and expense statements used by Revenue Canada), that is used to calculate the net income from your business. This form will encompass the results from a series of worksheets, including:

1. the statement of automobile expenses;

2. the statement of home-office expenses;

3. the statement of capital cost allowances; and

4. the statement of personal-use adjustments.

Once net income from the business is established, it forms part of the total income of the taxpayer on the "T1 General Tax Return". (A sample "T1 General Return" is shown in Appendix 5.) Any net profits will increase your taxable income, and will be subject to the calculation of Canada Pension Plan premiums on "Schedule 8" of the "T1 General". (*See* Appendix 6.) Such contributions — which include both the employer and employee's portion — must be remitted to the government when you file your tax return. You will find the appropriate lines for these purposes on page 3 of the return — "Line 310" and page 4 of the return — "Line 421".

However, should your business efforts produce a loss — that is, if your expenses exceed your revenues — the amount of the loss can be used to reduce all other income of the year. And, if there is an excess loss, it can be carried back to offset other income of the previous three years or carried forward to offset future income in the next seven years. Use "Form T1A" for this purpose. (*See* Appendix 7.)

For these reasons, it is very important to understand how your income will be taxed, and what your marginal tax rate is — that is, how much tax you'll pay on the next dollar of income you make.

On the following pages, you will find three tables:

1. Table 2-1 describes different income classifications;

2. Table 2-2 describes the basic federal and provincial tax rates in Canada; and

3. Table 2-3 describes approximate marginal tax rates. (These differ from province to province, so confirm your current rate with your tax professional.)

1. Income Classifications (Table 2-1)

You will note that some income sources are not taxable at all — for example, refundable provincial and federal tax credits, life insurance policy proceeds, private health insurance benefits and profits from the sale of a principal residence.

TABLE 2-1
INCOME CLASSIFICATIONS

SOME EXEMPT INCOME SOURCES	FULLY TAXABLE
Refundable Provincial Tax Credits	Employment Income
GSTC Prepayments	Commission Income
Child Tax Benefits	Pension Income
Income Earned by Status Indians on Reserves	Interest Income
Gifts or Inheritances	Net Rental Income
Life Insurance Policy Proceeds	Net Business Income
Personal Injury Awards	Alimony/Maintenance*
Private Health Insurance Payments	
Profit from the Sale of the Principal Residence	

SPECIAL TAX PROVISIONS	ASSET APPRECIATION
Dividends	Capital Gains Treatment
Certain Foreign Pensions	
Scholarships/Bursaries	
Income of an Indian	

*Starting May 1, 1997, child support payments will no longer be subject to tax inclusions for agreements made or altered after this date, based on tax proposals announced March 6, 1996. This rule, however, does not extend to spousal support, which continues to be taxable to the recipient and deductible to the payor.

From a tax planning point of view, you should set up your affairs to try to reach the income levels required to qualify for as many refundable tax credits as possible when you file your family returns, by reducing your income level with RRSP contributions, discretionary business expense deductions and income-splitting and tax-deferral techniques, where possible within the law.

The RRSP is a tool best suited for retirement planning purposes. As an estate planning tool, however, it has a serious drawback — and this is where many Canadians may make a mistake. A significant part of your RRSP accumulations could eventually be taxed away! Only one tax-free rollover is allowed within a family and that is from one spouse to the other (except when a single parent leaves RRSP accumulations to dependent children). After this, RRSP accumulations that are not used up by the surviving spouse must be included in that person's income on the final return. Often that means that Revenue Canada gets half of your life savings before your children do.

. . . your RRSP accumulations could eventually be taxed away . . .

By using life insurance policy proceeds to fund your legacy, you leave for your heirs a tax-free distribution which can help to pay the taxes owing on the deemed disposition of your assets upon your death, and much more. Trouble is, the best time to do your estate planning with life insurance policies is when you're insurable. For many of us, this means thinking about our estate in our younger years . . . when we all think we're invincible!

In addition, as an unincorporated small business owner, you must provide for the possibility of disability. Note that any premiums you pay to a private disability insurance plan will reap tax-free benefits should the unexpected happen. While the premiums are generally not tax-deductible, it is worth your while to insure yourself against the possibility that, for a period of time, you might not be able to run your business yourself. However, "overhead expense" insurance premiums may be deductible. (*See* IT 22.)

As previously discussed, it bears repeating that as a home-based business owner, it is also most important that you do not fall into a trap that could render the gains in your principal residence at least partially taxable. Do not claim Capital Cost Allowance on the undepreciated capital cost of your home. This will make the portion of capital gains attributable to your home office, subject to capital gains tax.

Finally, you will see in the following discussion, it is net profit, not gross revenues that is subject to tax. Should you earn dividends or capital gains income, you will be taxed personally, at special tax rates.

2. Effective Tax Rates (Approximate) (Table 2-2)

Except in Quebec, provincial taxes are based on a percentage of Basic Federal Tax, and these are collected on behalf of the provinces by Revenue Canada. There have been a variety of provincial tax changes over the years, and the table below reflects average federal/provincial tax rates within the past several years. Check with your tax advisor for the most current rates.

TABLE 2-2
EFFECTIVE TAX RATES (APPROXIMATE)

	Tax Rates	
INCOME LEVEL	AVERAGE FEDERAL	AVERAGE FEDERAL & PROVINCIAL
$ 0 to $ 6,456*	0%	0%
$ 6,457 to $29,590	17%	27%
$29,591 to $59,180	26%	42%
over $59,180	29%	50%+

*The Basic Personal Amount or "Tax-free Zone" everyone is entitled to is $6,456. However, some taxpayers will have a higher tax-free zone, depending on the amount of their total non-refundable credits, such as the Age Amount, Medical Expenses, Charitable Donations, and so on, found on page 3 of the Income Tax Return. (*See* Appendix 5.)

The taxes you will pay on your personal income are computed on "Schedule 1" of the "T1 General Return," an example of which is shown in Appendix 8. It is important to know at what point you will pay more tax, and to plan your income accordingly.

For example, if you pay your child to work in your home-based business, you should know that any earnings under the basic personal amount of $6,456 will be tax-free. If you pay your mother to babysit your children while you work, she will not be subject to tax if her income is under $6,457 (or, if she is a senior, up to $9,938 if she qualifies for the full Age Amount).

Should your taxable income hover around $30,000, an RRSP contribution may bring you back down into the 27% tax bracket. If your taxable income is in the $60,000 and up range, every new dollar you earn may cost you approximately 50 cents in taxes payable. Likewise, the meticulous keeping of receipts for every business expenditure may reap you tax savings of approximately 50 cents on the dollar. Obviously, at this level of income, scanty recordkeeping can be very expensive.

In fact, you should always be asking yourself whether there is a business purpose — an income producing activity — in every activity you undertake. For example, if your daughter has a tennis tournament in Montreal, can you write some business there in order to deduct at least a portion of the cost of the trip against business earnings? Or, if you are an artist or writer, consider whether there is a story or picture that can be produced from your last visit to the wilderness. If you can justify an income-producing purpose, a portion of your costs may be deductible. As mentioned earlier, it is important is to keep your Business Diary active on all excursions, because for most business people, the potential for earning income is as close as their next networking experience. If you can justify your deduction with your events summaries and personal-use allocation, you'll end up with more after-tax dollars in your pocket . . . legitimately.

. . . for most business people, the potential for earning income is as close as their next networking experience . . .

3. Your Marginal Tax Rates (Table 2-3)

While Table 2-2 illustrates the different tax rates you will pay at different income levels, Table 2-3 shows three income levels and the corresponding tax you will pay on the next dollar of income you make at each level.

You will see that in general, dividend and capital gains earnings are taxed more favorably than employment, pension, interest or net self-employment. However, because your home-based business income is taxed on a "net" basis, every legitimate expense you report will save you approximately 27¢, 42¢ or 50¢ on the dollar spent, depending on your tax bracket.

Dividends represent the distribution of after-tax profits of a corporation. In other words, because the corporation has already paid tax before the dividend is issued to the shareholders, the personal tax system will take this into

TABLE 2-3
APPROXIMATE MARGINAL TAX RATES (AVERAGE FEDERAL AND PROVINCIAL) 1992–1996*

Salary, Pension and Interest — 50%
42%
27%
Capital Gains — 35%
31%
21%
32%
Dividends
26%
8%

$15,000 $32,000 $65,000

*Subject to change, consult with your tax professional.

account . . . thereby allowing for special tax treatment on the "T1 General Return".

Capital gains — that is the increase in value of an income-producing asset over time — accrue tax-free until disposal . . . which can be in the form of a sale or transfer, or upon the deemed disposition at "fair market value" on death or emigration. If you own shares in a small business corporation that meets the eligibility criteria of the Capital Gains Deduction, on the first $500,000 of gains, subsequent dispositions could be tax-free. More about this later.

Basic Income and Expense Matching Rules

Because of the advantages of staying within a lower tax bracket, it is important for you to make tax-oriented decisions about when to spend money in your business. Often, people have a question about the "matching" of income and expenses. They need to know when expenses are claimable against income earned.

In general, income is reportable when "earned" and expenses are deductible when "incurred," within a fiscal period that ends on December 31 of the tax year. (*See* "Choosing a Fiscal Year-End," later in this chapter.)

In a recent court case (*Canderel,* Federal Court of Appeal) it was ruled that when expenses can be matched to income, they must be matched, to most accurately present the profit of the business, upon which the taxpayer is taxed. When in doubt, the guiding principle is that the method of computation that provides the truer picture of profit, will be the one that is acceptable for tax purposes.

> *. . . the . . . computation that provides the truer picture of profit, will be the one that is acceptable for tax purposes . . .*

However, in the case of "running expenses" — those that cannot be traced to specific income sources, but are necessary on a recurring basis to produce income from the business — amounts will be deductible when they are incurred.

Example

> *Matthew operates a typesetting business from his home, which is rented. He prepaid his rent to the end of the year and then gave another prepayment for January of the new year. In addition, he ordered all of his paper and toner supplies for next year in December, as he was able to get an incredibly good price from a printer who was closing shop. Finally, he prepaid the January salary of his assistant, Maggie, as a special before-Christmas bonus.*

In this case, his rent payment and the amounts paid to his assistant must be matched to income. Therefore, he would not be able to take the deductions when paid; rather he would have to claim the expenditures as they are used up in the business next year. However, because the supply items are "running expenses" of the business, he can claim the expenses against this year's income, even though they will be primarily used up next year.

When in doubt, contact your tax professional. It is important for you to have a relationship with a professional who is available to give you help in income classification questions, throughout the year. In that way, you can influence the size of your tax bill, with the timing of your business decisions.

THERE'S MORE THAN ONE WAY TO CALCULATE YOUR TAX

Now that you know how different income sources are taxed in Canada, it is just as important for you to understand that a tax return can be prepared in many different ways — each one mathematically valid, and each one acceptable to Revenue Canada. The key is to prepare personal and family returns correctly . . . and to your best tax benefit — both for this year, and the foreseeable future. This is where a relationship with a knowledgeable tax preparer with good communication skills can really pay off in the long run.

Let's take a look at a real life example, using fictious names and numbers, to illustrate this point.

Case Study #4

GLORIA AND HELMUT CALCULATE WISELY

Gloria Hewitt and her husband Helmut Schmidt have been together for several years. Last year they started their own home-based business after they both had the misfortune of losing their jobs in a printing company where they originally met. The company was forced to close its doors during the latter half of 1994.

Gloria decided to venture out and start her own consulting business when both of their Employment Insurance benefits ran out. This happened in mid-1995. Helmut continues to look for other work, but helps Gloria on a part-time basis to do the books for the business and answer the telephone. He is paid hourly for this work.

Gloria spends her time recruiting business from clients who need to have printing, typesetting and mailing work done. She then takes the work to other printers in town, who pay her a commission for bringing the jobs to them. In this way, she acts as a broker for the printing firm with the best quality and price.

In 1995, her first year of business, Gloria reported an operating loss from her business of $7,500 on her income tax return. This was primarily due to the advertising and auto expenses that she incurred networking with potential clients.

In 1996, working the full year on her business, she started to reap rewards. Her gross earnings were $26,350, after cost of goods sold, and after all other expenses, including the $4,500 she paid Helmut, she had a net income from the business of $6,067.

Looking back at last year's return, there are a few carry-forward provisions we need to take note of:

1. Gloria had made a $1,000 RRSP contribution in the first 60 days of 1996, which she did not need to take on her 1995 income tax return because of her business loss. Based on her 1996 results and her previous RRSP room, she has total RRSP room of $5,682 she can use sometime in the future.

2. Gloria did not claim the $1,500 of deductible home-office expenses on her return, because of the loss in 1995. However this was an error in filing. The home-office expenses should still have been calculated and scheduled, because they can be carried forward and claimed in a future year in which there is plenty of net income. An adjustment request should be filed with Revenue Canada to make this addition to Gloria's tax records for 1995. (*See* Appendix 2.)

Because Helmut's net income was only $4,500, a partial Spousal Amount can be claimed by Gloria on her return. The result is that Gloria and Helmut have no tax liability, but they do have to make a small Canada Pension Plan contribution based on their net earnings from the business. However, this will be completely offset by their GST Credit of $398 which will be forwarded to them quarterly, starting in July. Table 2-4 is an overview of their current tax position.

So, in 1996, Gloria and Helmut were ahead of the tax game. They contributed to the Canada Pension Plan, which in general is good, if you believe you'll be able to collect from this plan sometime in your future.

They wisely saved the $1,000 RRSP contribution Gloria previously made in February 1996 as an "undeducted contribution" for use in 1997, as they didn't need it to reduce their net income any further. (There may be some benefits in the size of refundable provincial and federal tax credits by reducing net income, but Gloria would get a better return on her RRSP contribution if she carried it forward for use against taxable income sources in the future.) Gloria also preserved the $7,500 non-capital loss from 1995 for use in a subsequent year, as it was not needed this year. (Non-capital or business losses can be carried forward up to seven tax years).

TABLE 2-4
GLORIA AND HELMUT'S 1996 TAX POSITION

DESCRIPTION	AMOUNT
Gross Income from the Business	$26,350.00
Expenses before Capital Cost Allowance	$13,125.00
Income before Auto Expenses	$13,225.00
Auto Expenses	$ 4,158.00
Income After Auto Expenses	$ 9,066.00
Home-Office Expenses	$ 3,000.00
Income after Office Expenses	$ 6,067.00
CPP Payable	$ 143.75
Total Non Refundable Amounts	$ 8,018.00
Total Payable Gloria	$ 143.72
Helmut (CPP)	$ 56.00
Total Family Liability	$ 199.72
Refundable Federal Credits: GSTC	$ 398.00

In 1997, Gloria's business grew again. Her gross income was $35,000. She was now required to register to collect GST on her sales. (For more information, *see* Chapter Three.) After cost of goods sold and the $5,000 she paid Helmut, who is still otherwise unemployed, the net income from her business is projected to be $14,093. However, she has not yet added her home-office expenses to this figure. She has, at her disposal, unused RRSP room of $5,682, and still is carrying forward her undeducted RRSP contribution of $1,000. In addition, she is thinking of buying a new computer before year-end (cost $2,335) so that Helmut can learn to do the books on it. Their 1997 tax position is shown in Table 2-5.

There are now several questions for Gloria to ask of her tax preparer, given that her total non-refundable tax credits will be about $7,778.

TABLE 2-5
GLORIA AND HELMUT'S 1997 TAX POSITION

DESCRIPTION	AMOUNT
Gross Income from the Business	$35,000
Income After Cost of Goods Sold	$28,210
Expenses before Capital Cost Allowance	$10,625.00
Capital Cost Allowance from Computer	$ 350.00
Income before Auto Expenses	$17,235.00
Auto Expenses	$ 3,492.00
Income After Auto Expenses	$13,743.00
Home-Office Expenses	$ 3,029.00
(includes carry-overs from prior years)	
Income after Office Expenses	$10,714.00
CPP Payable	$ 404.00
Total Non-Refundable Amounts	$ 7,778.00
(Basic Personal and Spousal Amounts)	

First, how much of an RRSP contribution should she take? If she contributes another $4,682 to maximize her opportunities to top up her RRSP room, her taxable income will come down to only $5,032.07. Given that her total non-refundable tax credits are $7,778 (her basic amount of $6,456; her Spousal Amount of $918 and her CPP contributions of $404), she is wasting $2,746 of her RRSP contribution ($7,778 − $5,032).

The optimum RRSP deduction in this case would be $2,936, which brings her net income down to $7,778; which is fully offset by her non-refundable tax credits, with the result that no taxes are payable and $2,746 of her RRSP contribution can be carried forward for use next year. Both parties would have a small CPP liability.

There are other ways this return could be correctly done. For example:

1. Gloria could choose not to take any capital cost allowance on her computer purchase or her automobile, preserving these deductions for future use. However, this would increase the net profits from her business and cause a bigger liability to the Canada Pension Plan. She would end up paying more into the plan now. Is this a good option if Gloria wishes to maximize her RRSP instead or invest that extra money into her business?

2. Gloria could choose to deduct only the $1,000 she previously contributed to her RRSP. If she finds herself in a situation where she cannot make any more contributions to an RRSP at this time, she can use a portion of her unused non-capital loss from 1995 to offset her income to come to the same results. Her unused RRSP room is preserved and she'll be able to take her RRSP deduction sometime in the future. This is a good option, if cash is tight now.

3. Helmut could make an RRSP contribution, which would increase the Spousal Amount Gloria can claim for him. If this happened, the optimum RRSP contribution would again be recalculated and reduced, again preserving more room for future years on Gloria's return.

As you can see, there are several ways to calculate this couple's returns — all legitimate and correct — but differing only as to the best tax advantages now and in the future. As a home-based business owner, it is most important that you now start looking at your tax-filing options over several tax years . . . never just the current one.

> *. . . it is most important that you now start looking at your tax-filing options over several tax years . . .*

FINANCING YOUR BUSINESS WITH START-UP LOSSES

In the previous story, it was evident that "forward planning" could save the taxpayer thousands of dollars in the taxes she would pay in the future. In certain cases, "backward planning" is just as lucrative. The following story illustrates how you can use your tax planning options to actually reach back and recover taxes you may have paid in the past.

Case Study #5

TOM O'BRIAN'S CARRY-BACK STRATEGY

In October of 1994 Tom O' Brian lost his executive position with a private company. That year, his taxable income was $68,000. In 1995, he started his own business, and incurred a non-capital loss of $13,000; $10,000 of which was left over after application to other income sources of the year.

With this excess $10,000, Tom has some tax planning opportunities. In 1996, he finds that he will break even in his business, so he really has no reason to use the loss this year. He is projecting a net income of $25,000 from his business in 1997, so it is possible to carry forward and utilize some of his loss to reduce income then.

However, because he will be in a tax bracket of only 27% in 1997, and because he was in a tax bracket of close to 50% in 1994, it makes more sense for Tom to carry back his loss to 1994. He can do this by requesting an adjustment to his 1994 income tax return and submitting a "Loss Carry Back Form" ("T1A"). A sample of this request follows.

The $10,000 loss will be applied to the 1994 tax return on "Line 253" and will reduce taxes payable by approximately $4,500. Revenue Canada will process this claim for the carry-back request and forward the overpaid taxes to Tom. Great news!

Now, what to do with the $4,500 of newly found money? Tom could pay down a bank loan, pay off his credit cards or other expensive non-deductible amounts. Or, he could put the $4,500 into his RRSP for use to offset the projected $25,000 net income in 1997. At a marginal tax rate of 27%, that $4,500 contribution could save Tom a further $1,200 on his tax liability for 1997.

Get the picture? A knowledge of your marginal tax rate, together with meticulous keeping of carry-over provisions from one tax year to the next will substantially reduce the taxes you pay over the long run.

In another example, let's assume the taxpayer, perhaps a homemaker, has not worked over the past several years, but now wishes to start a home-based business that generates a first-year operating loss. The loss carry-back provisions will not do this taxpayer much good, as she was not taxable in the past. However, business losses can be carried forward for up to seven years. So, should this taxpayer have a profitable tax report within this period, her prior year losses can reduce or eliminate her future tax burdens. Because of the time limit on the use of non-capital losses, it is best to try to use them up as quickly as possible.

Example

> *Susan manufactures and sells Christmas wreaths. In her first year she incurred an operating loss of $15,000. In her second year she had a profit of $14,000. Her operating loss could be used to offset her second-year profit, so Susan did not have to pay taxes on her profits that year. In addition, she could carry forward the excess loss for use as a deduction against her net income on next year's return.*

Here are some simple tax calculations (Table 2-6, Table 2-7, Table 2-8, and Table 2-9) that can help you to figure out the real returns on your business decisions:

TABLE 2-6
COMPUTING AFTER-TAX YIELD ON YOUR INVESTMENTS

Formula:

Current Investment Yield $\times$ (1 $-$ Your Marginal Tax Rate) = After-Tax Yield

Let's say:
  Your Current Investment Yield is 6%, and
  Your Marginal Tax Rate is 42%.

Then:
  6% $\times$ (1 $-$ .42) = After-Tax Yield
      1 $-$ .42 = .58
      6% $\times$ .58 = .0348

Your After-Tax Yield is .0348.

TABLE 2-7
COMPUTING BEFORE-TAX YIELD NEEDED ON
YOUR INVESTMENTS

Formula:

$$\text{Current Investment Yield} \div (1 - \text{Marginal Tax Rate}) = \frac{\text{Before-Tax Yield}}{\text{Needed}}$$

Let's say:
  Your Current Investment Yield is 6%, and
  Your Marginal Tax Rate is 42%.

Then:

$$\frac{.06}{(1 - .42)} = \frac{.06}{.58} = 10.35\%$$

Your Before-Tax Yield Needed is 10.35% for a true after-tax return of 6%.

TABLE 2-8
COMPUTING AN AFTER-TAX, REAL RATE OF RETURN TO
TAKE INTO ACCOUNT BOTH TAXES AND INFLATION

Formula:

$$\left(\begin{array}{c}\text{Rate of} \\ \text{Return}\end{array} + \begin{array}{c}\text{Expected Rate} \\ \text{of Inflation}\end{array}\right) \div \left(1 - \begin{array}{c}\text{Marginal} \\ \text{Tax Rate}\end{array}\right) = \begin{array}{c}\text{Rate of Return needed for} \\ \text{a true 6\% return after} \\ \text{taxes and inflation}\end{array}$$

Let's say:
  Your Rate of Return is 6%,
  Your Marginal Tax Rate is 42%, and
  The Expected Rate of Inflation is 2.5%.

Then:

$$\frac{(6\% + 2.5\%)}{(1 - .42)} = \frac{8.50\%}{.58} = 14.6552\%$$

The Rate of Return needed for a true 6% return after taxes and inflation is
14.6552%.

TABLE 2-9
COMPUTING THE BREAK-EVEN POINT AFTER TAXES AND INFLATION*

> Formula:
>   Expected inflation rate ÷ (1 − Marginal Tax Rate) = Rate of Return Needed
>
> Let's say:
>   The Expected Rate of Inflation is 2.5%, and
>   Your Marginal Tax Rate is 42%.
>
> Then:
> $$\frac{2.50\%}{(1 - .42)} = \frac{2.50\%}{0.58\%} = 4.31\%$$
>
> The Rate of Return Needed is 4.31%.

. . . with a good basic knowledge of your marginal tax position and . . . tax provisions . . . , you will be able to maximize your tax position . . .

Finally, following is a list of some carry-forward provisions you should keep track of each and every tax year, to maximize your tax planning opportunities. Armed with a good basic knowledge of your marginal tax position and the tax provisions you can tap into from year to year, you will be able to maximize your tax position as you weather the ups and downs of the business cycle.

TABLE 2-10
UNUSED CARRY-OVER PROVISIONS

> 1. Unused home-office expenses since 1988
> 2. Unused non-capital losses of prior years
> 3. Unused net capital losses of prior years
> 4. Capital Gains Deductions previously used
> 5. Cumulative Net Investment Loss balances
> 6. RRSP Contribution Room
> 7. Previously reported interest on compounding GICs and bonds
> 8. Unused charitable donations of the previous five years
> 9. Unused medical expenses of the immediately preceding year
> 10. Unused moving expenses of the immediately preceding year
> 11. Paid but unclaimed maintenance payments for up to one year before a written agreement or court order
> 12. Unused Business Investment Losses
> 13. Any Undepreciated Capital Cost Balances

*Thanks to Professor Larry A. Wood, Faculty of Management, University of Calgary, for his assistance with these calculations.

PROPRIETORSHIP OR INCORPORATION?

One of the first questions you will have to answer when you open your home-based business is: What kind of business organization should this be?

You could choose to open a sole-proprietorship (the terms self-employed or unincorporated small business would denote the same thing). Or, you could go into partnership with a family member or an unrelated party. Finally, you could incorporate your business.

What are the advantages and disadvantages of each from a tax point of view?

Proprietorships

A proprietorship is an unincorporated business that is owned by one person. That person's net profit or loss, which is arrived at by subtracting operating expenses from the revenues generated, is reported on the personal income tax return.

In the case of a proprietorship, there are a number of attractive advantages. Let's have a look at some of them.

SIMPLICITY

For a proprietorship, only one tax return — the "T1 General" — needs to be filed. The details of the income and expenses are recorded on "Form T2124" — "Statement of Business Activities". The net profits or losses are then transferred to the tax return on "Lines 135 to 143" (*See* "Form T2124" in Appendix 4 and the "T1 General" in Appendix 5.) Professionals who are sole-proprietors would use "Form T2032".

APPLICATION OF LOSSES

These will be deductible against other income of the current year, or they can be carried back to offset personal income over the past three years or up to seven years into the future. For this reason it is often best, from a tax point of view, to bear losses of start-up companies in a proprietorship, rather than a corporation.

RRSP ROOM

Eighteen percent (18%) of earned income of the business (of the previous year) qualifies for the purposes of making RRSP contributions for your future pension income. Note that maximum RRSP contributions are reached when your earned income reaches $75,000 (until 2003 under current budget proposals).

CPP CONTRIBUTIONS

A portion of net income may be used to calculate premiums that can be contributed to the Canada Pension Plan (both employer and employee shares must be submitted)

DRAWS

> *. . . money drawn out of the business by the owner is not taxed again as employment income . . .*

Since you are taxed on the net profits of the business, money drawn out of the business by the owner is not taxed again as employment income.

Example

Toby has started a home-based painting and decorating business. During the past year, gross earnings were $50,000 and net profits, after all operating expenses were calculated, amounted to $24,561. This figure was reported on the income tax return as net income from the business. During the year, Toby drew $2,000 a month out of the business earnings to pay for living expenses.

Toby must only report the net profit of the business ($24,561); he does not have to report the draws amounting to $24,000.

Toby's profits of $24,561 are added to his other income of the year. If there is no other income, Toby's liability for federal, provincial and Canada Pension Plan obligations can be expected to be approximately $6,100*. This will put Toby into an "instalment profile," which means that he will have to start remitting income tax payments to Revenue Canada throughout the year.

Tax Remittance Frequencies

As an individual, you may avoid remitting tax to Revenue Canada during the year if your taxes owing are less than $2,000. This would happen in the case of a single person, for example, when taxable income from the business is approximately $12,500*. If it's over this, at least one-quarter of last year's tax liability must be remitted on each of March 15, June 15, September 15 and December 15, to avoid additional interest charges.

The income tax return for a sole-proprietor and his or her spouse must be filed by June 15. If the amount of taxes owing exceeds $2,000 in both the current year and either of the two preceding years, quarterly instalment payments will have to be remitted. (*See* "Get Ready to Make Instalment Payments," later in this chapter.)

A sole-proprietor may voluntarily register to collect and remit GST. However, you are required to register when your gross sales exceed $30,000. (*See* Chapter Three.)

---

*Provincial rates subject to variation.

Partnerships

A partnership is a form of business organization where two or more people own the business and share in its profits and losses according to a partnership agreement. This topic will be discussed in more detail in Chapter Seven. Briefly, the revenues of the partnership are reduced by the operating expenses and the net profit or loss is then reported by each partner.

Example

Marissa and Louise own Campy Swap Shop, which they run out of Louise's home. It is a 50-50 partnership. At the end of the current year, the revenues of the business were $85,000, the operating expenses $30,000 and the net profit was $55,000. One-half of this ($27,500) is reported as income by each individual on their "T1 General Return".

However, this net income from the partnership can be further reduced by certain expenses that an individual partner may incur personally. These could be, for example, automobile or home-office expenses. Or, certain adjustments may be required when there is personal-use consumption of inventory of the partnership or drawing of revenues out of the partnership.

Example

Louise uses her own car in pursuing the various business activities of the Campy Swap Shop. From her share of the partnership income of $27,500, she will claim the business portion of the auto expenses and the business portion of the workspace in the home expenses. Therefore, her net income for tax purposes will be lower than Marissa's.

In addition, provided that the partnership is a GST Registrant, Louise could also claim a GST rebate on any GST paid on her business-related expenses. This is done on "Form GST-370". (*See* Appendix 9.) This is a refund of the business portion of GST paid by the individual partner on deductible expenses not normally recoverable under the GST Input Tax Credit system. (*See* "Understanding Your Obligations Under the GST," in Chapter Three.) The rebate is shown as a credit on the tax return on "Line 457".

. . . individual partnerships are like proprietorships when it comes to unlimited liability . . .

Individual partnerships are like proprietorships when it comes to unlimited liability. That is, should the business falter, each partner is personally liable for all the business debts.

When to Incorporate

As mentioned, it often makes sense to start your home-based business as a proprietorship, unless there are liability issues. It is important for you to speak to a lawyer about liability before you begin. Because a sole-proprietor or partner is responsible personally for all debts of the business, business failure or lawsuits resulting from the activities of the business must be paid for through the personal assets of the owner. It is for this reason, and the fact that certain small businesses qualify for advantageous tax positions once income starts flowing, that business owners often incorporate.

When a business is incorporated, it becomes a separate legal entity or "person" that must file an income tax return on its own. This is done on a "T2" Form. There are many similarities in the way net income from a business is computed for a corporation when compared to an unincorporated venture. There are also some significant tax advantages, including the $500,000 Capital Gains Exemption, currently available on the increase in value of a share that is an individual's qualifying small business corporation share. To qualify, all or substantially all of the assets of the corporation must be used in an active business in Canada.

Active business income of a corporation, does not include income that is "property," or income from investments. Should your corporation receive most of its income from interest, dividends, rents or royalties, it is considered to be a "specified investment business". This has implications on the level of taxation paid now and in the future on the sale of the assets of the corporation. A specified investment business can be considered to be an active business if it employs more than five full-time employees throughout the year.

A corporation that earns income from an active business is generally subject to a top combined federal and provincial marginal tax rate of about 47%. This is roughly equal to the top marginal tax rate for individuals in many provinces.

However, if your corporation earns active business income, a federal Small Business Deduction of 16% is allowed on the first $200,000 of taxable income. Once the Small Business Deduction and reduced provincial tax rates for small business income are taken into account, the combined federal and provincial corporate tax rate for a Small Canadian Controlled Private Corporation falls to about 20%. See Table 2-11 below.

Therefore, especially for those proprietorships whose taxable incomes exceed $59,180, incorporation can make sense, to minimize high personal tax rates on taxable income between $59,181 and $200,000. The challenge is how to withdraw money from your corporation and put it into your hands personally. You may choose to take a repayable shareholder's loan, salary, bonus,

TABLE 2-11
TAX RATES FOR SMALL BUSINESS CORPORATIONS: COMBINED FEDERAL AND PROVINCIAL RATES*

PROVINCE OR TERRITORY	NON-MANUFACTURING OR MANUFACTURING INCOME	OTHER CORPORATIONS (OVER $200,000 TAXABLE)	
		MANFACTURING	NON-MFG.
BC	22.1%	38.6%	45.65
AB	19.1%	36.6%	44.6%
SK	21.1%	39.1%	46.1%
MB	22.1%	39.1%	46.1%
ON	22.6%	35.6%	44.6%
PQ	18.9%	31.0%	38.0%
NB	20.1%	39.1%	46.1%
NS	18.1%	38.1%	45.1%
PEI	20.6%	29.6%	44.1%
NF	18.1%	27.1%	43.1%
YT	15.6%	24.6%	44.1%
NWT	18.1%	36.1%	43.1%

*Effective January 1, 1996

dividends, or sell shares, all of which can have implications on your personal tax return.

> *. . . you may pay yourself as an employee of your own corporation . . .*

To put income into your hands personally, for example, you may pay yourself as an employee of your own corporation. In such a case, you would deduct Canada Pension Plan premiums but not Employment Insurance (unless you own less than 40% of the shares of the company). In addition, you would deduct and remit income taxes, usually on a monthly basis, according to your personal tax rates. To maximize your RRSP room ($13,500 maximum from 1996–2003, under current rules), you should try to pay yourself at least $75,000 a year in salary.

You might consider certain taxable or tax-free benefits in your compensation package. These might include:

Taxable Benefits

- board and lodging at "fair market value";
- rent-free and low-rent housing;
- travel benefits for employee or his or her family;
- personal use of employer's motor vehicle;
- gifts that exceed $100;

- value of holidays, prizes and other awards;
- Frequent-Flyer Program points used for personal use;
- travelling expenses of employee's spouse unless he or she was also engaged in the business of the employer;
- premiums under a provincial hospital plan;
- tuition fees paid by employer, unless the course is taken on the employer's time, for the benefit of the employer;
- reimbursement of cost of tools;
- interest-free and low-interest loans (Note: Benefits of low-interest loans made to enable an employee to buy treasury shares of a corporation are excluded from income.);
- financial counselling and income-tax preparation services; and
- group sickness or accident insurance plans or group life insurance

(Note: Reimbursements of supplementary business insurance, parking or ferry/toll charges are not considered to be taxable benefits to the employee.)

Tax-Free Benefits

- board and lodging at a remote work site;
- wedding or Christmas gifts that do not exceed $100 and are not deducted by employer, to a maximum of one gift per year (two, in cases where the employee marries);
- discounts on merchandise;
- subsidized meals;
- uniforms, special clothing and their dry-cleaning costs;
- subsidized school services in remote areas;
- transportation to a special work site, or for security or other reasons;
- recreational facilities, including social or athletic club memberships;
- moving expenses if the move was required by the employer;
- premiums paid under private health services plans;
- employer's required contribution to provincial health and medical plans;
- transportation passes (if not paying less than 50% of fares on space-confirmed basis) or the full amount of bus and rail passes. Passes used by retired employees are not taxable;
- employee counselling services for mental or physical health or re-employment or retirement;
- transportation to and from work (including costs of parking near the work location) of blind or severely impaired employees;

- employer-paid costs for an attendant to assist an employee with a severe and prolonged mental or physical impairment in the performance of his or her duties; and

- employer-paid reasonable allowances to cover away-from-home education of the employee's child, if the child is in full-time attendance at a school not farther away than the nearest community where the employee is required to work.

Once you have determined your own compensation package, it is possible to take additional money out of your company if there are after-tax profits.

Take a Shareholder's Loan

. . . you may borrow money from your company . . .

You may borrow money from your company. A shareholder's loan must be repaid within one year of the end of the tax year in which it was made or the amounts are added to your income. Imputed interest charges must be calculated based on the prescribed rate of interest (*See* Table 2-12) and included as a taxable benefit to the shareholder. (The one year repayment referral could be jeopardized in cases where a series of loans or repayments is made.)

However, changes announced by the Department of Finance in April 1995 will allow loans made to shareholders who are also employees to be considered exempt from income inclusion if the loans were made because of the employment conditions (*i.e.,* a loan to acquire a company car), and bona fide repayments were arranged. Speak to your tax advisor about the planning opportunities.

TABLE 2-12
PRESCRIBED INTEREST RATES

PERIOD (1996)	ON TAX REFUNDS	ON OVERDUE TAX, INSTALLMENTS, SOURCE DEDUCTIONS, ETC.	DEEMED INTEREST ON EMPLOYEE/ SHAREHOLDERS LOANS
JAN TO MAR	9%	11%	7%
APR TO JUNE	8%	10%	6%
JULY TO SEPT	7%	9%	5%
OCT TO DEC	7%	9%	5%

Take Dividends

As a shareholder of your own company you may pay yourself dividends, which are the after-tax distribution of profits in the company. Let's say, for example, that your company pays corporate taxes of 20% on your profits of $100,000. That's $20,000, leaving $80,000 in after-tax profits that could be either retained within the company for expansion and growth or distributed out to the shareholders.

If you are already taking a salary of $75,000 out of your company, you might consider declaring a dividend for some of the after-tax profits. To take dividends into income personally, the actual amounts received must be grossed up by 25% to first put them on a pre-tax basis. Then, a dividend tax credit of 13.33% of the grossed up amounts is allowed. This is found on "Schedule 1," "Line 502". (*See* Appendix 8.) The result of these calculations on your personal return is that the dividends you take are taxed at a top personal tax rate of about 32% depending on where you live. When you add the tax you paid within the corporation on these earnings (about 20%), the combined tax on the corporate profits you take personally could be about 52%. Is this better in your province, than simply taking an employment bonus?

If not, you may wish to simply take profits out of your company as an employee performance bonus. This bonus is deductible to the company as a salary/wage expense. The company must remit the source deductions for income taxes on this bonus on your behalf, and the bonus treatment may help the company stay within the $200,000 threshold for taxation under the small business rules. You will usually end up with only half of the amount in your own pocket, depending on your personal marginal tax rate. However, this still may be a few percentage points better for you, than taking dividends. Speak to your tax professional about the best strategy in your particular case.

Dividends can also be paid to certain family members who are shareholders. These family members may not otherwise have a taxable income. For example, taxpayers may receive dividends of up to $20,000 or more in some provinces before they pay a personal tax liability. In those cases, income is distributed within the family for the price of the corporate tax rate only.

Example

> *Mallory Family Corporation paid dividends of $22,800 each to Tara and Jenna Mallory, shareholders in the firm. These dividends are distributed after the corporation pays tax of 20% on the profits.*

On their personal returns, the dividends received are grossed up to $28,500 ($22,800 × 1.25). The federal taxes payable on this amount are $4,845. An offsetting dividend tax credit of $3,800 is allowed and together with the federal credit resulting from the basic personal amount (17% of $6,456 = $1,097.52), taxes on the dividends are nil. (Credits are $3,800 + $1,097.52 = $4,897.52.)

This means the Mallory girls were able to receive $22,800 in after-tax corporate distributions and pay nothing more personally to receive this money.

(Note: In provinces that have a net income tax, such as Manitoba, a small tax liability would have resulted from this transaction.)

Capital Gains

▶ *. . . it is not uncommon to issue one share, usually for a dollar . . .*

Earlier in this chapter we discussed the concept of wealth creation through the building of equity within your business. When you start a Small Business Corporation, it is not uncommon to issue one share, usually for a dollar.

When you sell your company down the road, someone may give you $500,000 for your share. (Wouldn't that be great?) Should that happen, your capital gain of $499,999 would be received virtually tax-free under rules in effect at the time of writing. This is because you would still qualify for the $500,000 Capital Gains Deduction on Qualifying Small Business Corporations.

It is important to note that each individual taxpayer qualifies for their own $500,000 Capital Gains Deduction once in a lifetime. This means if you have a company whose resale value is projected to be $2 million, and the shares are held equally by four family members, the entire disposition of the company might be received on a tax-free basis by the family unit as a whole.

You may wish to transfer some shares to your adult children. This would normally be done at their "fair market value," which may create a tax consequence on your return. (This in turn, may be sheltered by the $500,000 Capital Gains Deduction.) Future capital appreciation will then be shared by each shareholder.

There are many other planning issues that should be discussed with a qualified tax professional. For example, it is usually best to make this type of transfer to adult children. This is because dividends paid to minor children, on property that was transferred to them by the parent, are attributed back to the parent for tax purposes, until the child turns 18. (*See* discussion of Attribution Rules on the following pages.) There may also be legal issues on the acquisition and sale of shares held by minors. Your tax professional can help you make these decisions, while keeping your plans onside with the GAAR — General Anti-Avoidance Rules — that is, your business transactions must have a bona fide business purpose, or Revenue Canada could ignore them for tax purposes.

Losses

Should your corporate activities result in operating losses, it will not be possible to distribute these losses to you personally. In other words, corporate losses cannot be applied to your personal return. They can however be carried forward for up to seven years and applied to corporate profits in that period, or carried back up to three years, in a similar manner as previously described. Many business owners are surprised to find that their corporate losses will not help them on their personal returns. For this reason the timing of incorporation could be influenced by the profitability within the business.

Example

> *In his first seven months of business, Jack Heindriks incurred an operating loss of $13,000 from his home-based carpentry business. However, from the eighth month onward it is expected that his profitability will soar, as he won a significant long-term contract with a construction company. He started to hire staff to help him build the first project, a housing development.*
>
> *Jack's tax advisor suggested that incorporation take place at the start of the eighth month. The $13,000 in losses from the proprietorship could be claimed personally to recover any taxes paid in the current year or the carry-over years.*

In the situation above, certain assets may have to be "rolled over" from the proprietorship to the corporation, which is discussed in later chapters.

This has been a very brief overview of how different business organizations are taxed in Canada. It is meant to enlighten you to various planning possibilities. You should seek additional information from your tax professional.

The decision to form a certain type of business organization need not be a permanent one. For example, you may start your home-based business as a proprietorship, taking advantage of the low overhead costs and the tax advantages of writing off your workspace-in-the-home. (For specific details, *see* "Write Off Your Home-Office Expenses," in Chapter Four.)

Once your business grows, you may make the decision to move into a commercial space which you rent or own. You may wish to incorporate at this time, as the risk factors in obtaining a lease, telephone, systems, and other such expenditures, grow. Incorporation may coincide with new income sources that flow specifically through the company while, the proprietorship within the home office is still needed to preserve existing income sources . . . and so on.

The reality is, all of these options can be easily managed to minimize your tax burden, with a solid long-term plan and an understanding of your business statements. (For more information about reading your business statements, *see* "Understanding Your Balance Sheet and Income Statements," later in this chapter.)

FAMILY MATTERS

From the previous discussions of wealth creation with your home-based business, you can probably tell that a small business owner can multiply his or her after-tax efforts several-fold, with proper tax planning. The development of a small home-based business into possibly a corporate entity over time, will allow you to split income among family members, defer taxes with the timing of income distributions or reduce taxes with income diversification, including the creation of salary, dividends and capital gains sources.

> *. . . you and your tax advisor must be aware of the Attribution Rules . . .*

To do so, you and your tax advisor must be aware of the Attribution Rules. These rules generally state that one must pay the tax on any earnings from property transferred to a spouse or minor children. However, there are exceptions to these rules which will allow you to transfer assets to your children on a legitimate basis.

Splitting Income With Spouse

You may transfer property to your spouse on a tax-free basis upon your demise, to accomplish what's known as a tax-free rollover of assets. However, if you transfer assets to your spouse during your lifetime, resulting interest, dividends or capital gains will generally be taxed back to you, unless the transfer of the assets take place at "fair market value".

Example

Sylvia owns a duplex from which she derives rental income. Should she pass away, the property could be transferred tax-free to her husband, Mark, at her adjusted cost base. (That is, the cost of the property, plus improvements) Sylvia wants to transfer one-half of the property to Mark now, though. If she does so at "fair market value," she will incur a tax consequence, and Mark will be free to report future gains on the disposal of the property on his return. If she transfers the property at its adjusted cost base without assuming the tax consequence, any resulting income or capital gains on future dispositions will be taxed back to her.

Business income and/or losses, however, can be shared, as it is possible to avoid attribution on income/losses earned on a business given to a spouse. Here are ways to transfer assets to the spouse, in a tax-wise manner:

1. Gifts, including money to buy consumer goods, pay for education or other non-income-producing activities will not generate a tax consequence.

2. Gifts of capital assets to the spouse will not attract a tax consequence until disposition of the asset. Capital gains that result from the disposition will be taxed in the hands of the transferor.

3. The financing of your spouse's business venture will not attract tax consequences in the hands of the transferor. Rather, the spouse will report income and expenses.

4. Any salary that you pay to your spouse out of your own business venture is a legitimate tax deduction to you (and income to your spouse) if certain criteria are met:

    a. the amounts were paid for work that was actually done by the spouse,

    b. the amounts paid were reasonable and similar to what you would have paid a stranger to do the same work,

    c. an employment contract will help you verify the employer-employee relationship should your spouse ever wish to collect Employment Insurance, and

    d. a "T4 Slip" must be issued for the remuneration paid to family members if over $500 a year.

5. You may transfer assets to your spouse and avoid the attribution rules on interest, dividends or capital gains if you set up a bona fide business loan, with interest payable at prescribed rates no later than January 31.

6. You may contribute to a Spousal RRSP; that is, make your RRSP contribution in the name of your spouse. You will still get the RRSP deduction (if you have RRSP "Room"), but your spouse is the annuitant of the plan. If the money is kept in the Spousal RRSP for at least three years from the last spousal contribution, resulting withdrawals are taxed in the spouse's hands. As your business grows, it is important that retirement income be equalized in order to minimize the tax you pay as a family down the road.

7. Wherever possible, after RRSP contributions have been maximized, have your lower income-earning spouse invest income sources that can be attributed directly to him or her: inheritances, windfalls such as lottery winnings, Child Tax Benefit payments, Goods and Services Tax Credit Payments or any salary or wages earned from your business or other part-time employment activities. Interest, dividends or capital gains that are earned on such services, outside the RRSP will then be taxed to your spouse.

Splitting Income With Your Child

. . . resulting capital gains on the disposition of assets transferred to a child will be taxed in the hands of the child . . .

While interest, dividends and capital gains earned on property transferred to your spouse will be attributed back and taxed in your hands, there is one important exception to these attribution rules when it comes to money transferred to a minor child. That is, the resulting capital gains on the disposition of assets transferred to a child will be taxed in the hands of the child and not the parent. This means that if you buy a mutual fund for your child, resulting interest and dividends will be taxed back to you, but any capital gains will be taxed in the hands of your child.

Let's have a look at some additional ways to put money into the hands of your child, tax-free:

1. You can start saving for your child's education by investing in a separate account, any money received from the Child Tax Benefit. Resulting investment earnings will also be taxed in the child's hands.

2. Pay your child for working in your business.

3. If you transferred interest or dividend income from investments to a child and were subject to tax on this income, have your child re-invest that interest or dividend income. The earnings made on the re-investment of those tranferred amounts are called "second-generation earnings" and will be taxed in the hands of the child this time.

4. Create unused contribution room to an RRSP by filing a tax return for your child who works in your business. The unused RRSP room created by the child's actively earned income, can be topped up to keep the child's net income below the Basic Personal Amount of $6,456.

Example

Last year Joan earned $5,000 working in her dad's business stuffing envelopes and mailing inventory to his clients. When she filed her tax return this year, she noticed that she had $900 in unused RRSP room, which resulted from these earnings (18% of $5,000).

This year Joan, who finishes high school in June, estimates that she will make $7,000 working for her dad. This will put her earnings over the tax-free zone of $6,456. So, by making an RRSP contribution of $900, her net income will drop to $6,100 and she can avoid paying tax. In addition, because she is a university student, making the RRSP contribution will allow her dad to transfer all of her tuition and education credits to his tax return, because she is not taxable.

In fact, if dad gives Joan the $900 as a gift, resulting earnings stay inside Joan's RRSP until she withdraws it, which will likely be much past her 18th birthday. The withdrawals will be taxed to her.

5. A bona fide loan drawn up between parent and child for investment purposes will satisfy Revenue Canada's auditors that money has not been transferred from parent to child for the express purposes of avoiding tax at the parent's high marginal tax rates. Interest charged at prescribed rates must actually be paid, at least by the end of January each year to validate the loan for money outstanding during the previous 12 months.

6. A parent can hold a child's mortgage to keep wealth in the family. For example, if you buy your child's tax-free principal residence, and decide to charge only for the repayment of the principal, there are no

tax consequences. If you charge interest on the mortgage you hold, you will have to report this interest on your return.

7. Give your child the money to start his or her own business. Resulting profits are taxed to the child, not to you.

8. There is no income attribution on interest or dividends earned on money received by the child from non-resident grandparents.

UNDERSTANDING YOUR FINANCIAL STATEMENTS

Some home-based business owners enjoy recording the income and expense transactions of their activities; others learn quickly that someone will be needed to record these transactions on an ongoing basis in order for the preparation of financial statements to occur. Your financial statements — the Profit and Loss Statement and the Balance Sheet — should be prepared monthly as a summary of activities within your enterprise. For tax purposes, however, only the final summary of each is required at year-end.

> *. . . your financial statements . . . should be prepared monthly . . .*

It is not necessary for you to have formal training in accounting or bookkeeping to read your financial statements and decide whether the computation of your profit and loss is accurate. Some training will be helpful, however. You will need to spend a little time familiarizing yourself with the basic concepts in order to meet your obligations under the Income Tax Act, and to use your financial data to make important short and long-term decisions about your business activities. Consider taking a basic bookkeeping and basic tax course.

The Basic Accounting Equation

The accounting process, which ends in the preparation of the financial statements, begins with the Basic Accounting Equation:

Assets = Liabilities + Owner's Equity

This equation, expresses the results summarized in the Balance Sheet — a look at the financial position of your business as of a particular date in time. The purpose of the Income and Expense Statement, on the other hand, is to show whether the business operations are profitable. That profit or loss, as the case may be, forms a part of the Owner's Equity in the firm.

The Income and Expense Statement

Here's an example of an Income and Expense Statement, which shows the primary account categories: Assets; Liabilities; and Owner's Equity; and some typical sub-categories.

TABLE 2-13
L. OWNER'S INCOME AND EXPENSE STATEMENT

ASSETS	LIABILITIES	OWNER'S EQUITY
Short-Term Assets	**Short-Term Liabilities**	L. Owner, Capital (Start)
Cash	Accounts Payable	Net Income/Loss from
Accounts Receivable	Short-Term Notes Payable	Income and Expense
Inventory	Wages Payable	Statement
Long-Term Assets	**Long-Term Liabilities**	Less personal withdrawals
Equipment	Bank Loan Payable	Income/loss after
Building	Mortgage Payable	withdrawals
Land		L. Owner, Capital (End)
Total Assets	**Total Liabilities**	Total Equity

All transactions that happen in a business will either increase or decrease one of the primary account categories in the basic accounting equation.

To increase or decrease an account, one will either debit it or credit it. This is where most people get a little confused. Assets, the resources owned by the business, have a debit balance. This means that to increase an asset account, such as Cash, you will "debit" it.

Liabilities and Equity accounts have Credit Balances. This means to increase a Liability or Equity account you would "credit" it.

Example

Morgan started a business with $5,000 in cash. To record this transaction:

The Cash account is debited (Increased)   *$5,000*
Owner's Equity is credited (Increased)   *$5,000*

Both the Cash account and the Owner's Equity account have been increased by this transaction and the debit transaction equals the credit transaction. This is mandatory in double-entry accounting: all debits and credits must be equal for the books to balance.

Remember that the Profit and Loss from the Income Statement forms a part of the Owner's Equity, which has a credit balance. What this means, is that a net profit will increase Owner's Equity, and it will generally also increase your cash position. It may, on the other hand decrease your Liabilities if you can pay off some debt with your profits. Here's what a typical income transaction might look like in your books:

1. The firm has sales of $1,000.
   Debit Cash $1,000
   Credit Sales $1,000

   Both the cash account, which is increased by the deposit of the money, and the revenue account, which is increased by the sale, are adjusted upward.

2. The owner decides to pay an outstanding bill of $500.
   Debit Accounts Payable $ 500
   Credit Cash $ 500

   Both the cash account and the accounts payable are decreased by this transaction. The balances in the accounting equation are best summarized, then, as follows:

TABLE 2-14
YOUR BALANCE SHEET

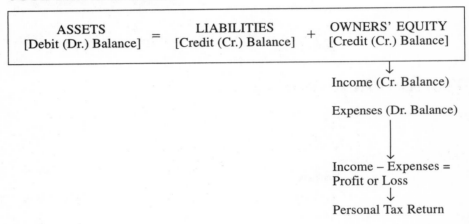

To prepare your books, follow these steps:

1. Name and number your accounts. Assets usually have 1000 series numbers, Liabilities 2000, Equity 3000, Sales or Revenues 4000 and Expenses 5000.

2. Set up a journal to record the daily transactions.

3. Transfer the journal results to a ledger, which records the cumulative balances in each separate account.

4. Prepare a Trial Balance, which is a listing of all the accounts in your business and their cumulative balance, with the debit balances on one side and the credit balances on the other. If equal, your books are usually correct, although mistakes can occur when amounts are posted in the wrong account types or numbers are transposed.

TABLE 2-15
TRIAL BALANCE FOR L. OWNER'S SCHOOL SUPPLY SHOPPE

ACCOUNTS	DEBIT	CREDIT
Cash	$1,500	
Supplies Expense	$1,000	
Auto Expense	$ 200	
Accounts Payable	—	$1,000
L. Owner, Capital	—	$1,700
Total	$2,700	$2,700

5. Prepare your Income Statement (from the totals in the ledger for all revenue accounts, and expense accounts)

6. Prepare your Balance Sheet (from the totals for all asset, liability and equity accounts).

7. Compare your financial statements to your forecasts, to last month's performance and to your predictions for the future.

Year-End Adjustments

At year-end, you will be required to make a number of adjusting entries as you close out your books in preparation for the next fiscal year. This could include the following adjustments:

1. The recording of depreciation on the assets of the business,

2. The recording of prepaid rent or other accrued expenses,

3. The recording of unearned revenues paid in advance of performance, or

4. The recording of accrued revenues (amounts have been earned but not paid).

These adjustments are generally made for accounting purposes. However, there are also adjustments required strictly for tax purposes.

Depreciation is a good example. For accounting purposes, the useful life of an asset is determined in advance (*e.g.,* 10 years, 3 years, 5 years) and then the original value of the asset is reduced in equal amounts over its useful life to account for the decline in value as it is used within the business. This is called the "straight-line method" of accounting for the "book value" of the asset.

Example

Bob buys a truck for his business, Bob's Towing. It costs him $40,000 and he expects it to have a useful life of five years. His *accountant will claim depreciation on the accounting statements of $8,000 per year to write down the value of this depreciable asset.*

For tax purposes, however, Bob will find a completely different figure on his Income and Expense Statement. That's because the decline in value of the income-producing asset, over time, qualifies as a deduction, in computing profit or loss. The calculation, for tax purposes is based on a "declining-balance method" — that is, each depreciable asset is assigned to a special Class, which has a Capital Cost Allowance (CCA) rate assigned to it.

Example

Bob's truck, is classified as a Class 10 Asset with a 30% CCA rate.

Normally, the CCA deduction, which is always taken at the taxpayer's option, would be 30% of $40,000 or $12,000. However, in the year of acquisition, the rate allowed for tax purposes falls to 50% of its normal rate (which would make the deduction in this case $6,000). This is called the "half-year rule" and is one of several restrictions that Revenue Canada makes to your tax deductions.

Other restrictions include:

1. *Meals and Entertainment:* Tax-deductible amounts allowed are 50% of expense

2. *Charitable Donations:* These must be claimed personally as a donations credit on the "T1 General Return," unless there is promotional component.

3. *Advertising in Foreign publications:* generally not deductible

4. *Costs of tax-free benefits* given to employees are generally not deductible

These and other deductions will be discussed in greater detail in later chapters.

. . . it's a good idea for every small business owner to have a basic knowledge of the accounting process . . .

It's a good idea for every small business owner to have a basic knowledge of the accounting process. Some day you might have an accountant or even a vice-president of finance working for you . . . and you will have to be sharp enough to check the work and make sure the statements and tax returns being prepared for you make sense in relation to the cash you have on hand and the commitments you know you've made.

In fact, one the biggest contrasts between an accountant and a business owner is this: in general, your accountant will be recording history . . . events that have already happened. You, the owner, on the other hand, are in the hot seat, responsible for producing future revenues. While the knowledge of what has already transpired is critical, you must put your energies into creating a successful future. To do so, make sure you have the documented history of your company's performance at hand as soon as possible.

WHEN IS IT A BUSINESS?

It is not unusual for a hobby to turn into a business. As soon as a profit motive is apparent, you are considered to be in business for yourself, and you should be keeping track of income and expenses in the formal way previously discussed.

The Income Tax Act does have a definition of what a business is, although it is rather vague. It includes a profession, calling, trade, manufacture or undertaking of any kind whatever and includes . . . "an adventure or concern in the nature of trade".

Interpretation Bulletin 459 (IT 459) states that " it is a general principle that when a person habitually does a thing that is capable of producing a profit, then he or she is carrying on a trade or business notwithstanding that these activities may be quite separate and apart from his or her ordinary occupation". (Interpretation Bulletins or ITs are published by Revenue Canada.)

It is possible and common, for example, for a taxpayer to hold a job as an employee, and then run a home-based, for-profit business. However, in these cases, if the taxpayer continuously claims business losses that offset and reduce the tax payable on the employment income, Revenue Canada may be skeptical about whether a profit motive really exists. More about this later.

You should also know, especially if you own real estate, that a person who does certain activities infrequently — even once — may be engaged in an "adventure or concern in the nature of trade". The most common situation when income is considered "business income" for tax purposes under this provision is when transactions involve the sale of real estate.

In determining whether a transaction will be considered "an adventure or concern in the nature of trade," all circumstances must be considered, but there are three principal tests:

1. A taxpayer's conduct: Has he or she dealt in the same manner as a dealer?

2. The nature of the property: Was the only purpose of acquisition a resale?

3. A taxpayer's intention: Is it to hold the property as an investment or for resale?

If the taxpayer is considered to hold real estate as inventory for resale, rather than as an investment, resulting losses are deductible as business losses and resulting profits are reported as business income.

Are You Trying to Earn Income?

A business is considered to have started when some significant activity is undertaken to be a regular part of the income-earning process. There must be a specific organizational structure. It is a good idea to separate all business and personal affairs at this time by opening a separate bank account in which to deposit business income, establish separate communication lines, and a home workspace area, if you are operating your business from your home. Should any family members help you in the business, time cards or employment contracts for employee status; or a sub-contracting agreement should be set out.

Hobby or Business?

. . . if . . . the continued losses reported from your ventures constitute a "not-for-profit" activity, such losses will not be deductible . . .

The main difference between a hobby and a business is that there is no reasonable expectation of profit from a hobby. If Revenue Canada considers that the continued losses reported from your ventures constitute a "not-for-profit" activity, such losses will not be deductible. However, any time your income from the venture exceeds expenses, the net profits will have to be reported.

Reasonable expectation of profit is discussed in detail in IT 504R for "Visual artists and writers" and can be used as a guideline for other businesses. Relevant factors in each case must be determined. For example, it is noted by Revenue Canada that a considerable period of time may need to pass before an artist or writer becomes established and profitable, and therefore a longer period of loss deductibility can be tolerated. The business owner will have to demonstrate some or all of the following activities to prove that a business does in fact exist:

a.   there is considerable time devoted to the business activities;

b.   the works of the business or artistic enterprise is actively presented for sale;

c.   the taxpayer is represented by outside third parties, such as agents, publishers, retail outlets, and so on;

d.   time and effort is spent on promoting the business;

e.   there is revenue from sales, commissions, royalties, fees, grants or other awards;

f.   the taxpayer is well qualified to pursue the business activities and continually seeks improvement and/or is recognized through honors, awards, prizes, and/or critical appraisal;

g.   there is membership in a professional association that has specific standards;

h.   there is growth in gross revenues; and/or

i.   distribution of products, or creations in not restricted.

From this list of factors, it must again be mentioned that business owners would be wise to keep a scrapbook of newspaper or other reviews of their works or establishment, a log of the activities pursued in the making of business contracts, government awards or grants, connections or other activities with the view to making sales in the future. Should Revenue Canada ever question "reasonable expectation of profit" after several years of losses, you will have a better chance of proving your case with your "business diary".

The Income Tax Act broadly states that a deduction will be allowed if it was made for the purpose of gaining income from business or property. What is significant here is that it is not necessary to show that income actually resulted from the particular outlay or expense itself. It is sufficient for the taxpayer to show that the outlay or expense was a part of the income-producing process. Further, an expense will generally not be disallowed because the income-earning process produced a loss, as long as the intention of making the expenditure was to produce income.

Finally, a recent court case underscored that when a business is considered to be started and how long it takes to become profitable is not set out in stone. The court ruled that each business must be looked over for its own profitability trends and that in fact, there is no set rule stating how many years of operation are required to show that a business has a reasonable expectation of profit. (*Mattison,*1995, Tax Court of Canada)

This has sent a clear message to Revenue Canada, that once it can be shown that a commercial activity exists with a profit motive, losses cannot be disallowed by the department prematurely.

AMOUNTS TO BE INCLUDED IN INCOME FOR TAX PURPOSES

We have previously defined income from a business to be the profit thereon: the difference between the revenues you create and the expenses you have incurred, computed according to Generally Accepted Accounting Principles. You will learn in this chapter, that the Income Tax Act does not always follow these rules.

...always start by depositing that revenue into a separate business account ...

To report income from your home-based business, always start by depositing that revenue into a separate business account. At the end of each month, reconcile your bank account: match the individual deposit records you have to the bank statement entries. Then match your bank balance with your balance in your cheque book register. This cheque book register also doubles as your cash-flow manager.

The Cash-Flow Manager

It is necessary to keep on top of every dollar that comes and goes in your business to make decisions about when to buy, when to pay and when to borrow. Here's a tip: buy a three ring binder; keep a series of ruled sheets that look something like this in it, to keep track of all banking transactions:

TABLE 2-16
CASH-FLOW MANAGER FOR ABC CONSULTING SERVICES

	Deposits						Expenditures			
DAY	CASH	CHEQUE	VISA	MC	AMEX	TOTAL DEPOSIT	CH #	PAID TO	$ AMT	$ BAL. FWD
1										
2										
3										
4										
5										
6										
7										
8										
9										
10										
11										
12										
13										
14										
15										
16										
17										
18										
19										
20										
21										
22										
23										
24										
25										
26										
27										
28										
29										
30										
31										

Income Classification

There are a variety of Interpretation Bulletins set out by Revenue Canada describing the department's position on a variety of business issues. Among these are:

IT 92	Income of contractors
IT 95	Foreign exchange gains and losses
IT 99	Legal and accounting fees
IT 102	Conversion of property, other than real property, from or to inventory
IT 129	Lawyer's trust accounts and disbursements
IT 182	Compensation for loss of business income or of property used in business
IT 200	Surface rentals and farming operations
IT 218	Profit, capital gains and losses from the sale of real estate
IT 223	Overhead expense insurance vs. income insurance
IT 233	Lease option agreements; sale leaseback agreements
IT 257	Canada Council Grants
IT 261	Prepayment of rents
IT 273	Government Assistance — general comments
IT 417	Prepaid expenses and deferred charges
IT 425	Miscellaneous farm income
IT 434	Rental of real property by individual
IT 454	Business transactions prior to incorporation
IT 490	Barter transactions
IT 525	Performing artists

You may wish to obtain some or all of these to read up on transactions specific to your business.

Auxiliary Tax Forms

Besides your "T1 General Tax Return," specific tax forms that will be used in computing income from a business include the following:

T2032	Statement of Professional Activities
T2042	Statement of Farming Income and Expenses
T2121	Statement of Fishing Income and Expenses
T2124	Statement of Business Activities

T2130   Reconciliation of net income per financial statements with net income for tax purposes

(Samples of these forms can be found in the Appendices.)

Additional Working Papers

Most small businesses will require the use of some additional working papers to properly report income and expenses. These may include:

A statement to justify a Business Investment Loss;

A statement that describes automobile expenses for the year;

A statement that describes home workspace expenses;

A statement that describes capital acquisitions, dispositions and the deduction for capital cost allowances; and/or

A statement to overview the wages and source remittances paid to employees.

In addition, working papers should reconcile income reported with bank deposits for the business.

On the "T1 General" Tax Return

The net profit from a business enterprise is reported on "Lines 135 to 143". In addition, the following lines on the "T1 General" may be addressed in specific circumstances:

Line 217   Allowable Business Investment Loss

Line 252   Non-capital Losses of Other Years

Line 310   Contributions payable on self-employment earnings ("Schedule 8")

Line 412   Investment Tax Credit

Line 421   Canada Pension Plan contributions payable on self-employment earnings from "Schedule 8"

Line 454   Refund of Investment Tax Credit

Line 476   Tax paid by Instalments

Business income or losses do not include any capital gain or losses from the disposition of income-producing assets. This is reported on "Schedule 3" — "Capital Gains or Losses".

Net income or loss from a business is computed in a fiscal period that ends in a taxation year. Such a fiscal period is — after the 1994 tax year — generally considered to end on December 31. If a valid, non-tax reason exists for establishing or maintaining a non-calendar year-end, an election may be made to do so. (*See* "Choosing a Fiscal Year-End," later in this chapter.)

Your Accounting Method

Earlier in this chapter (*See* "How Income Is Taxed in Canada"), we talked about various income classifications in describing basic taxation rules. You learned that net business income is calculated according to the Generally Accepted Accounting Principals and that normally, expenses must be matched to income to present the truest picture of profit over a specific period of time.

When does business income have to be recognized and reported for tax purposes? This largely depends on whether you are on a cash, accrual or modified accrual reporting method.

CASH

Farmers, fishermen and self-employed commission sales agents may report their income using the cash method of accounting. That is, income is reported in the year in which they are received and expenses are deducted in the year in which they are paid.

ACCRUAL

Most other self-employed persons will report income on an accrual method. That is, income is reported in the fiscal period when you earned it, even if you did not yet actually receive the funds. Expenses are deducted when they are incurred, even if you did not yet actually pay for them.

MODIFIED

Professional businesses, which earn their income primarily from fees, will include all amounts received for professional services, whether the services are provided during the current year or after the current year-end. They must also include all amounts receivable at the end of the current tax year for professional services provided during the current year, less all amounts receivable at the end of the previous year. For work-in-progress — work that has not been completed — you must include the value of such work in your business income for the year, unless a special election is made. Work in progress may be excluded from income of an accountant, dentist, lawyer, medical doctor, chiropractor or veterinarian. No special election form exists, rather, a letter is simply attached to the return to indicate that work-in-progress should be excluded from income. Examples follow later in this chapter.

Amounts to Be Included on Form T2124

At tax time, you will be required to record income from your business activities, including a profession, calling, trade, manufacture or an "adventure or concern in the nature of trade", on your tax return. Income from a business does not include income from employment or investment property.

> ... *income from a business does not include income from employment or investment property* ...

INCOME FROM SALES, COMMISSIONS OR FEES

Gross Income from your business is defined as Net Sales, after deducting remittances of Provincial Sales Tax (PST) or Goods and Services Tax (GST) ("Line 8123" of the "Business Activities Statement"), plus any reserves deducted last year, plus any other income. The result is shown on "Line 8124", of Form T2124, "Statement of Business Activities".

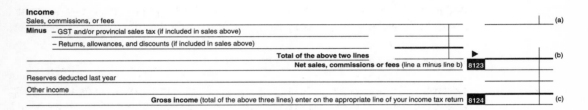

Amounts to Be Included in "Other Income"

The following income sources may be included under "Other Income".

RESERVES

When amounts of money are received in a tax year for goods or services that will be supplied in a future year, a reserve can be set up to defer the tax on these amounts. A reserve is a mechanism by which certain income is excluded in the current tax calculations and deferred to next year. Any reserve deducted out of income this year must generally be reported next year. Examples of reserves are:

1. Ten-year transitional reserve for income in the qualifying period ending December 31, 1995 resulting from the requirement for businesses to report income on a calendar year-end (*See* "Choosing a Fiscal Year-End," later in this chapter.)

2. Amounts due from sale of property (*i.e.,* vendor holds a mortgage)

3. Reserve for Doubtful Accounts (*See* IT 69)

4. Reserve for undelivered goods, services not rendered, rent received in advance and returnable containers other than bottles (*See* ITs 92, 154 and 165)

5. Reserve in respect of instalment sales of land (*See* IT 152)

6. Reserve in respect of the sale of property other than real estate (*See* IT 154)

7. Reserve for unearned commissions of insurance agents and brokers other than life insurance

8. Reserve for credit risks such as arm's length guarantees

Probably one of the most common reserves is a reasonable amount for doubtful accounts. Any amounts identified as doubtful accounts in one year will be deductible from income in that year; and then reported as income in the following year. When the debt, in fact, becomes a bad debt, it can then be deducted. Where debts are forgiven or settled for less than the amounts owing, the debt forgiveness rules, discussed below, will take effect.

COMMISSIONS

Section 20(1)(m) of the Act allows for a reasonable amount to be claimed as a reserve for an "unearned" receipt that is otherwise required to be included in income, for services that are rendered after the end of the year.

Commissions earned by self-employed agents will be considered business income in the same manner, as the Act does not allow a broker or agent to take a tax deduction for any unearned commissions. However, it is possible under certain insurance contracts, that portions of unearned commissions applying to services such as client support services, be rendered after the end of the year. For example, under paragraph 32 (1) a reserve may be set up and deducted in respect of unearned commissions of an insurance agent or broker, relating to policies still in force. This reserve cannot be set up for life insurance policies, and cannot be claimed in the year a broker passes away. The reserve (or amount excluded from income) is the lesser of:

1. a prorata portion of the commissions based on the part of the term that falls into subsequent years (number of days in the period provided in the insurance contract that fall in years after the end of the tax year over total number of days in the period of insurance in total), or

2. the amount that would have been deductible under section 20 (1) (m), which is a reserve for services that will be rendered after the end of the year, if such a deduction were available to insurance agents and brokers.

Any reserve deducted from income in one year must be included in income in the next.

DEBT FORGIVENESS

Recent economic times have had disastrous consequences for some investors whose properties were repossessed or debts forgiven outright because of an inability to pay. These events will have a tax consequence if the taxpayer was not bankrupt at the time the debt was cancelled or forgiven. In certain instances, it may be required that a portion of a forgiven debt be included in income. New rules introduced in the February 22, 1994 budget affect two key sections of the Income Tax Act.

. . . it may be required that a portion of a forgiven debt be included in income . . .

On mortgage foreclosures and conditional sales repossessions, tax consequences may include a capital gain, or recaptured deductions for depreciable assets. In the case of a mortgage foreclosure, for example, any amount of debt that was extinguished (plus related unpaid interest on the debt for property acquired after February 21, 1994) is added to the "Proceeds of Disposition" of the asset.

Therefore, if you acquired a property for $100,000 and had it repossessed when the outstanding debt plus unpaid interest amounted to $106,000, your tax consequence would be:

$$\frac{Proceeds\ of\ Disposition}{\$106,000} - \frac{Adjusted\ Cost\ Base}{\$100,000} = \frac{Capital\ Gain}{6,000}$$

If you subsequently repay the debt, it will be classified as a capital loss if it relates to non-depreciable capital property.

Filing Tip

For the purposes of determining the family's net income for GST and Child Tax Benefit Calculations elsewhere on the tax return, capital gains that result from the surrender of property by a debtor to a creditor on mortgage foreclosures and conditional sales repossessions, will be excluded.

When a debt is extinguished, settled or forgiven, the excess of the debt remaining over what you actually paid has a tax consequence. The unpaid or forgiven amounts were previously used to reduce the following "tax attributes" to which you are normally entitled:

1. Your non-capital losses of prior years,

2. Your net capital losses of prior years,

3. Your farm losses of prior years,

4. Your restricted farm losses of prior years,

5. The capital cost of your depreciable property, and

6. The adjusted cost base of non-depreciable capital property you own.

New rules introduced in the February 22, 1994 budget changed these existing rules in a number of ways including:

1. The adjusted cost base of non-depreciable capital property may be reduced as described above, by forgiven amounts, except for "restricted property" (such as shares of a corporation related to the taxpayer). Some exceptions exist to this rule.

2. Where such reductions in adjusted cost base are made, a capital gain (or loss) will be calculated upon subsequent disposition of the property.

3. Forgiven amounts may be used to reduce the capital cost of depreciable property as before, but not to create a negative balance.

4. Three-quarters of unused forgiven amounts can be further used against the cumulative eligible capital account.

5. Undeducted resource balances, cumulative Canadian development expense and oil and gas property expense will be reduced by the forgiven amounts.

6. Unapplied forgiven amounts may not be applied to the Adjusted Cost Base of the following types of capital properties: personal-use properties, interest in partnerships related to the debtor and other specific properties of corporations.

Finally, the new rules state that amounts still undeducted after all the procedures described above, will be added to income. Tax relief, however, has been provided because the debtor will be allowed to offset any income resulting from these changes with a reserve mechanism. That is, income arising out of the settlement of a debt need only be reported to the extent of 20% of income over $40,000, or in a five-year period generally.

BAD DEBTS

A taxpayer who recovers bad debts that were previously deducted as uncollectible amounts will be required to include these amounts as income in the year they are received. It does not matter whether the amount is paid in cash or in kind. If the debt arose on account of eligible capital property (intangibles such as goodwill, customer lists, milk quotas, etc.) only three-quarters of the bad debt may be deducted, and likewise only three-quarters of any subsequent recovery should be included in income. In the case of qualifying farm properties, any amounts recovered in excess of the deductions previously taken will qualify as a capital gain eligible for the $500,000 capital gains deduction.

BARTER TRANSACTIONS

A barter transaction occurs when goods and/or services are traded or exchanged between taxpayers. No money usually exchanges hands in these situations, but Revenue Canada still considers or "imputes" that it did for tax purposes. Therefore the "fair market value" of the goods or services must be added to income, or in the case of capital property, the value of the asset at "fair market value" must be recognized.

FARMING AND FISHING

Farmers and fishermen are discussed in more detail in Chapter Seven. Briefly, farmers and fishermen may calculate their income on either a cash or accrual basis (*See* below). Fishing income may be reported on a T4F slip. You might receive income from the sale of fish products, marine products, grants, credit and rebates, subsidies, insurance proceeds and patronage dividends, all of which will be considered taxable. If you pay off debts with a part of your catch, the "fair market value" of the catch must be included in income. File Form T2121 to record income from fishing enterprises.

Farmers will report income received from the activities of soil tilling, livestock production or showing, maintenance of race horses, poultry or dairy farming, fur farming, tree and Christmas tree farming, fruit growing, beekeeping, operation of a feedlot or a wild-game preserve and hydroponics. In some cases, fish farming, market gardening and the operation of a nursery or greenhouse will qualify as farming income as well. Record Income and Expenses on Form T2042.

INTEREST INCOME

Interest received from a bank account or other term deposit is considered income of the business and reported on the Income and Expense Statement if it results from amounts invested on behalf of the business. Amounts invested by the individual are reported on "Schedule 4 — Investment Income".

PARTNERSHIP INCOME

Partnerships are discussed in more detail in Chapter Seven. A partnership describes the relationship that two or more people have in conducting a common business for profit. Partnerships are generally governed under provincial statutes. The partnership itself will not pay tax on its income; rather the amounts are flowed through to each partner, who must file an income tax return to report his or her share of the net income or loss.

... partnerships are generally governed under provincial statutes ...

A partnership with six or more members must file "Form T5013". A partnership with five or fewer members throughout the year, that has none of the members involved in another partnership need not file a special information slip. Should one of the partners of the group of five or fewer also belong to another partnership, a "Partnership Information Return" must also be filed.

PROFESSIONAL INCOME

Professionals earn business income in the form of professional fees, and a modified-accrual method of accounting is used to report income (*See* "Your Accounting Method," earlier in this chapter). Certain professionals — accountants, dentists, lawyers, medical doctors, veterinarians or chiropractors — may choose to either include or exclude work-in-progress in income. The election is made simply through the filing of a tax return. The election will still be valid if the return is filed late; but will not be accepted on an amendment or adjustment to a prior filed return.

Work-in-Progress of a Professional

Work-in-progress is not specifically defined in the Income Tax Act. It generally refers to goods or services that have only been partially rendered. Where an election has not been made to exclude income for such services, the income must be included on the normal accrual basis. That is, the income inclusion is based on the expenses incurred in relation to the services performed, or on the basis of what the billing would be if an invoice had been prepared.

. . . work-in-progress of a professional is seen . . . as having the same characteristics as inventory . . .

In general, work-in-progress of a professional is seen by Revenue Canada as having the same characteristics as inventory. The value that is placed on this unfinished work is the "fair market value" of the amount that can reasonably be expected to become receivable after the year-end.

This is handled on "Form T2032" as follows:

With ongoing election to exclude Work-in-Progress:

1. *On the Line: Work-in-Progress, beginning of Year:* record whatever was the "Work-in-Progress" at the end of the last year. Enter nil if this is the first year of business.

2. *On the Line: Work-in-Progress, end of the year:* record the value of your "Work-in-Progress" at the end of the year.

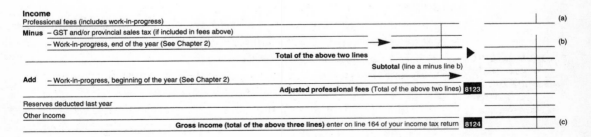

Qualifying taxpayers who choose to exclude work-in-progress from income must live by that decision. It may not be reversed unless the election

■◆■ Revenue   Revenu
Canada   Canada

STATEMENT OF PARTNERSHIP INCOME
ÉTAT DES REVENUS D'UNE SOCIÉTÉ DE PERSONNES

Fiscal period end	10	Partnership's identification number	11	Partnership code	12	Business code
Month Year		Numéro d'identification de la société de personnes		Code du genre de société de personnes		Code du genre d'activité
Mois Année						
Exercice se terminant le						

| 13 | Partner's share (%) of partnership income (loss) Quote-part (%) de l'associé des revenus (pertes) de la société de personnes | 14 | Recipient type Type de bénéficiaire | 15 | Country code Code du pays | 16 | Member code Code du genre de membre | 17 | Recipient's identification number Numéro d'identification du bénéficiaire |

Partner's name (surname first) and full address
Nom, prénom et adresse complète de l'associé

Partnership's name and full address
Raison sociale et adresse complète de la société de personnes

| 18 | Canadian and foreign net business income (loss) Revenu net (perte nette) d'entreprise canadien et étranger | 19 | Foreign net business income (loss) Revenu net (perte nette) d'entreprise étranger | 20 | Canadian and foreign net rental income (loss) Revenu net (perte nette) de location canadien et étranger | 21 | Foreign net rental income (loss) Revenu net (perte nette) de location étranger | 22 | Capital cost allowance Déduction pour amortissement |

| 23 | Limited partnership loss available for carryforward Perte comme commanditaire disponible à reporter | 24 | Actual amount of Canadian dividends Montant réel des dividendes de source canadienne | 25 | Interest from Canadian sources Intérêts de source canadienne | 26 | Foreign dividend and interest income Revenu étranger en dividendes et en intérêts | 27 | Capital gains (losses) Gains (pertes) en capital |

| 28 | Capital gains reserve Réserve relative aux gains en capital | 29 | Business investment loss Perte au titre d'un placement d'entreprise | 30 | Income tax deducted Impôt sur le revenu retenu | 31 | Partnership's total gross income Revenu brut total de la société de personnes | 32 | Carrying charges Frais financiers |

| 33 | Foreign tax paid Impôt étranger payé | 34 | Charitable donations Dons de bienfaisance | 35 | Gifts to Canada or a province Dons au Canada ou à une province | 36 | Federal political contributions Contributions politiques fédérales | 37 | Provincial political contributions Contributions politiques provinciales |

| 38 | Investment tax credit Crédit d'impôt à l'investissement | 39 | Canadian exploration expenses Frais d'exploration au Canada | 40 | Canadian development expenses Frais d'aménagement au Canada | 41 | Canadian oil and gas property expenses Frais à l'égard de biens canadiens relatifs au pétrole et au gaz | 42 | Foreign exploration and development expenses Frais d'exploration et d'aménagement à l'étranger |

| Details – Détails | 43 | Recapture of earned depletion Récupération de la déduction pour épuisement gagnée | 44 | Amount eligible for resource allowance deduction Montant donnant droit à la déduction relative aux ressources | 45 | Limited partner's at-risk amount Fraction à risques de la participation du commanditaire |

Privacy Act personal information bank number RCT/P-PU-005
Loi sur la protection des renseignements personnels, Fichier de renseignements personnels numéro RCT/P-PU-005

For tax centre
Pour le centre fiscal   **1**

T5013 Supplementary/Supplémentaire (96)

2794

Canadä

is formally revoked with the permission of Revenue Canada. Permission will be granted if the taxpayer can prove a valid non-tax reason for the change that does not result in an undue tax advantage. In the year of death, any deferral of work-in-progress may be reported on a "Rights or Things" return.

Attach a note to your tax return notifying Revenue Canada of your election.

REBATES AND REIMBURSEMENTS

Any inducements, reimbursements, contributions, allowances or assistance received by a taxpayer in a business will be included in business income unless the amounts pertain to a capital asset, in which case the cost of that capital asset will be reduced for depreciation purposes. However, such amounts will only be included in income to the extent that it does not reflect a reduction of outlays and expenditures resulting from the disposition of a capital asset.

RECAPTURED DEPRECIATION

When an asset, upon which depreciation was previously claimed, is disposed of for more than its Undepreciated Capital Cost, the amounts of the deductions previously taken will be "recaptured" or added to business income. This includes amounts for eligible capital properties. (*See* Chapter Five.)

What Income or Losses Are not Included for Tax Purposes?

CERTAIN ORGANIZATIONS AND CLUBS

Non-profit status, and therefore tax-exempt status will be given to a qualifying organization. To comply with the exempt status, the organization:

1. must not be a charity,

2. must be organized exclusively for social welfare, civic improvement, pleasure, recreation or any other purpose except profit,

3. must be exclusively operating for the purposes described above, and

4. no part of its income may be paid, payable or otherwise made available for the personal benefit of any proprietor, member or shareholder, except in connection with the promotion of amateur athletics in Canada.

See IT 496 for more information about Non-Profit Organizations.

DAMAGES FOR BREACH OF CONTRACT

Breach of contract damages will not be taxable unless they are considered to be a substitute for profits.

HOLDBACKS

Where a certificate must be obtained to verify that work has been satisfactorily completed, no amounts need to be included in income until that happens, but then, the amounts become receivable immediately.

INDUCEMENT PAYMENTS/GOVERNMENT ASSISTANCE

Government assistance that enables a taxpayer to acquire capital property will not be considered income, but rather will be used to reduce the adjusted cost base of the property.

INSURANCE PROCEEDS

Compensation for loss of profits or destruction of inventory is generally considered to be income from a business. Business interruption insurance is generally considered to be income from the business. However, where an insurance policy compensates the taxpayer for damage to depreciable assets, provided the amounts are not spent on simply repairing the damage (in which case they will be treated as income), the amounts received will be considered to be the proceeds of disposition of the asset.

PREPAID EXPENSES

In general, the accrual method of accounting will prevail in deducting prepaid expenses . . . that is they are generally only deductible in the year to which they relate. New rules apply to farmers. More on this in later chapters.

VOLUNTARY PAYMENTS

Amounts received from lotteries, gifts or windfalls will generally not be considered as income of an individual, unless the individual is in the business of running a gambling enterprise in which case revenues will generally be considered taxable income of a business. Also value of prizes or other awards given to you because of your business activities are considered income of the business.

SALE OF INVENTORY

When a business ceases, the sale of inventory will be considered to be normal business income in the year received, for tax purposes.

CHOOSING A FISCAL YEAR-END

For home-based businesses that started after December 31, 1994, it became mandatory to report net profits for tax purposes on a calendar-year basis —

▶ *. . . after*
December 31,
1994, it became
mandatory to
report net
profits for tax
purposes on a
calendar-year
basis . . .

January 1 to December 31 — the period we use to report all other income and deductions of individuals.

There is only one exception: if you have a valid non-tax reason for choosing a reporting period other than the calendar year, you may be allowed to make a special election when you file your return to keep your non-calendar year-end. However, should you do this, an adjustment would have to be made each and every year to bring your income from the business to a calendar year-end projection. This is called the "Alternative Method".

Example

Margaux started her business "A Christmas Miracle" in July this year. She sells fine Christmas ornaments on a year-round basis, but her busiest time is in the month of December and the after-Christmas sale-period. From July to December her profit from the business was $27,500.

Margaux can choose to report the income and expenses of her business on the mandatory calendar year-end basis. In this case, because she just started during the year, she would report all income and expenses for six months only. This would mean, prorating her auto, home office and capital cost allowance expenses to take into account this short fiscal year. The net profit of $27,500 would be added to her 1996 tax return.

However, Margaux would have a valid reason for electing a January 31 year-end, given her busy activities in December. If her fiscal year ended on January 31, 1997, Margaux would not have to report this business income until the following tax year (deadline June 15, 1998). However, she would then have to make a special adjustment to her tax return:

A. Business income from July 1996 to January 31 1997 $35,000 (1)

B. Number of days in the period, Feb. 1, 1997
to December 31, 1997   334

C. Number of days in the fiscal period that ends in 1997
(July 1, 1996 to January 31, 1997)   215

Adjustment: A × B ÷ C = Additional Income Inclusion $54,372 (2)

Income to be reported on the 1997 return (1) + (2) $89,372

Next year, when the new additional income inclusion is calculated based on this formula, the $54,372 is subtracted.

A. Business income from Feb. 1, 1997 to January 31, 1998 $85,000 (1)

B. Number of days in the period Feb. 1, 1998
to December 31, 1998   334

C. Number of days in the fiscal period that ends in 1998   365

Adjustment: A × B ÷ C = Additional Income Inclusion $77,781 (2)

(1) + (2) $162,781

Less prior year income inclusion $ 54,372

Income to be reported on 1998 return $108,409

So, as you can see, the decision to report on an off-calendar-year basis would mean that no income from the business is required to be reported on the 1996 tax return. That is all deferred until the 1997 tax-filing year. However, at that time, Margaux must add an additional income adjustment of $54,372 to her income to bring it in line with the calendar year-end. She may simply decide that this is too complicated and too expensive under the circumstances.

Existing businesses that were in place on December 31, 1994, were required to make a similar adjustment to add income earned in the "stub period" from the end of the normal non-calendar fiscal year to December 31, 1995. However, only for these businesses was tax relief available. This came in the form of a Ten-Year Transitional Reserve, that would bring the additional income inclusion into other income of the year over a 10-year period.

This provision is discussed in detail in *Jacks on Tax Savings,* 1997 edition.

...corporations, on the other hand, are still allowed to choose any 12-month period ... for tax reporting purposes ...

Corporations, on the other hand, are still allowed to choose any 12-month period ending in the tax year as the fiscal year for tax reporting purposes, without having to make this new "additional income inclusion". Margaux may decide to incorporate her business, if this makes sense otherwise, on February 1, 1997.

This would have the effect of giving her a tax deferral on the income from the proprietorship, which would be reported on the 1997 return ($35,000 in profits from the period July 1996 to January 31, 1997).

The new company would choose a fiscal year-end of January 31, 1998, thereby deferring tax consequences to the 1998 year. (Profits for the period February 1, 1997 to January 31, 1998).

Therefore, choosing your fiscal year-end is important and should be discussed in detail with your tax advisor in the year you start your home-based business.

ACCOUNTING FOR INVENTORY

When a business is started, certain supplies or purchases may be made for the express purpose of resale. Stock in trade, items to be consumed in rendering services, any items whose cost is relevant in computing income from a business can be considered to be inventory, in accordance with generally accepted accounting principles. These principles give us general valuation guidelines.

General Valuation Guidelines

> ... *"fair market value" will generally mean, replacement cost* ...

The Income Tax Act requires inventory to be valued at its cost to the taxpayer or at its "fair market value," whichever is lower. "Fair market value" will generally mean, replacement cost.

WORK-IN-PROGRESS

For work-in-progress, the Income Tax Act defines such inventory to be the "fair market value" of amounts that can reasonably be expected to become receivable after the end of the year.

PROPERTIES OTHER THAN WORK-IN-PROGRESS

For advertising or packaging materials, parts, supplies or other properties, other than work-in-progress, the "fair market value" of inventory is considered to be its replacement cost. However such items used primarily for advertising or packaging are not considered to be items held for sale or lease, in which case they can be written off as expenses rather than inventory.

LAND HELD IN INVENTORY

Land held in inventory can be valued to include "fair market value" plus the cost of any otherwise non-deductible amounts, such as interest and taxes. However, on June 20, 1996 it was proposed that land held in "an adventure or concern in the nature of trade" must be valued at its historical cost, rather than the lower of cost or "fair market value". This means that accrued losses will only be recognized on actual disposition, not on a "rollover".

THREE METHODS FOR CALCULATING DIFFICULT VALUATION

Where it is difficult to determine cost of inventory, valuation can be accomplished using one of the following methods:

1. Average cost

2. First In, First Out (FIFO): First items purchased are deemed to be disposed first.

3. Last In, First Out (LIFO): Last items purchased are deemed disposed of first.

Revenue Canada does not recognize the LIFO method for tax purposes. It is required that inventory recorded at the start of a year is valued using the same amount as the end-of-year valuation last year.

▶ *. . . it will be your responsibility to determine the value of the inventory on hand at the end of each year . . .*

It will be your responsibility to determine the value of the inventory on hand at the end of each year for tax-filing purposes. This is information your tax practitioner will ask you for.

Filing Tip

Where goods are acquired for resale, and therefore held in inventory, obtain the following information for tax return filing:

1. value of inventory at the start of the fiscal period,

2. value of inventory at the end of the fiscal period, and

3. cost of purchases, net of any discounts, for the fiscal period.

Opening inventory is claimed on "Line 8200" of the "Business Activities Statement," based on an actual stock count, unless a perpetual inventory system is used. First year businesses will enter nil on this line.

"Line 8201" is used to record purchases during the year. Exclude any items taken from inventory and used for personal consumption. "Line 8202" will record any direct costs of hiring outside help to perform tasks specifically related to the goods sold; while, "Line 8245" will record amounts paid to employees who work directly in manufacturing the goods held for resale. Finally, record the value of closing inventory including raw materials, goods in process and finished good on "Line 8203". This amount is subtracted from inventory, purchases and direct costs of production, as shown below:

Calculation of cost of goods sold (enter business portion only)

Opening inventory (include raw materials, goods in process, and finished goods)	8200
Purchases during the year (net of returns, allowances, and discounts)	8201
Sub-contracts	8202
Direct wage costs	8245
Other costs	
Total of the above five lines	
Minus – Closing inventory (include raw materials, goods in process, and finished goods)	8203
Cost of goods sold ▶	(d)
Gross profit (line c minus line d) 8125	(e)

▶ *. . . Revenue Canada will not allow a reduction in inventory value to reflect losses that are anticipated after year-end . . .*

To value items that are damaged or obsolete, use the "replacement cost". If items cannot be disposed of in the normal merchandising manner because of their deterioration during the year, use "net realizable value" — that is, the estimated selling price in the ordinary course of business less reasonably predictable preparation and marketing costs. Revenue Canada will not allow a reduction in inventory value to reflect losses that are anticipated after year-end.

Here's an interesting variation for retail operations: Revenue Canada will allow a "retail inventory method" if all of the following circumstances are in place:

1. The method is used only where there are many different commodities for resale, as in a grocery or department store,

2. The values are established in accordance with generally accepted accounting principles, and

3. The values are used for both the tax and financial statements.

(For more details, *see* IT 473.)

Valuation Guidelines for Specific Situations

There are a number of special cases that have specific rules for determining the valuation of inventory.

LAND DEVELOPERS

In the case of land developers, vacant land is considered to be held as "inventory for resale" if the primary reason for holding it is resale or development. Subsequent sales will be considered income gains (100% taxable) as opposed to capital gains (subject to 75% income inclusion after capital losses of the year are applied).

If such vacant land incurs costs of interest or property taxes, these amounts will be deducted from any net income generated by the property during the year. Where there is no income from property, or the expenses exceed the net income, they are added to adjusted cost base of the property. Where the land is held for speculation investment purposes only, with no hope of earning income in the meantime, no deduction for interest and property taxes is allowed. (*See* IT 153R.)

Subdivision and development costs; including the costs of roads, sewers, watermains, streetlighting, sidewalks, landscaping and recreational facilities, are considered to be a cost of inventory. Costs that are directly attributable to the development of the land, such as legal, consulting, mortgage and survey fees are added to the cost of the land in the tax year in which they are incurred.

STOCK TRADERS

Stock traders could be considered to be in the business of buying and selling stock, in which case, the stock they own forms part of their inventory. In general, inventory of shares held at the end of the year are considered to be valued according to their average cost.

Taxpayers who take futures positions or trade in futures or commodities will generally create fully taxable income or fully deductible losses, if they are connected with the commodities in the normal course of their businesses. Canada Pension Plan contributions can be made on the net income, as under normal business reporting rules. Speculators who are not connected with the commodities in the normal course of their business may apply capital gains and loss treatment to their dispositions.

Note that the cost of a seat on a Canadian stock exchange is considered to be a capital property.

VALUATION OF ANIMALS

In farming enterprises, the cost of animals, feed, seeds and plants and other items used for resale are expensed at their cost. However, where a cash-basis loss results from the operation, a Mandatory Inventory Adjustment must be made to add back to income the amount of the "fair market value" of the animals to the extent that the loss is extinguished. Any amount added to income this year is deducted next year. This is discussed in more detail in "Farmers and Fishermen," in Chapter Seven.

VALUATION OF WORKS OF VISUAL ARTISTS AND WRITERS

Taxpayers who are in the business of creating paintings, prints, etchings, drawings, sculptures or other works of art, not including reproducing works or art, may choose to value ending inventory as nil on "Line 8203".

If works from inventory are donated, it is not necessary to report a profit on the tax return from such a disposition, if the gifts are defined as total cultural gifts donated to an institution or public body named under the Cultural Property Export and Import Act. In such a case Revenue Canada will consider that you have disposed of the item at its cost provided that it is a work you have created and it was previously included in inventory. (For more information, *see* IT 504.)

ACCOUNTING FOR PERSONAL USE

We started the discussion of home-based businesses with a thorough examination of audit-proofing techniques. One of the key concepts in staying onside with Revenue Canada, is to separate your business affairs from your personal ones.

To begin, personal and business funds should never be mixed. To make sure you have a paper trail that clearly differentiates between the two:

1. Open a separate bank account for the business.

2. Have a separate charge card for the business.

In this way, your carrying charges are fully tax-deductible as a business expense and your bookkeeping costs will be greatly reduced. Be sure to keep all individual charge card vouchers, as the monthly statements themselves may not be enough to satisfy the tax auditor.

Always make sure that any personal-use component of expenses you run through the business is accounted for on your income tax return.

Example

Steve and Karin run a health food store. They write off all the purchases of inventory on their income tax return when accounting for their cost of goods sold. Often, Steve and Karin take foods, vitamin supplements and other items home for personal consumption.

In this situation, Steve and Karin should add back the cost of the items consumed personally to the net profit calculated for their business. If this is not done, the tax auditor may estimate the personal-use consumption on his or her own, and Steve and Karin will be left to prove otherwise.

Here's another example.

Example

Barbara sells Tavon Cosmetics and Upperware Kitchen Helps by setting up home parties in her neighborhood. She buys these goods for resale through two leading direct selling companies. Her clients generally buy these goods on the spot, and her "hostesses" receive marvellous gifts of merchandise for hosting the selling party.

Barbara should be writing off the costs of the purchases she makes from the companies for resale. This is legitimate. However, any cosmetics that Barbara uses personally, or any of the Upperware products she uses in her home for personal use, must be added back into her income.

Example

Mike and Martha raise pheasants on their farm in rural Ontario. Martha has her own business selling crafts made of the prize pheasant feathers, while Mike sells the pheasants to the local grocery store for human consumption. At year-end, Make and Martha both account for any of the products they use personally, and reduce their expense costs accordingly.

As you can see, anyone who runs a grocery store, a farm, a vegetable gardening centre, a bakery, a cleaning products resale business, cosmetic sales, a candy store, a television repair shop, a video store, and so on, should audit-proof their tax returns by adding back into income the value of personal-use consumption, or reducing their expenses by this amount.

Personal-use components of automobile and home-office expenses must also be accounted for. These are discussed in more detail in "Write Off Your Home-Office Expenses," and "Six Simple Steps to Minimizing Your Auto Claims," in Chapter Four.

Those who claim meals and entertainment as a cost of doing business will also be subject to a restriction for personal use. This is discussed in detail in "Maximizing Entertainment and Promotion Claims," in Chapter Four.

GET READY TO MAKE INSTALMENT PAYMENTS

As a home-based business owner, the presence of Revenue Canada may be felt from a cash-flow point of view, very soon after you are profitable.

The majority of taxpayers in Canada have income tax deducted at "source". This is because they are employees, whose employers are required to make source deductions and remittances on their behalf for income taxes, Canada Pension Plan premiums and Employment Insurance (formerly Unemployment Insurance) premiums.

. . quarterly instalment payments are due March 15, June 15, September 15 and December 15 . . .

However, other Canadians, primarily unincorporated self-employeds and pensioners, may have to make their own income tax remittances directly to Revenue Canada. Quarterly instalment payments are due March 15, June 15, September 15 and December 15 for those who fit into the "instalment payment profile". Farmers, notably, may remit one instalment payment on December 31, based on two-thirds of the estimated amount due on the instalment payment base otherwise calculated.

When you file your income tax return, the total instalment payments made during the year become a credit to you, and are used to offset the actual amount of taxes owing. Record these instalment payments on "Line 476" on page 4 of the "T1 General".

Instalment Payment Profiles

An individual will be required to make quarterly instalment payments if the difference between the tax payable and amounts withheld at source is greater than $2,000 in both the current year and either of the two preceding years.

Losses carried back from subsequent years will not count towards the threshold calculation; nor will CPP overpayments, EI (formerly UIC) overpayments, employee and partner GST rebates, child tax benefits or GST credits. However, your provincial tax credits can be used in determining the instalment base, and so can child tax credits of prior years and investment tax credits.

Calculating Quarterly Payments

Revenue Canada will generally start sending you instalment billing notices or reminders, based on the tax payment base you have had in the current year and two prior years. However, it is important to note, that instalment payments

. . . There are three methods for calculating how much you may have to pay quarterly . . .

need not be made according to this formula. There are three methods for calculating how much you may have to pay quarterly.

REVENUE CANADA'S BILLING OPTION

Revenue Canada automatically sends out instalment billing notices which state the amount of instalment payments due. Under this system, when a taxpayer enters the instalment profile for the first time, instalment payments for the full year would have to be caught up and paid in September and December of the current year. If you pay according to your billing notice, no interest or penalties will be charged if additional taxes are owing when you complete your actual tax return, and pay any balance due by April 30. In other words, if Revenue Canada mistakenly bills you for fewer tax dollars than you'll have to pay when you complete your tax return, no interest will be charged on the deficiency.

This method is recommended if your income appears to be increasing from year to year. However, if the opposite happens, and your income actually decreases relative to the two previous years, the Revenue Canada billing method will collect too much pre-paid tax. In such cases, you may want to use one of two other methods of instalment calculation: the prior-year method or the current-year method.

THE PRIOR-YEAR OPTION

Under this method of computing instalment payments, equal quarterly instalments are based on taxes owed in the tax year immediatly prior to the current year. That is, if you owed $4,000 in taxes when you filed your return last year, you'll be able to remit $1,000 each quarter under this option, to offset next year's liability. However, if your current year's tax bill is higher than your instalment prepayment, interest will be charged on the deficiency when your tax return is assessed.

THE CURRENT-YEAR OPTION

This option is based on an estimation of income you expect to earn in the current year. Using this option, you can ask the tax department to reduce the amount of instalment tax on the billing notices that are automatically sent to you, because you expect your income to drop over what it was in the past.

You can use the "Instalment Payment Calculation Worksheet," "Form T1033," available from the local Tax Services Office, to help you compute the estimated tax liability for the current year.

Deficiencies

... remember, errors in your instalment account can be costly ...

Remember, errors in your instalment account can be costly. You may be required to pay an interest penalty under all three options if quarterly payments are deficient or late, and under the current-year or prior-year options if the final total paid by instalment does not equal the actual tax liability due on April 30.

Interest Rates

Interest is calculated at the prescribed rate, which consists of the average interest rate paid on 90-day treasury bills plus 2 percentage points, for amounts outstanding before July 1995. The interest rate was increased to the average interest rate paid on 90-day treasury bills plus 4 percentage points starting in July of 1995. It is expected that this change will increase interest revenues by $75 million in 1995-96 and $110 million in 1996-97.

... a taxpayer can eliminate interest charges ... by prepaying or overpaying other instalments ...

Interest is compounded daily. If your instalment interest charge is more than $1,000, a further penalty is assessed, equal to 50% of the greater of $1,000 or 25% of the instalment interest, calculated as if you had made no instalment payment at all for that year.

A recent Technical Amendment has clarified that for individuals, the minimum instalment required to be paid on each due date is the amount that brings the total instalments to date equal to the lowest total amount the individual is required to pay by that date.

Interest owing on late or deficient instalments can be offset, however. That is, a taxpayer can eliminate interest charges on late or deficient tax instalments by prepaying or overpaying other instalments. The new higher interest rate will be charged only on net deficient instalments.

It is important to be aware that instalment interest may not by eliminated by using the carry-back of a loss or other amount that reduces the tax payable for the year or the immediately preceding year to $1,000 or less. An addition to this rule was recently announced. Where contributions were made to a Registered Pension Plan for prior-year service, or a "buy-back," the deduction for such contributions may have been limited to certain maximums, with any undeducted contribution available for carry-forward purposes. In the year of death, it will now be possible (for deaths after 1992) to apply such undeducted contribution balances to the year of death and the immediately preceding year. Income taxes payable in that prior year will be calculated before taking into account this carry-over amount.

To ensure that your instalment payments are credited to the correct tax year, always put your social insurance number and the period your payment covers on the cheque or money order.

CHAPTER THREE

Coping with the GST

He who obtains has little. He who scatters has much.
— *Lao-Tzu*

UNDERSTANDING YOUR GST OBLIGATIONS

Just what are your obligations under the GST? Well, it all depends! But, we can start to answer that question, by first having a closer look at the GST.

Understanding the GST

The GST is a tax on consumption. That is, every time you need to buy a good or service in Canada, after December 31, 1990, it will be subject to a GST tax rate of 7% if the good or service is taxable. (Note: Some goods and services are GST-exempt; others will be zero-rated; these will be discussed later.)

The GST is a "value added" tax because it is charged at every stage of production, and thus on the value added all the way down the production chain.

> ... *GST is a "value added" tax because it is charged at every stage of production* ...

For example, assume that a furniture maker purchases raw materials directly from a supplier to make wooden furniture for $5,000. The GST that would be payable on this purchase is $350. The furniture maker now makes wooden tables, which he sells to a wholesaler for $10,000 plus GST of $700. Finally, the tables are sold to retailers for $20,000 plus GST of $1,400. The final consumer will pay $30,000 for these tables, plus GST of $2,100.

Therefore, at every stage of production one can see that GST was charged on the "value added". However, it is only the final consumer who will pay the tax to the government, because all of the businesses in the production chain will be allowed to claim a refund of the GST paid on their supplies, (called an Input Tax Credit) provided they are GST registrants.

This is illustrated in Table 3-1 below.

TABLE 3-1
GST: VALUE-ADDED TAX

INPUT	VALUE	INPUT TAX	TAX ON OUTPUT	NET
Wood	$ 5,000	0	$ 350	$ 350
Furniture	$10,000	$ 350	$ 700	$ 350
Wholesaler	$20,000	$ 700	$1,400	$ 700
Retailer	$30,000	$1,400	$2,100	$ 700
Tax on Final consumer remitted to government				$2,100

Therefore, the basic GST remittance equation is:

GST Collected − GST Paid = GST Remittance

In this context, the GST tax is simple. There is a basic matching principle, and the tax is easily identifiable on invoices provided by suppliers.

. . . GST will not be applied uniformly to all goods and services . . .

However, in Canada, the GST will not be applied uniformly to all goods and services. Instead some outputs or "supplies" will be taxable, at rate of 7%, others will be taxable at a rate of 0% (called zero-rated supplies), still others will be exempt.

A "supply" of goods or services, which may be subject to the GST collection rules, can be provided in any of the following ways:

1. sale

2. rental

3. transfer

4. barter

5. exchange

6. license

7. lease

8. gift

9. as a taxable benefit to an employee

As mentioned, GST is only chargeable on taxable goods and services, but in fact, the federal government has introduced three categories of supplies: two "taxable" and one exempt.

Taxable Supplies

There are two categories of taxable supplies:

Category 1. Taxable supplies upon which the 7% GST is charged, and

Category 2. Zero-rated supplies, upon which GST is charged, but at 0%.

SEVEN-PERCENT SUPPLIES

This category includes any property, real or personal; movable or immovable; tangible or intangible; corporeal or incorporeal; a right or interest of any kind; or a share and a chose in action.

Real Property, Tangible Personal Property, Specified Tangible Personal Property, and Intangible Personal Property are further classified.

Real Property

Real Property is land and buildings, and fixtures thereof, as well as rights to purchase land and the lease of real property. (Note: Where a supply of real property includes both an exempt residential complex and other real property, the residential complex will be treated as a separate supply that continues to be exempt.)

Tangible Personal Property

Tangible Personal Property is any good that can be touched or felt, other than money. This type of property usually depreciates in value. This category may contain used goods, or "capital personal properties," which are assets used primarily — 50% or more — in a commercial activity.

Specified Tangible Personal Property

Specified Tangible Personal Property includes items that are considered "listed personal properties" under the Income Tax Act, and usually appreciate in value, such as rare manuscripts, art, or stamp and coin collections. These properties will generally receive the same GST treatment as other tangible personal property.

Intangible Personal Property

Intangible Personal Property is property that cannot be touched or felt, but that is a right, option, share, or intellectual property such as patents, trade secret, trademarks, trade names and know-how.

A taxable service is anything other than the provision of the properties described above, money or services rendered by an employee to an employer.

ZERO-RATED SUPPLIES

Zero-Rated supplies do not require GST collections, but qualify for the claiming of input tax credits. They include:

1. Prescription drugs

2. Medical devices

3. Basic groceries

4. Agricultural and fishing products, machinery/equipment designed for use by farmers and fishermen and lease of farmland under a crop-share arrangement

5. Travel Services to international points

6. International transportation services

7. Supplies to international organizations and officials

8. Export of property and services

9. Financial services provided to non-residents

10. Precious metals sales

TAX-EXEMPT SUPPLIES

Exempt supplies are not subject to GST, and do not qualify for input tax credits and can include:

1. Sale of used residential housing and rental of residences

2. Health care services

3. Educational services

4. Child care and Personal care services

5. Legal Aid services

6. Certain services of public sector bodies

7. Certain Financial services

8. Ferry, road and bridge tolls

Table 3-2 illustrates what these provisions mean to the consumer.

TABLE 3-2
GST PAYABLE BY CONSUMER

Type of Supply Purchased	GST Payable
Taxable	Yes at 7%
Zero-rated	No
Exempt	No

To the business registrant, however, these classifications will affect whether or not GST paid on inputs is recoverable. This is illustrated below in Table 3-3.

TABLE 3-3
GST PAYABLE BY BUSINESS REGISTRANT

Type of Supply	GST Collectible	Input Tax Credit Claimable
Taxable at 7%	Yes	Yes
Zero-rated	No	Yes
Exempt	No	No

This means that business registrants who make exempt supplies will not be allowed to recover input tax credits on GST paid to make such supplies. To the consumer this means that the increased costs in making exempt supplies will be passed on, where market conditions allow, to the final consumer.

SUMMARY

TAXABLE SUPPLIES	EXEMPT SUPPLIES
at 7% or at 0%	no GST collected

Who Must Register for GST Purposes?

Now that you know what the GST is, the key question is whether or not you should be collecting and remitting it. Here are some basic rules:

1. All goods and services made in a commercial activity in Canada are called "supplies".

2. The Goods and Services Tax, will be charged on most taxable supplies provided by a registrant.

. . . a registrant . . . is someone who is required to register to collect and remit the GST . . .

3. A registrant, for GST purposes is someone who is required to register to collect and remit the GST. This is:
   (i) any person* or organization engaged in commercial activities with annual sales and revenues of GST-taxable goods and services over $30,000. ($50,000 for public service bodies effective April 26, 1996);

*including a partnership, corporation, trust, association

(ii) a small trader: any person, business, or organization with annual sales of GST-taxable goods and services of less than $30,000, who volunteers to register; and

(iii) property owners: any person who sells real property that is not an exempt property, is required to remit GST, even if that person is otherwise not a GST registrant with sales over $30,000. (In such cases, there is no "small trader" exemption.)

How do You Determine the Correct Income Thresholds?

GST is imposed by the registrant on the recipient of the taxable goods or services, and the amount of the tax is calculated on the "consideration payable" for the supply.

> ▶ *. . . the consideration payable is the amount, before GST, that is payable by a recipient of a supply . . .*

In general, the consideration payable is the amount, before GST, that is payable by a recipient of a supply, to a supplier. The value of supplies is usually the sale price of the item, expressed in monetary terms. However, where there is a barter transaction, the value is determined as the "fair market value" of the supply at the time it is supplied or similar reasonable value. This general "fair market value" rule would also be applied at any time that the consideration is property and not money.

Special Circumstances in Determining the Value of a Supply

There are often special circumstances that will determine the value of a supply. Let's have a look at some of them.

EXCHANGE OF PROPERTY BETWEEN TWO REGISTRANTS

There may be cases where property used exclusively in a commercial activity (*e.g.,* inventory) is exchanged between two registrants. In this type of "product-for-product exchange," registrants do not have to calculate and collect GST on the value of property exchanged.

VALUE BEFORE OR AFTER DUTIES OR PROVINCIAL TAXES

The value of a supply includes any tax, duty or fee imposed by an Act of Parliament or legislature of a provincial government. This means that GST would be charged on the value of the supply plus customs duties, excise duties and air transportation taxes. GST will not be charged on provincial retail sales taxes or other provincial taxes that are to be prescribed by legislation, except when calculating taxable benefits for employees or shareholders with auto or other taxable benefits.

VALUE OF SUPPLIES NOT TRANSFERRED AT ARM'S LENGTH

This refers to transfers of supplies between related persons. Two specific rules apply here:

1. Transfers to non-registrants (*i.e.,* small traders) consumers, or makers of exempt supplies for less than "fair market value". In this case, tax is calculated on the "fair market value".

2. Supplies between two non-arm's length parties, where the recipient is a registrant and the supply is used in the course of a commercial activity. In this case, the tax is calculated on the amount of the consideration, not the "fair market value". This means that if there is a transfer for no consideration, no GST is payable.

ELECTION FOR NIL CONSIDERATION

Transactions between a parent corporation and its closely related corporations are treated as "zero-rated". This means that the GST paid on the inputs will be eligible for "input tax credits," but GST is not charged on supplies provided between the corporations. To qualify for this zero-rating, the members in the group of closely related corporations must file a special election. (Note: Sales of real property or any supply not used exclusively in a commercial activity cannot qualify for zero-rating.)

GIFT CERTIFICATES

. . . where a supplier issues gift certificates for no consideration, the value of the supply is reduced . . .

Where a supplier issues gift certificates, they do not attract GST as the supply acquired will have tax applied in the usual way, and the gift certificate will be used as cash.

Example

A $50 gift certificate is given to a customer to apply against a restaurant meal. At the time the gift certificate is given, no GST is charged. When the customer buys the meal, GST is charged on the total bill for the meal less the gift certificate.

The same rules hold true in cases where a gift certificate is sold to the customer.

Example

A customer buys a gift certificate for the provision of cosmetic application services. At the time the gift certificate is purchased, no GST is charged.

When the gift certificate is redeemed: GST is charged on the full price of the supply, before the gift certificate is applied. The certificate is, therefore, treated just like cash.

TAX REFUND DISCOUNTING

When a taxpayer assigns his or her rights to an income tax refund to a tax discounter in return for immediate payment, the discount transaction has two components:

(i)   a taxable component, which is the preparation of the tax return itself. This is computed as 2/3 of the discount (amount kept by the discounter) to a maximum of $30. This means that any refunds in excess of $300 will contain a GST charge of $2.10 ($300 × 7%); and

(ii) a tax-exempt component, which is the amount of the fee that is considered to be a financial service. This component will have a bearing on the amount of input tax credits claimable by tax discounters.

TRANSACTIONS IN FOREIGN CURRENCIES

Where payment for a supply is made in a foreign currency, the value of the supply is expressed in Canadian funds, and GST is calculated on this value.

The value of consideration then, is the Canadian dollar equivalent on the date the consideration is payable. Alternatively, the Revenue Minister may allow the exchange value to be determined on the day the foreign currency was acquired or the date of payment, if such methods are reasonable and applied on a consistent basis.

COIN-OPERATED DEVICES

In the case of vending machines, the customer must pay the GST when he or she puts the money in the machine. However, the supplier only remits the GST when the coins are removed from the machine.

EARLY OR LATE PAYMENTS

Sometimes, recipients of supplies can receive a discount for early payment of an invoice. If the invoice is written for the full price, GST is charged on the value of the supply before applying the discount. If the invoice is issued net of a discount, GST is paid on that net amount. The same rule applies where there is a penalty for late payment. Again, GST is charged on the original value of the supply only.

NATURAL RESOURCE ROYALTIES

Resource royalties are generally not subject to GST. However, rights provided to non-registrants for personal use or enjoyment (such as recreational fishing licences or the right to cut trees by a small supplier for resale to consumers) will be subject to GST.

TOUR PACKAGES

The costs of the package that relate to domestic transportation or accommodation will be subject to GST. Therefore, a prorated GST will be charged in cases where all inclusive packages to international destinations are sold to Canadians.

DONATIONS TO CHARITIES OR REGISTERED POLITICAL PARTIES

Such supplies are not subject to the GST. However, if a portion of a fund-raising event's ticket applies to the cost of a meal, for example, 7/107 of the cost of the ticket that is not a donation would be charged.

CREDIT NOTES

Where a supplier gives credit for GST charged in error and the GST has been remitted, the registrant is allowed to deduct tax applicable to the credit note in the remittance period in which the credit note is given. Where the amount was charged but not collected, the supplier may adjust the tax charged and claim a refund up to two years from the day of the charge or collection

DEPOSITS

. . . where a customer leaves a deposit, GST is not payable . . .

Where a customer leaves a deposit, GST is not payable until the deposit is applied against the full purchase price of the supply. If and when a deposit is forfeited, the supplier must remit GST in an amount equal to 7/107 of the amount forfeited.

More Than One Business

Individuals who own one or more business may register for the GST and will receive one number for all businesses. An incorporated company will register for the GST on behalf of all of its businesses. A partnership, not its individual partners, will register for the GST. Individual partners may qualify for special rebating provisions, as discussed below.

The New Business Numbers

Revenue Canada has recently introduced a new Business Number (BN). Its purposes is to provide a single identification number for businesses regardless of the number of "accounts" they have with Revenue Canada. The BN will begin with four departments at Revenue Canada:

1. Corporate Income Tax   Department RC

2. Import/Export   Department RM

3. Payroll Deductions   Department RP

4. GST Remittances   Department RT

Implementation of the new numbers began in February of 1995. The first nine digits of the number are the same as the GST Registration numbers that existing businesses already have. The next two numbers will identify a specific department at Revenue Canada and the last four numbers are reference numbers.

New businesses should call for information at 1-800-959-5525. A BN can be received for registration in any one of the four areas above. Existing businesses will not have to change any aspect of their current accounting systems to accommodate the new numbering system; and as long as the account identifier numbers are used (the last five digits) Revenue Canada will be able to cross match existing accounts.

Sole-proprietors and partners will continue to use their existing Social Insurance Numbers to file their income tax returns. The new BN will be mandatory by January 1, 1997.

Now that you know the basics of when to charge and collect GST, it's most important for you to take the next step: claiming back the GST you pay on your inputs.

Input Tax Credits

The way the GST is structured, no tax should be borne by the cost of the inputs used by a registrant in the course of a commercial activity. That is, only the final consumer pays the GST. In order to ensure that GST is not paid on the making of taxable supplies, a full refundable credit of GST paid is allowed. This credit is called the Input Tax Credit (ITC).

Input Tax Credits are subtracted from GST collected on taxable supplies. However, Input Tax Credits are also claimable for GST paid in the making of zero-rated supplies. There are no input tax credits on inputs used to make exempt supplies. To claim back the cost of the GST, the calculations that follow are made on your GST return.

TAXABLE SUPPLIES REMITTANCE EQUATION

TABLE 3-4
BASIC GST REMITTANCE EQUATION: TAXABLE SUPPLIES

$$\text{Net GST Charged on Outputs} - \frac{\text{Net GST Paid}}{\text{on Inputs}} = \frac{\text{GST Refund}}{\text{or Balance Due}}$$

ZERO-RATED SUPPLIES REMITTANCE EQUATION

TABLE 3-5
BASIC GST REMITTANCE EQUATION: ZERO-RATED SUPPLIES

$$\text{Net GST Charged on Outputs (0\%)} - \text{Net GST Paid on Inputs} = \text{GST Refund}$$

EXEMPT SUPPLIES REMITTANCE EQUATION

TABLE 3-6
BASIC GST REMITTANCE EQUATION: EXEMPT SUPPLIES

$$\frac{\text{No GST is Charged}}{\text{on Outputs}} \quad \frac{\text{Net GST Paid on Outputs}}{\text{Is Not Recoverable}} = \frac{\text{No GST Balances or}}{\text{Refunds}}$$

Non-Classified Goods and Services

The following are not considered to be supplies for GST purposes, and so GST is neither collected nor remitted, nor are input tax credits claimable:

(a) Sales of an individual's personal effects,

(b) Sales of exempt supplies,

(c) Sales under $30,000 unless an election is made to be a registrant or where real property is sold by a "small supplier"* in the course of a commercial activity,

(d) Persons who sell real estate outside of a commercial activity, unless the transaction is considered an adventure or concern in the nature of trade,

(e) Supplies made outside Canada by non-residents who do not carry on business in Canada, and

(f) Supplies of rights to explore or exploit a natural resource.

(*Note: A small supplier is one whose gross sales are under $30,000. Effective April 26, 1996, public service bodies including charities and non-profit organizations will have a small supplier threshold of $50,000.)

File for your input tax credits when you complete your GST return, which will be automatically sent to you by the federal government.

Adjustments for the Claiming of Meals and Entertainment

Where the registrant pays GST on the cost of food, beverages, and entertainment in the course of his or her commercial activities, input tax credits can be claimed in full in the normal reporting period. However, at the end of the fiscal year, an adjustment will be required to "recapture" or pay back 50% of these input tax credits. (On the GST remittance form, this would be addressed on "Line 104").

The types of entertainment expenses that would be subject to the recapture rules are:

(a) the cost of food and beverages, including cover charges or any tips included in an all inclusive price, for which GST is charged on the total;

(b) the cost of food and beverages consumed at a convention or seminar, calculated at $50 per day where the fees paid are all-inclusive; and

(c) the cost of admissions to sporting events, fashion shows, private boxes or concerts.

The following would *not* be subject to the 50% recapture rules, meaning that full input tax credits would be claimable for any GST paid:

(a) food, beverages or entertainment provided in the course of the commercial activity, such as in a train, or plane;

(b) amounts included in the employee's taxable income in cases where the food was provided at a remote worksite; and

. . . where tips are paid . . . separately from the billings . . . there is no GST liability . . .

(c) food, beverages and entertainment costs provided at functions held for all employees (*i.e.,*staff dinners or Christmas parties).

(Note: Where tips are paid to service personnel separately from the billings for the meals or entertainment, there is no GST liability, and therefore, no input tax credits claimable.)

GST CONSEQUENCES ON REAL PROPERTY TRANSACTIONS

Taxpayers often make costly errors in ignoring the GST consequences of real estate transactions. Whether you are buying a new home or selling a piece of land, here is what you need to know to stay out of the GST auditor's way.

Real estate transactions will generally be subject to GST remittance requirements even if the vendor is otherwise a small supplier, who is not required to register for GST purposes. There are certain exceptions to this general rule. The following transactions are not subject to the GST, and persons supplying these goods are not allowed to claim input tax credits.

Tax-Exempt Real Property Transactions

Real Property that is tax-exempt include:

1. Long-term residential rents;

2. Short-term accommodations where rent is not more than $20 per day or $140 per week;

3. Sales of used residential housing, including single family homes, condominiums and apartment buildings,

   Exception:

   (a) where sale takes place in the course of a business that resells such dwellings, or
   (b) where such used dwellings are substantially renovated and resold;

4. Sales of personal use real property by an individual or trust;

5. Most sales and rentals of real property by charities, non-profit organizations and certain public sector organizations;

6. Sales of summer cottages; vacation homes or hobby farms not used in a commercial activity; and

7. Sales of farmland to related persons for their personal use and enjoyment.

GST-Exempt Residential Complexes

Residential complexes that are GST-exempt will include used residential real property and rentals such as:

(a) owner-occupied single family homes;

(b) semi-detached homes;

(c) condominiums;

(d) multi-unit apartment buildings;

(e) the related land and common areas associated with the buildings listed above;

(f) non-profit and private-for-profit nursing homes;

(g) student residences at a university, college or other schools;

(h) group homes for the mentally or physically disabled;

(i) residential accommodation supplied at a special or remote worksite;

(j) supplies of parking spaces that are incidental to exempt residential complexes; and

(k) rental of land on a long-term basis to a mobile home owner or lessee, including pad rentals.

Supplies of the residential complexes defined above will be GST-exempt even where the owner used the property up to 50% of the time for commercial use. This would be the case for most home-based businesses. No input tax credits or rebates are claimable on any of the supplies outlined above.

Taxable Supplies of Real Property

Let's examine the taxable supplies of real property, which generally includes sales of new residential housing and vacant land, as well as most commercial real estate.

THE SUPPLY OF REAL PROPERTY BY A SMALL TRADER

> *. . . the normal exemptions for small traders . . . will not apply when it comes to real property . . .*

The normal exemptions for small traders (those with revenues under $30,000) will not apply when it comes to certain real property transactions. That is, any time real property is sold, or transferred by a person involved in a commercial activity, GST is payable, even if the amounts involved are below the small trader's threshold.

However, receipts from such sales will not be included in the definition of "revenue" for the requirement of GST registration. Therefore, while GST must be remitted on these transactions, the transaction itself will not push a small trader over the $30,000 threshold so as to require him or her to be a registrant. (This will not hold true, however, if the small trader is in the business of buying and selling real estate, or in providing commercial rents.)

It is the purchaser who must file a GST return within the normal GST reporting period to record the purchase of the property and pay the tax directly

▶ *. . . it is the purchaser who must file a GST return . . . to record the purchase of the property and pay the tax . . .*

to Revenue Canada. If the purchaser, who is a registrant, acquires real property from a vendor who is not a registrant, the purchaser must file a prescribed "Form 60" — "GST Return for Acquisition of Real Property".

Effective January 1, 1997, registrants purchasing property from those who are not required to collect tax on sale will not have to file the special "Form 60," provided that the property was purchased for use or supply primarily in the course of the registrant's commercial activities. In these cases, tax will be reported in the registrant's regular return for the reporting period in which the tax became payable. The registrant will pay the tax no later than the filing-due date of the return. In all other cases — for example, where the purchaser is not a registrant or where the property is not acquired for supply or use primarily in commercial activities of the purchaser — the requirement that a special return be filed will remain and the tax will have to be paid by the end of the month following the calendar month in which it becomes payable.

Where a non-registrant, who previously paid GST on the purchase of the commercial real property, subsequently sells this property, a special rebate is available. A special election of "GST Form 22" will allow a registered vendor to claim an input tax credit, or an unregistered vendor to claim a rebate, equal to the tax paid on the original acquisition cost or improvements to the real property, or the tax payable on the sale of the real property, whichever amount is less.

FARMLAND

The GST does apply to sales of farmland to developers or individuals who are not related to the vendor. If it is sold as a part of an ongoing operation, the vendor and purchaser can file an election stating that they agree the transaction is not subject to GST. In such cases, either the vendor or the purchaser can claim input tax credit for expenses that relate to the sale and purchase of the property.

SUBDIVIDED LAND

The April 23, 1996 GST Reform proposals brought forward new rules for individuals who sell subdivided lots. The sale of subdivided land by an individual will be taxable, except where the subdivision creates no more than two lots and the person has not previously subdivided nor severed the property from another parcel of land. The subdivided land will also not be taxable if the individual is transferring it to related individuals. A rebate will be available for the taxes paid in relation to land purchases and improvements made on subdivided land that is subsequently sold on a taxable basis by a non-registrant.

THE PURCHASE OF NEW RESIDENTIAL HOUSING

GST will apply directly to the sale of a newly-constructed home purchased from a builder, owner built homes, substantially renovated residential condominium units or purchases in shares of a co-operative housing corporation. This includes residential condominium units built on leased land.

REBATE FOR NEW HOMES PURCHASED FROM BUILDERS

This rebate will apply to single unit residential complexes such as detached homes, semi-detached homes, row houses and duplexes, as well as to residential condominium units. It will apply to homes purchased from a "builder" — defined to be anyone who buys unoccupied new houses for resale purposes. This means that a rebate may be claimable even if the new home is purchased from a person who didn't actually build it.

The rebate will also be allowed on the purchases of "substantially renovated" properties. This is an important concept because substantial renovations — renovations where all or substantially all of the building, other than the foundation, exterior walls, interior supporting walls, floors, roof and staircases have been removed or replaced — will render the building to be considered "newly-constructed".

(Note: The rebate is only allowed for primary residences; therefore, it will not be available on the purchase of investment properties or recreational cottages; unless, the latter are used as a primary residence. In addition, new rules introduced on April 23, 1996 deny the new housing rebate in situations where the builder is not required to self-assess the GST and remit it because of another law or Act of Parliament. What this means is "buyer beware"! You'll have to find out whether a new housing rebate is payable to you, based on the builder's status.)

The rebate cannot be claimed until the GST is paid on the home, and title has passed, except in the cases of condo units, which may be occupied by the purchaser before title passes.

The rebate also applies to mobile homes, including mini homes. In such cases, purchasers may be able to assign their new housing rebate to the vendor to offset the purchase price.

The new housing rebate is not available on homes priced over $450,000. The rebate is equal to 2.5 percentage points of tax or 36% of the total tax paid to a maximum of $8,750. On homes prices between $350,000 and $450,000, the rebate is reduced.

HOUSING REBATE UP TO $350,000

Value of house: up to $350,000
Rebate: 36% of GST paid, or about 2.5% of the purchase price.

Example

New home purchased at $80,000

GST = $80,000 × 7%   *= $5,600 × 36% = $2,016 Rebate*
Net GST paid   *= $3,584*

Example

New home purchased at $250,000

GST = $250,000 × 7%   *= $17,500 × 36% = $6,300 Rebate*
Net GST paid   *= $11,200*

Example

New home purchased at $350,000

GST = $350,000 × 7%   *= $24,500 × 36% = $8,820 Rebate*
Maximum   *= $ 8,750*
Net GST paid   *= $15,750*

HOUSING REBATE BETWEEN $350,000 AND $450,000

Value of House: between $350,000 and $450,000
      Rebate: the lesser of :
                (a) $8,750, or
                (b) 36% of GST paid multiplied by
                     ($450,000 − selling price) ÷ $100,000

Example

New home purchased at $380,000

a.   *GST = $380,000 × 7%*   *= $26,600*
b.   *Lessor of (a) $8,750 or (b) 36% × $26,600*   *= $ 8,750*
c.   *Rebate = $8,750 × ($450,000 − $380,000)*
    divided by $100,000   *= $ 6,125*
    Net GST paid   *= $20,475*

Example

New home purchased at $420,000

a.   *GST = $420,000 × 7%*   *= $29,400*
b.   *Lesser of (a) $8,750 or (b) 36% × $29,400*   *= $10,584*
c.   *Rebate = $8,750 × ($450,000 − $420,000)*
    divided by $100,000   *= $ 2,625*
    Net GST Paid   *= $26,775*

(Note: Subsections 254(4) and (5) of the Excise Tax Act permit the vendor, at the time of sale, to pay the rebate to the purchaser or credit the amount of the rebate against the tax owing by the purchaser. However, if the purchaser does not credit the rebate against GST payable on purchase, then he or she may apply for the rebate directly from Revenue Canada for up to four years from date of purchase. You must apply for this rebate within two years of the time you acquire ownership of the newly-constructed home, effective for houses acquired after June 1996.)

Also note that GST paid on a new home purchase does not qualify as a moving expense.

REBATES FOR CO-OP HOUSING

Where an individual purchases a share in a co-op housing corporation in order to use a residential unit therein as a primary place of residence, a rebate will be allowed if the corporation paid GST when it acquired the complex. As well, the maximum price that can be paid by the individual for the share must be less than $481,500. This limit corresponds to the $450,000 limit on new homes built by builder, except it takes into account the GST paid by the corporation.

The possession of the unit must be given to the first purchaser after it is substantially complete but before it is occupied, in order to qualify for the rebate. The formula for computing this rebate is the same as the one for new homes built by builders, except that all amounts must be converted to "tax included" amounts.

REBATES FOR OWNER-BUILT HOMES

Where an individual builds or substantially renews his or her own principle place of residence, or hires someone to do this, a new housing rebate will also be available to offset the GST liability. The value of the rebate will depend on the cost of the property, which includes the house and the land, however, the rebate will depend upon whether GST was paid on the land.

Example

An individual buys land for $50,000 and pays GST thereon, and builds a house for $150,000, paying GST on all building supplies and services

"Fair market value" of house and land	*$200,000*
Total GST Paid	*$ 14,000*
Rebate: lesser of	*(a) $ 8,750 or (b) 36% × $14,000*
Rebate =	*$ 5,040*
Net GST Paid	*$ 8,960*

Example

An individual constructs $150,000 house on land valued at $50,000, but no GST was paid on the land.

Total GST paid ($150,000 × 7%)	*$ 10,500*
Rebate = lesser of (a) $1720 and (b) 10% of GST:	*$ 1,050*
Net GST Paid	*$ 9,450*

The rebate is phased out on homes valued between $350,000 and $450,000. The owner is not required to obtain a formal appraisal of the property for the purposes of claiming the new housing rebate, if the property's value is well below $350,000. However, if the value of the property is close to $350,000, the purchaser will be required to obtain a formal appraisal.

A different statute of limitations also applies. That is, the rebate must be claimed within two years of the earlier of: (a) the day the home is first occupied by the individual (or ownership is transferred to another individual before the home is occupied), or (b) the day construction or substantial renovation of the home is substantially completed.

SIMPLIFIED GST REPORTING PROCEDURES

When you file your income and expense statement for income tax purposes, your will generally report income, after GST has been removed, as this amount is remitted to the government. In addition, you will remove the GST component from your expenses, as this is generally netted out against the GST you must remit. Therefore, if you are a home-based proprietor, it is important that you have your GST returns at hand when you file your personal income tax return every year, to balance GST remittances with input tax credits.

▶ *. . . it is important that you have your GST returns at hand when you file your personal income tax return . . .*

There are a number of methods of remitting GST and accounting for input tax credits. Here are the reporting requirements.

GST registrants will be required to keep books and records, including supporting invoices for all GST collected and input tax credits claimed. Such books and records must be maintained in Canada, although permission to maintain records elsewhere may be granted. The mandatory retention period for keeping this documentation is six years from the end of the year to which it relates.

Keeping track of GST collected, and input tax creditable amounts would be a relatively simple task if all businesses fell into "pure" categories. That is, they only produced goods and services that were either taxable at 7%, zero-rated or exempt. In such cases, a simple accounting of GST charged and GST paid should be virtually all that's necessary to account for the tax.

Unfortunately, this becomes much more difficult when commercial activities engaged in include the sale of both taxable and zero-rated items (*e.g.,* a drug store or convenience store) or taxable and exempt items (*e.g.,* a tax preparation service that provides both income tax preparation and tax discounting services).

In response to these very real problems of apportionment of both the tax collected and input tax credits claimable, the government accepts different accounting methods for GST collection.

Regular Accounting Method

Under regular accounting methods, a business adds a separate column to its sales and disbursements journal to record GST charged and GST paid as separate items. At the end of the reporting period the taxes would be summarized as in Table 3-7 below.

TABLE 3-7
GST SUMMARY — REGULAR ACCOUNTING METHOD

Total GST Collected per Sales Journal	$ 5,000
Total GST Paid per Expenses Journal	($ 3,000)
Total GST paid on Capital Assets	($ 3,000)
Total GST Refundable Credit	$ 1,000

If that business produced both taxable and zero-rated goods (*e.g.,* a sheep farmer who also sells home made sweaters in a shop situated on the farm) zero-rated sales (the raw wool) may be recorded separately from the taxable sales (the sweaters), although the GST paid on inputs purchased to produce both supplies would qualify fully for input tax credits in this case.

On the outset, this appears to be a relatively straightforward matter, were it not for the fact that provincial sales taxes must be accounted for separately. For some businesses this would mean that the federal and provincial tax status of each good sold would have to be separately identified. It is for those reasons that the following simplified accounting systems have been introduced.

The Quick Method

This accounting method was unveiled on May 31, 1990 and applies a set percentage to total sales. It basically eliminates the need to list and apportion GST collected and paid separately.

WHO'S ELIGIBLE?

Most businesses with total annual sales of less than $200,000 are eligible. Legal, accounting or financial consulting businesses are excluded from eligibility.

BASIC PROCEDURES

Under this method, registrants will collect GST in the normal manner based on previously discussed invoice formats and identification of tax status of all supplies.

Then:

(a) All GST-included sales for a filing period will be totaled (specifically excluded are zero-rated sales and sales to Indians).

(b) This total will be multiplied by the "Quick Method Percentage" applicable to each business.

(c) GST paid on capital purchases will be subtracted.

(d) The GST form will be completed, and remittance sent in (or a credit will be applied for).

RATES

The predetermined percentages to be applied to total sales are illustrated in Table 3-8 below. Sales figures must include the GST collected on those sales, but not the provincial sales taxes.

TABLE 3-8
PREDETERMINED GST PERCENTAGES

Type of Business	Sales Limit	Amount of GST to be Remitted*
Manufacturing/services	under $200,000	5%
Retailers/wholesalers	under $200,000	2.5%

*Note: These rates are 1% lower on the first $30,000 of gross sales.

Once chosen, the business must use this system for one year. Input tax credits would not be separately computed under this methods, except for GST paid on capital property. An election form must be completed if this method is chosen.

The cash-flow implications of choosing this method should be carefully analyzed by the registrant, before it is chosen, because changes cannot be made for a full year thereafter.

Frequency of GST Remittances

. . . once a business has chosen a bookkeeping system . . . it must remit on time . . .

Once a business has chosen a bookkeeping system to record the collection of the GST, has redesigned its invoices, and is in fact in the tax collection business, then it must remit on time. There are three filing frequencies:

1. Annual Sales over $6 million: Remit GST monthly.

2. Annual Sales under $6 million but over half a million: Remit GST at least quarterly, but you may elect to remit monthly.

3. Annual Sales under $500,000   File GST form annually, but remit quarterly instalments, unless instalment base is less than $1,000. You may elect to file monthly.

These reporting periods will be determined on the registrant's threshold sales amount. This sales amount takes into account taxable supplies (at 7% or 0%) made in the preceding fiscal year or quarter.

Persons who are filing the GST return annually or quarterly may elect to file monthly. This election must take effect on the first day of the fiscal year, if the person is already registered. New registrants may have the monthly remittances take effect immediately. Monthly registrations are of benefit to those who export goods or make other zero-rated sales (*e.g.,* farmers, fishermen, drug stores or convenience stores).

In cases where a person's reporting period was the fiscal year but the sales revenues of a fiscal quarter during the year exceed $500,000, the person must begin filing quarterly for the rest of the year (but may elect to file monthly).

Monthly filers who find their annual sales have dropped below the $6 million threshold may elect to file quarterly. This quarterly filing election will remain in effect until the earliest of:

(a) the day a replacement election comes into effect,

(b) the first day of the first fiscal quarter for which the $6 million threshold amount is exceeded, or

(c) the first day of the first fiscal year for which the $6 million threshold amount is exceeded.

The threshold amount is calculated by taking the total value of sales on taxable supplies, other than the sales of financial services and sales of capital real property made in the immediately preceding fiscal year. Finally, where a person is a non-registrant, the reporting period for remitting GST is the calendar month.

Reporting Periods

In the 1995 tax year, if the business does not make an election to retain its non-calendar year end and conforms to the common December 31, 1995 year end, the GST reporting methods will not be affected until 1996.

The Harmonized Sales Tax (HST)

Effective April 1, 1997, the federal government and the provinces of Nova Scotia, New Brunswick and Newfoundland and Labrador will harmonize federal and provincial sales taxes, and bring the combined sales tax rate down to 15%. Federal rebates and the GST Credit Prepayment will continue to be available to taxpayers in those areas, and those businesses that have previously registered for the GST will automatically be registered for the HST.

Under this new scheme, businesses across Canada will be required to collect and remit the 15% HST on sales into the three participating provinces. There are also new rates and rules for the Nova Scotia New Housing Rebate.

If you sell goods and services into these provinces, see your tax professional about the implications to your business of the new rules.

GENERAL ANTI-AVOIDANCE RULES

You may have guessed . . . there are consequences for being a GST delinquent.

You'll Have to Pay Interest

. . . You may have guessed . . . there are consequences for being a GST delinquent . . .

Persons who do not pay the GST or remit instalments will be charged interest based on the prescribed rate of interest as well as a penalty of 6% per year. The penalty and interest will be calculated from the time the tax was required to be remitted to the day the tax is actually remitted. The same 6% penalty plus interest at the prescribed rate will be charged on late of deficient instalments. These charges will be calculated from the time the instalment was required to be paid until the earlier of:

(a) the day on which the instalment, penalty and interest is paid, or

(b) the day on which the amount should have been paid.

The "Offset" Rule

Businesses will be allowed to take advantage of an "offset rule," in which GST remittances in one period can be overpaid to offset deficiencies of another. Penalty and interest charges will be waived if they amount to less than $25.

Avoid Penalties With Voluntary Compliance

The penalty can be avoided by those who voluntarily come forward to correct errors or omissions in filing. However interest will continue to be charged in this period.

If Asked to File — File

The Revenue Minister may demand that a person file a GST return, and failure to comply to such a demand will result in a penalty equal to the greater of $250 or 5% of the outstanding tax.

Should a person fail to provide any information or document, a penalty of $100 for each such default can be levied if no reasonable attempt is made by the person to comply.

No False Statements or Omissions!

If a person knowingly makes a false statement or omission, a penalty equal to the greater of $250 or 25% of the amount by which the tax owing was reduced or the refund increased by the false statement, will be charged. (Also see discussion of "Offences" later.)

You Must Provide the Required Information

Section 289 of the Excise Tax Act states that the Revenue Minister may require any person to provide any information or document for any purpose relating to the administration or enforcement of the Act. However, such requirements can only be made with the authorization of a judge, where they relate to "unnamed persons". This is an important aspect of the enforcement of the Act, as is explained below.

Revenue Canada could issue a requirement to a trader for the names of persons to whom the trader paid GST and the amounts that were paid to this person. The tax department could then use the information to verify if the suppliers were reporting the same amount on their GST remittances.

The person upon whom this requirement is served may have this authorization reviewed. Such a review must be applied for within 15 days of the day on which the requirement was served.

Can the Government Search my Premises?

. . owners of the goods in question are entitled to inspect them and obtain photocopies . . .

As well, the Revenue Minister may apply to a judge for a warrant to enter and search any building, receptacle or place and seize any documents or things that may be evidence of an offence, provided there are reasonable grounds to believe an offence has been committed. Seizure may, in fact extend to any documents or things that could be used as evidence, even if such things or documents are not itemized in the search warrant. Owners of the goods in question are entitled to inspect them and obtain photocopies of them.

Documents that are seized, inspected, examined or provided may be photocopied by the person who took them or another officer of the Department. Such a copy will have the same "probative value" as the original, as stated in Subsection 291(1). The Act goes on to say that a person shall not hinder, molest or interfere with a person authorized to seize, inspect or examine any document.

Where a Revenue Canada officer is set to seize documents that are being held by a lawyer for the person, and the lawyer claims that a solicitor-client privilege exists, the documents shall be seized and packaged and sealed without inspection, and placed in the custody of a sheriff or other custodian. There are several procedures that follow to determine whether such a privilege did in fact exist, including an *in camera* sitting with a judge, who has the right to inspect the articles. If the claim of privilege is upheld, the items are returned to the lawyer. Otherwise, they will be delivered to the examiner at Revenue Canada. Reasons for the decision will be given.

Will the Government Ensure Confidentiality?

The Act also contains confidentiality rules that prohibit Revenue Canada officials from communicating or allowing access to any information obtained from the business. There are exceptions to this rule. Information may be communicated to another authorized person in the course of performing the duties of enforcement. As well, it may be communicated under prescribed conditions and on a reciprocal basis to the government of a province or any foreign state for the purposes of administering a sales tax, or similar tax. Information may also be communicated to an official of the Department of Finance for the purposes of evaluating and formulating tax policy. Revenue Canada officials who break the confidentiality rules can be found guilty of an offence and on conviction could face fines of up to $5,000 or imprisonment of up to one year, or both.

Are There Time Limits?

The statute of limitations on assessments or reassessments will be four years after the day on which an application for rebate was filed, unless there was a misrepresentation or fraud.

Limitation periods will be reduced to two years for rebates of tax paid in error, new housing and other special real property rebates and imported goods subject to abatement or refund, effective after April 23, 1996. In addition, the period of time which a GST registrant may refund or provide a credit for tax paid in error by a customer, and limitation periods for claiming deductions for price adjustments, bad debts and exclusive products of a direct seller, have all been reduced to two years.

Persons who are dissatisfied with assessment may file a Notice of Objection with the Revenue Minister within 90 days of the day of mailing of the Notice of Assessment. Further appeals may be made to the Tax Court of Canada.

If You Are Guilty of an Offence

. . . it is under the category of offences that we find the severest penalties for those who do not comply . . .

It is under the category of offences that we find the severest penalties for those who do not comply.

For example, anyone who willfully fails to pay, collect or remit an amount of tax could be found guilty of an offence, and subject to fines not exceeding the aggregate of $1,000 and an amount equal to 20% of the amount of tax that should have been remitted, and or a prison term of up to six months.

It gets worse! Every person who fails to file a return or fails to comply with a requirement to keep accurate records or fails to give reasonable access to documents or property will be found guilty of an offence. If convicted, fines could be levied in amounts not less than $1,000 and not more than $25,000, and a prison term not exceeding one year may be levied.

A person is guilty of an offence if he or she has participated in making false or deceptive statements in a return filed; or employed any fraudulent or destructive means to evade the payment of GST or obtain refunds of rebates; or conspired with any person to commit any such willful acts. Conviction of these offences will carry fines of not less than 50% and not more than 200% of the tax sought to be evaded or the rebate or refund sought to be gained, or a fine of not less than $1,000 and not more than $25,000. These fines could be levied in addition to a prison term of not more than two years.

Further, the Attorney General of Canada could proceed to charge the tax evader by indictment. If convicted, fines of not less than 100% and not more than 200% of the amount of tax being evaded or rebates sought could be levied, or fines of not less than $2,000 and not more than $25,000, or prison terms of up to five years.

Finally, similar to the Income Tax Act, there will be an anti-avoidance provision in the Excise Tax Act. This general provision states that where a transaction is an avoidance transaction, the tax consequences of this transaction are to be determined as is reasonable in the circumstances in order to deny the tax benefit that has resulted from the transaction.

New for 1996 and Future Years

If you find that you have paid or remitted an amount of tax, penalty or interest in error, some of you now have only two years in which to claim your money back. This includes those filing for rebates of tax paid in error, new housing and other real property and imported goods subject to rebate or adjustment. (This was four years prior to June of 1996.) The Minister of National Revenue may take into account amounts that a person has failed to claim as an input tax credit, deduction, refund or rebate and may refund an overpayment or apply it against other liabilities for up to four years back. The Minister may also apply an overpayment of net tax against a net tax liability in another reporting period, whether or not the GST return was actually filed. Interest on the overpayment may also be applied. This interest accrues from 21 days after the later of the due date of the return and the day the return was filed.

SPECIAL GST RULES FOR UNIQUE BUSINESSES

If you are participating in a network marketing business, sell on consignment, are an artist or musician, operate a grocery store, or work in the health care industries, there are special GST rules for you. These are summarized below.

Independent Sales Contractors and Agents

Independent sales contractors who sell consumer products to others on a person-to-person basis, door to door, through sales parties or by appointment in someone else's home, will usually sign up with a particular direct selling company to sell its product line. These people can also be known as independent sales contractors, consultants, dealers, demonstrators, representatives or sales representatives. If their only source of income (other than employment income) is from direct selling, and the direct selling firm has been approved to use the Alternate Collection Method, there is no need for the independent to register and collect the GST.

The Alternate Collection Method has the agent pay GST on inventory purchases based on the suggested retail price rather than the cost price of the products purchased for resale. The agent then keeps the GST collected from the customers on the products. A direct seller or distributor is not required to charge GST on sales aids supplied for independent sales contractors.

As a result of the Alternative Collection Method, most independent sales contractors will not need to be registered and will not need to include the sale of the direct seller's products in determining whether they have met the $30,000 threshold. To determine whether or not the sales agent must register for GST purchases under the $30,000 threshold limit, compute the money earned from the enterprise less:

1. product sales,

2. performance bonuses based on volume of sales or purchases, and

3. employment earnings.

You must, however, include performance bonuses that are based on factors other than volume of purchases and sales and other sources of business income that are not connected to the Alternative Collection Method. If the direct selling organization does not use the Alternative Collection Method, the agent must register for, and remit GST in the normal manner.

. . . agents . . . will also have GST liabilities . . .

Agents, who are used as the "go between" in the completion of a business transaction, will also have GST liabilities, but this will generally depend on who has title to the property being sold. Usually, title will pass directly from the vendor, who is a registrant, to the purchaser, through the hands of the agent, who throughout this whole venture, never has title to the goods in question.

The GST will have to be charged on the goods supplied by the agents and auctioneers acting on behalf of those who would be required to collect the tax, even if some of these goods are tangible personal properties according to recent tax changes. This takes pressure off the agent or auctioneer who no longer must "classify" the assets to be sold.

Consignment Sales

Where goods are sold on consignment, title does not pass to the registrant who took the goods on consignment until he or she in fact sells the goods, (or if the consignee used the goods for personal use). The liability for the GST arises on the earlier of the time the consignee makes payment for the goods, or the time the consignor invoices for the goods.

Where the invoicing is delayed, an "override rule" may apply. This rule states that a GST liability may not go beyond one month following the month in which the supply is completed. In the case of consignment sales, the supply is considered completed on the day on which the consignee supplies the goods to another person. If the goods are not sold or are returned to the consignor, there is no GST liability. Where does this leave the claiming of input tax credits?

The consignor (the registrant supplying the goods) can claim an input tax credit when the goods are invoiced to the consignee. The consignee, on the other hand, will claim an input tax credit when the goods are paid for.

Indians

Tax relief is provided to Indians who live and work on the reserve on both income tax and GST. Indians who live on one of the eligible settlements will not have to pay GST on goods bought on the settlement, goods bought off the settlement and delivered to the settlement by the vendor or an agent of the vendor, and services that are performed totally on the settlement.

In the case of Indian bands, the band does not have to pay GST on goods bought on the settlement, goods bought off the settlement by the vendor or agent, or services for real property located on the settlement. Services for band management activities are relieved of GST regardless of where they are performed.

To obtain relief, the person must show the Certificate of Indian Service Card. The vendor then must write the registry number or band name and family number on the invoice, and keep proof of delivery to the settlement. Indian bands must supply the vendor with a signed statement.

GST must be paid, though, in cases where the property is imported and where the property is purchased off the reserve and transported to the reserve by the Indian or other person empowered by the band. Tax relief can apply to purchases made in certain "remote stores." Indians are eligible for the GST credit.

Vending Machines

The price of food or beverages sold through a vending machine is considered to be GST-included and the vendor is considered to have officially collected the tax on the day the money is removed from the vending machine.

Supplies by Non-Registrants

If a Canadian resident makes payments for supplies purchased from a non-resident, no GST is paid and no input tax credits will be claimed unless the non-resident:

1. Makes taxable supplies of real property situated in Canada by way of lease; or

2. Makes supplies through a permanent commercial establishment in Canada.

Imports

. . . the GST is collected at the same time as customs duties and excise taxes . . .

The GST is calculated on the total value of taxable goods that are imported, including customs duties and excise taxes. The GST is collected at the same time as customs duties and excise taxes. Imported services, such as consulting services are not subject to the GST when they are imported for use exclusively (90% or more) for use in taxable business activities.

Artists and Entertainers

In the case of a group of musicians, the legal relationship between the members of the band and the band leader determines who must register. If the individual members are employees of the band leader, the band leader must register; if the band is a corporate entity, then the band has to register or if the individual is self-employed and enters into a contract with the band for services, the individual must charge and collect GST from the band. Sales of goods and services by performing artists include sales of music, art, books, films and videos, services and tickets to professional events and concerts. GST does not apply to goods and services provided outside of Canada.

Farmers and Fishermen

Where gross revenues exceed $30,000, or where the individual registers voluntarily, GST must be collected on goods and services provided by the farming operation. Many farm products, however, such as milk, sharecropping and feeder-cattle purchases are zero-rated, which means no GST is paid on purchase and no GST is charged when the items are sold to customers. Zero-rated fishing products include bait and any fish used for human consumption. Zero-rated fishing equipment includes fishing boats, and nets.

Grocery Store Operators

The normal rules discussed above will apply. In addition, franchise fees are taxable under the GST rules, and amounts paid will qualify for an input tax credit. It is a requirement that GST is charged to your clients in this instance, except in the case of exempt supplies such as financial services, if, for example, you are advancing credit. As well, municipal taxes are not subject to the GST. When a soft drink is sold in a returnable container, the amount of the deposit is added to the GST-included price of the soft drink. No GST is required on the charge for the deposit:

. . . municipal taxes are not subject to the GST . . .

Cost of Soft Drink	$1.00
GST	.07
Deposit	.40
Total	$1.47

When the empty bottle is returned, the deposit of 40¢ is refunded; the bottle is returned to the supplier and no GST is charged in these calculations. If prepared foods are sold in the store, GST must be charged on anything available for immediate consumption, including sandwiches, prepared salads, hot beverages and soda fountain beverages.

Coupons presented by customers for goods in the store will be handled as follows: the full value of the coupon will be deducted from the goods. When the vendor accepts a coupon for a taxable good, an input tax credit is claimed for the amount of the GST in the coupon, based on 7/107 of the value of the coupon redeemed. A manufacturer's coupon is used to offset goods for full value as explained above, but the individual vendor cannot claim the input tax credit on the GST remittance form in those cases. Instead, the manufacturer will give back the full amount of the coupon plus GST to the vendor.

Video games in the store or other coin-operated machines will be required to collect the 7% GST, as will all food and beverage vending machines. The price of the goods or services are deemed to include the GST and tax is considered to be paid at the time of sale. The tax to be remitted is 7/107 of the total amounts collected.

. . . if you . . . charge a delivery fee, GST must be paid on the delivery fee . . .

If you deliver items to your customers and charge a delivery fee, GST must be paid on the delivery fee.

Health Care Professionals

Most services provided by health care professionals will be tax-exempt, if one of two criteria are met:

1. the service must be covered by a provincial health care plan in two or more provinces; or

2. the service must be provided in the practice of a profession that is regulated by a health care profession in five or more provinces.

Dieticians, for example, will be able to provide their services on a tax-exempt basis as of January 1, 1997.

However, the following will be considered taxable:

1. Cosmetic medical and dental services performed exclusively for appearance purposes including facelifts and color veneer applied by dentists.

2. Professional services that do not relate directly to the individual's health, such as court testimony or appraisals of health standards in a work environment.

3. Services provided by acupuncturists, herbalists, homeopaths, midwives, moxabustists, musculo-skeletal therapists, polarity therapists and reflexologists.

Note that hospital fees are tax-exempt, including laboratory and radiological services.

The following services are zero-rated, which means no GST is charged, but input tax credits may be claimed:

1. Drugs dispensed for human use (Note that over-the-counter medications are taxed, unless a prescription is given by a medical doctor.);

2. Artificial teeth, dentures, bridges, crowns made by dentists or labs;

3. Communication devices for those with speech or hearing disabilities;

4. Eye glass or contact lenses;

5. Special chairs or other devices for disabled persons; and

6. Most other expenditures deductible by the patient on the income tax return.

. . . no GST is charged when a drug manufacturer gives the doctor free samples . . .

Services provided to a non-resident patient are treated in the same manner as those given to Canadians. No GST is charged when a drug manufacturer gives the doctor free samples of drugs or other medications.

Insurance Agents and Brokers

Insurance agents and brokers generally provide tax-exempt financial services. Commissions earned in the sale of such products are also tax-exempt. If other services are provided, such as advice on estate planning, risk-control or insurance evaluation, the amounts paid will be entirely GST-exempt if the services are covered by the insurance policies and account for less than 50% of the entire remuneration. Otherwise any separate fee charged is GST taxable.

Property Managers

Services provided that are taxable include office space and other commercial rental accommodation, short-term hotel and motel accommodation and real estate services, such as fees paid to lawyers, surveyors and real estate agents.

Examples of zero-rated goods and services include the leasing of farmland to a registrant in exchange for a share of the zero-rated produce from the land.

Examples of tax-exempt goods and services are the resale of an individual's home, long-term residential rental accommodation, low-cost residential rental accommodation and long-term residential rentals by a public service or public sector body, or rentals in a student residence.

In the case of mobile homes, GST will not apply to long-term mobile home rentals, or to a lease or rental of land for at least one month. Monthly pad rentals in a mobile home park are tax-exempt, but if the mobile home is used for commercial or business reasons, rental fees will be taxable in the normal manner.

For motels and hotels, GST will be charged on restaurant meals, room service, parking, coat-check fees, pay-per-view movies, telephone charges, but not voluntary gratuities.

For those who provide meeting facilities, GST will be charged on convention space and meeting rooms, baggage services, management fees, parking, restaurant and room service. Exempt supplies include long-term residential accommodation and accommodation rented for no more than $20 for each day of occupancy.

Residential Builders and Developers

When builders construct or substantially renovate their residential rental properties which they own, they will be treated as having sold and immediately repurchased the properties when completed. GST is then calculated on the "fair market value" of the properties at that time and remitted in the normal manner. These are called the "self-supply" rules. Specifically excluded from the self-supply rules are religious communal organizations. (*See also* "GST Consequences on Real Property Transactions," earlier in this chapter).

 CHAPTER FOUR

Deductions for Home-Based Businesses

Any person who contributes to prosperity must prosper in return.

— Earl Nightingale

WRITE OFF YOUR HOME-OFFICE EXPENSES

A recent development in the province of Quebec may serve as an omen for the hundreds of thousands of people who write off home-office expenses on their personal income tax returns every year. Starting this year, residents of Quebec will only be allowed to claim one-half of their allowable home workspace expenses in a move that is intended to raise extra money for the government there.

While this has not yet come to pass for those who live in the rest of the country, the federal government has said that it is looking at home workspace rules very carefully, to see whether it should follow Quebec's lead.

... be sure you are claiming all that you are entitled to ...

So, the rules for claiming home-office expenses, federally at least, could very well be a tax advantage that is with us only temporarily, so be sure you are claiming all that you are entitled to.

To make your claim, prepare a separate worksheet, possibly entitled "Home Workspace Costs." It will be necessary for you to do two things on this statement:

1. Gather information about the total expenditures for the year.

2. Prorate these expenses by the fraction that you obtain with the following information:

$$\frac{\text{Square footage of the home workspace}}{\text{Square footage of the entire living area of home}} \times \frac{\text{Total}}{\text{Costs}} = \frac{\text{Deductible}}{\text{Portion}}$$

The categories of allowable expenditures you will be able to claim depend on whether you are an employee, an employee earning commissions, or self-employed.

Only the self-employed may claim capital cost allowance and mortgage interest paid as home workspace expenses in addition to the other allowable home workspace expenses:

- utilities (heat, electricity, water),
- maintenance and repairs,
- rent,
- property taxes,
- insurance, and
- cleaning supplies.

Prior to the 1987, home workspace expenses could be used to offset other income earned in the year without restriction. Under the new rules effective 1988 and future years, home workspace expenses are deductible under only two specific conditions: (a) the office must be used exclusively to earn business income on a regular and continuous basis for meeting clients, customers or patients; or (b) the office must the principal place of business of the individual.

Your Workspace Is Used Exclusively for Business

. . . there must be a segregated area in the home used for no other purpose but the business . . .

Taxpayers whose business circumstances fit under the first criterion must use the workspace "exclusively" to earn income from a business. This means there must be a segregated area in the home used for no other purpose but the business. As well, the space must be used to regularly meet customers at some level of frequency, which will be determined according to the type of business and individual facts of each taxpayer upon audit. Therefore, it is most important to keep a log of appointments to justify these claims.

Example

Cordell is a chiropractor. He practices out of his home, to which he had a separate addition built. His clients have their own entrance, and are attended by his receptionist, daughter Christina.

Because this office space is used on a regular and continuous basis to meet clients of the practice, and it is set aside for no other purposes, the portion of the home expenses that relate to this office area are deductible on Cordell's personal income tax return.

Your Workspace Is Your Primary Place of Business

Taxpayers whose business circumstances fit under the second criterion may have two places of business, but the workspace must be the principal or main place of business.

Example

Cordell makes housecalls. This means he has to work at locations away from the home office, but returns to the home office to take appointments, do administrative work, and so on. In such cases, it is not necessary for the home-office space to be used "exclusively" for the business, but it is necessary for the space to be segregated from the rest of the living area in the home.

Restrictions

▶ *. . . The deduction for the home-office space . . . cannot create or increase a loss . . .*

The deduction for the home-office space may be used only to offset business income earned in a year. It cannot create or increase a loss. Unused deductions under these rules may be carried forward and used to offset business income in a subsequent year.

In addition, it is important to point out that claiming Capital Cost Allowance (CCA) on the building is an option for the self-employed, but it is not a good idea. On the plus side, a deduction for the declining value in the building (if this is in fact the case), will result in an additional home-office expense of 4% of the building's value, if the building falls into Class 1 for CCA purposes. This deduction will reduce the net income from your business, and therefore the taxes you'll have to pay.

However, on the negative side, any claim for Capital Cost Allowance and/or possible recapture on a principal residence will compromise the tax exempt status you have on this property. Therefore, when you sell your home, taxable capital gains will result on the portion of the building that was depreciated under the Capital Cost Allowance provisions, if you sell it for more than the original cost, plus additions and improvements.

Example

The value of Cordell's building in which he lives and works, is $50,000 without the land. (Land is not a depreciable asset.) It is classified as Class 1 with a CCA rate of 4%. This would reap a tax *deduction of $2,000, which must be prorated to remove any personal use component. Cordell, however, decides to forego this deduction to preserve the tax exempt status of his principle residence.*

Claim home workspace expenses on the "Business Income and Expense Statement" allocated to their enterprise: "T2032," "T2042," "T2121" or "T2124, as shown below:

A. HOME WORKSPACE COSTS (EXHIBIT 4-1)

1. **Personal Use Component:**
    Fraction of Total Expenses to be Subtracted from Total:

Square Footage of Living Area without Home Workspace:	800	
Square Footage of Total Living Area of Home:	1000	
	= 80%	(A)

2. **Expenses** (Record totals for the year):

a.	Heat	650
b.	Electricity	490
c.	Water	280
d.	Property Taxes	2560
e.	Insurance	880
f.	Mortgage Interest	9950
g.	Capital Cost Allowance	N/A
h.	Other	
	Other	

3. Total Expenses $ 14810   (B)

4. Less Personal Component:
    Total in (3) times (A) $ 11848   (C)

5. Amount Claimable (B–C) $ 2962

B. ON THE STATEMENT OF INCOME AND EXPENSES (EXHIBIT 4-2):

```
┌─ Calculation of business-use-of-home expenses ─────────────────────────────────────
│ Heat
├────────────────────────────────────────────────────────────────────────────────────
│ Electricity
├────────────────────────────────────────────────────────────────────────────────────
│ Insurance
├────────────────────────────────────────────────────────────────────────────────────
│ Maintenance
├────────────────────────────────────────────────────────────────────────────────────
│ Mortgage interest
├────────────────────────────────────────────────────────────────────────────────────
│ Property taxes
├────────────────────────────────────────────────────────────────────────────────────
│ Other expenses
│                                                                        Subtotal
├────────────────────────────────────────────────────────────────────────────────────
│ **Minus** – Personal use portion
│                                                                        Subtotal
├────────────────────────────────────────────────────────────────────────────────────
│ **Plus** – Amount carried forward from previous year
│                                                                        Subtotal      1
├────────────────────────────────────────────────────────────────────────────────────
│ **Minus** – Net income (loss) after adjustments from line j above (if negative, enter "0")   2
├────────────────────────────────────────────────────────────────────────────────────
│ Business-use-of-home expenses available for carry forward (line 1 minus line 2) if negative, enter "0"
├────────────────────────────────────────────────────────────────────────────────────
│ **Allowable claim** (the lower of amounts 1 or 2 above) enter this amount on line 8235 above
```

Home Office Claim Restrictions

You will notice on the statement a space for any home-office expenses that were carried forward from a previous year. This is usually due to the restriction that states one cannot increase or create a business loss with home-office expenses. However, such unclaimed amounts may be carried forward and claimed in subsequent tax years. Unfortunately these carry forward rules are rigid. That is, unclaimed home-office expenses must be used up in any year there is business income, to reduce income to zero.

Example

Debbie had a business loss last year, and so was unable to deduct her home-office expenses of $2,500. She has carried them forward for use on this year's return. This year Debbie was profitable; but her net income was only $3,500 from the business.

Despite the fact that she will not be taxable (her Basic Personal Amount of $6,456 will wipe out federal and provincial taxes payable on her income), she must make the claim for the carried forward home-office expenses. This will reduce her net income to $1,000. If she has home-office expenses again this year, she must use these to reduce her income to zero and then carry forward any balance.

Audit-Proofing

For the purposes of satisfying a tax auditor about the size of the space, sketch out the office area and its relationship to the living area in the rest of the house.

. . . sketch out the office area and its relationship to the living area in the rest of the house . . .

Keep this in your tax files in case of a tax audit, to be used to justify the percentage of tax-deductible expenditures that you have claimed. In all cases, expenses claimed as deductions must be reasonable.

For your information, deductions for a home workspace are similar for persons who are qualified employees, differing slightly in the type of tax-deductible expenditures available.

Employees — Salary Only

If you are an employee who earns salary only, you may claim part of your rent or, if you own a home, part of the fuel, electricity and water bill, as well as cleaning materials and minor repairs for the office. You may not claim capital cost allowance on your home, property taxes, insurance payments or mortgage interest.

Employees may claim "home workspace" expenses only if:

1. It is required under the contract of employment that the employee maintain an office in a self-contained domestic establishment. (Form T2200 Declaration of Employment Conditions must be filed.)

2. It is required that the employee pay for the expenses without reimbursement by the employer.

3. One or more rooms are set aside solely to earn income.

As well, the home must be either the principal place of employment or used by the employer exclusively for the purpose of earning income from an office or employment. It must be used on a regular and continuous basis for meeting customers or others in the ordinary course of performing duties. Claim home workspace expenses on "Form T777".

Employees — Salary and Commission

If you are an employee who earns part salary and part commission, or someone who earns commission only, you may claim all of the expenses listed above, including property taxes and insurance. Capital cost allowance or mortgage interest paid will generally not be allowed.

(Note: Amounts claimed for home workspace deductions for employees cannot exceed income from employment. If they do, they may be carried forward and claimed next year. This carry-forward is allowed indefinitely, until used up. Again, make the home workspace claim on "Form T777".)

SIX SIMPLE STEPS TO MAXIMIZING YOUR AUTO CLAIMS

... keeping track of your business travels can be very lucrative from a tax point of view ...

All home-based business owners need transportation from their home to their business-related appointments. For most people, this will mean the use of a passenger vehicle will be required; however, for others, there is public transportation or other means. Keeping track of your business travels can be very lucrative from a tax point of view, yet many home-based business owners either under-claim their auto expenses, or claim them under the "best-guess method" — which of course won't fly with a tax auditor. Here are six simple steps to maximizing your claims.

STEP1 — Keep Track of Public Transportation Charges

If you should do your travelling through taxis, buses, subways or other public transportation, these travelling costs should be fully deductible, if you can show from your Daily Diary that the trip had a solely business purpose.

If the trip had both a personal and a business purpose, prorate the expense according to the appropriate use.

Example

Sheri has started a gardening business out of her home called Creative Gardens. She designs flower gardens for people by providing them with sketches, recommendations for plant acquisitions and their related budgets, and then she hires university students to carry out her plans. She does not have a car at this time. She takes a taxi to and from her clients' homes whenever she makes a presentation, or follows up with her recommendations or contract fulfillment.

In Sheri's case, because her trips are always directly from the home to the client's home and back, 100% of the costs of the taxi fares will be tax-deductible. Sheri should keep all of her cash receipts, charge card statements or monthly billings from the cab company to verify her claims.

STEP 2 — Claim 100% of Business Only Vehicles

... very few 100% claims for auto expenses are allowed ...

If you own or lease a car, the bookkeeping required to stay onside with Revenue Canada is somewhat more complicated. First, you need to know that very few 100% claims for auto expenses are allowed. However, this can happen if you can show you own or lease a vehicle for no other purpose whatsoever but business driving.

Example

Mac owns a shut-in meal delivery service. He leases a van to do this. The van is painted purple and covered with his business name and logo "The Purple People Pleaser." (Mac is quite a character!) The van comes equipped with a hot oven, so at night he also delivers pizza on a freelance basis for other firms, to supplement his income. For personal driving, Mac owns a 1979 Camaro. (It's barely breathing.)

In this case, provided that Mac can show he never uses the van for personal use purposes (*i.e.,* picking up milk, driving to the cottage, driving to the cleaner's to pick up his wife's suits, *etc.*) all expenses of the van will be claimable on his personal tax return.

STEP 3 — Keep a Log of Your Travels if There is a Personal Use Component

For most people, life is not as cut and dried as Mac's situation. Most home-based business owners use their vehicles both for business and personal use. To compute how much of the total expenses of the vehicle are deductible for tax purposes, there is only one acceptable way: a record of distance driven for business purposes compared to distance driven for the entire year. Yes, that means a "cents-per-mile" basis of computing auto expenses will not be good enough. Rather, the taxpayer must do these things:

1. Save all receipts for operating and fixed expenditures.

2. Determine the total distance driven during the year for business use.

3. Determine the total distance driven during the year.

4. Prorate the total expenses for the year to reflect the portion for business driving only.

For example, assume that Sheri, who acquires a vehicle mid-way through her fiscal year, drove 12,000 km this year for business purposes, out of 20,000 km driven in total. Her total expenses for the car were $7,000. Using the following formula, Sheri could compute the tax-deductible portion of this expenses:

$$\frac{\text{Total Business Kilometers}}{\text{Total Kilometers Driven in the Year}} \times \frac{\text{Total}}{\text{Expenses}} = \frac{\text{Tax-deductible}}{\text{Expenses}}$$

$$\frac{12,000}{20,000} \times \$7,000 = \$4,200$$

This is the method that must be used, and the only way to make it work for you is to keep track of the business driving you do. This is a burden for most business people, but well worth it during tax audit time. Some people keep an auto log in their car; others keep track of their business driving right in their daybooks. Even if you haven't kept accurate track of past driving, begin immediately to establish your driving trends with proper records. This may work in your favour when Revenue Canada asks for records from two or three tax years. To help you, a sample Auto Log format is shown in Appendix 10.

Finally, if you use both your car and your spouse's car for business purposes, you will have to try to keep track of the deductible expenses with your distance records. This can get very confusing at tax time. It's generally best to allocate one vehicle to business use for simplicity's sake.

STEP 4 — Save Receipts for all Tax-deductible Expenditures

The types of expenditures you can claim fall into two groups:

1. Operating Expenses:
   Gas and Oil;
   Maintenance and Repairs;
   Tires;
   Car Washes;
   Insurance;
   License Fees;
   Auto Club; and
   Parking (usually claimed in full).

2. Fixed Expenses:
   Lease Costs;
   Interest Costs; and
   Capital Cost Allowances.

▶ *. . . Revenue Canada assumes that parking is a necessary part of your normal business activities . . .*

The operating expenses incurred by the business owner are usually fairly straightforward. A reasonable estimate of unreceipted expenditures, such as coin parking or car washes may be claimed, and can be justified by keeping a written log of these expenses and when they occurred. Note that 100% of parking expenses are usually allowed: Revenue Canada assumes that parking is a necessary part of your normal business activities and so do not require proration.

STEP 5 — Know the Difference Between a Luxury Vehicle and a Motor Vehicle

In tax jargon, a "luxury vehicle" is also known as a "passenger vehicle". This means that the normal tax deductions you can claim for fixed expenditures such as leasing costs, interest and capital cost allowance will be restricted if you acquired the vehicle after June 17, 1987.

A "motor vehicle," on the other hand is one whose fixed costs will generally not be restricted. There are some specific usage rules to consolidate these definitions. For example, in order to be classified as "motor vehicles" not subject to the luxury vehicle restrictions, a pick-up truck that seats one to three people would have to be used more than 50% of the time to transport goods or equipment. A pick-up truck, sport utility or other van that seats four to nine people would have to be used 90% of the time or more to transport goods, equipment or passengers to avoid the restrictions, which are described below:

Restricted Deductions:	**Vehicles acquired**	**Vehicles acquired**
(PST and GST may be added to maximums listed)	after June 17, 1987 and before Sept. 1, 1989	after August 31, 1989 and before January 1, 1997*
Capital Cost Allowances: maximum values	$20,000	$24,000
Leasing costs based on values of	$600 a month	$650 a month
Interest costs based on values of	$8.33 a day	$10 a day

Back to Mac. Let's say that Mac had leased the van he's using for business purposes. If he could not meet the 90% rule, and if his leasing costs were $700 a month, his tax deduction for leasing costs will be limited to a maximum of $650 a month before taxes.

Let's say that Sheri, on the other hand, bought a BMW for $55,000. If her interest costs are more than $10 per day, her maximum deduction for interest will be $10 a day. And, the capital cost that can be used on Sheri's CCA schedule will be limited to $24,000 plus PST and GST.

STEP 6 — Make Decisions to Acquire or Dispose of Vehicles with Capital Cost Allowance Provisions in Mind

The CCA classification used for a Motor Vehicle (costing less than $24,000) is Class 10, with a depreciation rate of 30%. For a Passenger Vehicle, Class 10.1 is used, which also has a depreciation rate of 30%. However, all Class 10.1 assets must be listed separately, rather than pooled together in one class, as is the case with Class 10 vehicles. This rule will have a tax effect on disposition of the asset. (*See* Chapter Five.)

---

* After 1996, maximum leasing costs are $550 a month and the maximum allowable interest deduction is $250 per month. The maximum CCA ceiling will increase to $25,000 plus PST/GST.

In the year of acquisition, the normal "half-year rules" apply to both Class 10 and Class 10.1. That is, only 50% of the normal capital cost allowance is claimed in the year of acquisition. Generally a purchase in the last half of the tax year would give you the most immediate tax benefits, given this restriction.

Remember that your CCA deduction is always claimed at your option, so if your other business expenses are already enough to reduce income to the desired non-taxable level, you can choose to "save" the Undepreciated Capital Cost of your vehicle for another year, to maximize your claims.

Example

Sheri shows a business income of $15,500 after all expenses before CCA on her auto. She has an RRSP contribution of $9,000 this tax year, which is good planning because her net income will be reduced to $6,500. After deducting her safety deposit box fees of $75, Sheri's income is below the basic personal amount of $6,456. Therefore, she would be wise not to claim any CCA on her BMW this year. She will have taken the half-year restriction into account, and next year can claim the full 30% deduction on a capital cost of $24,000* plus GST and PST.

DISPOSITIONS

The introduction of Class 10.1 for vehicles affects the tax treatment of the vehicle when it comes time for a disposition. First, there is a "half-year rule on sale". That is, you will be able to claim 50% of the capital cost allowance that would be normally allowed if you owned the vehicle at the end of the year. Because of this rule, terminal loss is not deductible and recapture is not reportable on Class 10.1 vehicles. For Class 10 vehicles, there is no half-year rule on sale, but as mentioned, no terminal loss is allowed if you didn't take enough depreciation. Recapture on Class 10 assets will, however, have to be accounted for. (*See* "Capital Expenses," in Chapter Five.)

MAXIMIZING CLAIMS FOR ENTERTAINMENT AND PROMOTION

▶ *. . . ask any successful business person — networking is a necessary part of business activities . . .*

Ask any successful business person — networking is a necessary part of business activities. It's what will bring you the contacts to sell your services or goods. It's a fact of business life that your skill at "schmoozing" (a nineties term for networking) may bring about those "big deals" you are dreaming about. People generally like doing business with the people they like having lunch with.

---

*25,000 after 1996.

Revenue Canada recognizes this business fact . . . grudgingly. Since the tax reforms of 1988, Revenue Canada has followed our taxing neighbors to the south in bringing in restrictions to the deduction that is claimable for meals and entertainment in the context of pursuing your business profits.

Prior to 1988, 100% of your costs of meals and entertainment were claimable; from 1988 to February 22, 1994, 80% of these expenses could be claimed, and after this date only 50% of your expenses in this category will be used to reduce income from your business.

What's important is that you keep all receipts for any meals, coffee stops, or entertainment activities you engage in with your clients and business associates. Make sure that you have a record of all tips you leave; if in cash, keep this information in your Company Diary; if paying by credit card, you'll have this record on each voucher.

In addition, you should know how special types of networking situations will be handled with regard to the 50% limitation, because there are some exceptions to the general rules.

Gift Certificates

The 50% limitation will apply to restaurant gift certificates and also to gratuities, cover charges, room rentals at hotel or resort to provide entertainment, and costs of private boxes at sports facilities.

Conventions

. . . remember that a self-employed person may attend only two tax-deductible conventions each year . . .

The 50% limitation will apply to the cost of meals while travelling or attending a convention, conference, seminar or similar function. Where a flat fee is paid for the convention, $50 a day will be deemed to be paid towards food, beverages and entertainment. To the extent that a taxpayer is reimbursed for the business meal or entertainment, the limitation will apply to the person who makes the reimbursement. Remember that a self-employed person may attend only two tax-deductible conventions each year.

Exceptions

The following expenses will be exempt from the limitation:

(a) Where an amount is paid by the taxpayer for food, beverages or entertainment in the ordinary course of business (*e.g.,* restaurants, airlines hotels), such amounts will be exempt if costs are incurred to provide food for consumption.

(b) Where expenses relate to a specific fund-raising event to benefit a registered charity. However, expenses for meals or entertainment expenses incurred at a meeting to organize the event will be subject to the 50% rule.

(c) Where a taxpayer spends money for food, beverages or entertainment for which he or she will ultimately bill the client if the amount is identified in the account submitted to the client. The 50% rule will then apply to the client.

(d) Amounts paid for food or beverages for employees in a remote location where the employee could not be expected to maintain a self-contained domestic establishment will not be restricted.

(e) Where the amount is incurred to provide food, beverages or entertainment to all employees who consume these items at a particular location (*e.g.,* Christmas parties).

(f) Where amounts are paid for travel on an airplane, train or bus, no amount of the fee is considered to be on account of food, beverages or entertainment.

These rules also flow through to your GST return. Where a GST registrant pays GST on the cost of food, beverages and entertainment in the course of commercial activities, input tax credits can be claimed in full in the normal reporting period. However, at the end of the fiscal year, an adjustment will have to be made to "recapture" or pay back 50% of these credits. Where tips are paid to service personnel separately from the billings for the meals or entertainment there is no GST liability and therefore no input tax credits claimable. This would be another reason why it would make sense to pay tips on your credit card.

. . . it would make sense to pay tips on your credit card . . .

OTHER TAX-DEDUCTIBLE EXPENDITURES

We have previously discussed that a home-based business owner has few limitations to claiming operating expenses in an active business. In general, the expenses must be reasonable, incurred to earn income from a business that has a reasonable expectation of profit and supported by documentation. Based upon this, every spending decision you make in your business should be eyeballed with a view to its tax consequences.

There are two types of expenditures for tax purposes: Operating Expenses and Capital Expenses.

What is an Operating Expense?

Operating expenses are those that are required in the ongoing operations of the business. The items purchased are generally used up in the operations of the business, so there is little, if any useful life. Examples are office supplies, advertising, telephone, rent and salaries.

Operating expenses are fully deductible from income of the business; with the exception of certain restricted expenses, such as meals and entertainment.

What Is a Capital Expense?

These are amounts expended to acquire tangible or intangible assets of the business . . . those items that have a useful life of more than one year, and are used to produce the goods or services sold in the business. Examples are equipment, building, furniture and fixtures, automobiles, trucks, and so on, each of which has a useful life of more than one year, and generally costs more than $200.

▶ *. . . capital expenditures cannot be written off in full . . .*

Capital expenditures cannot be written off in full. They are placed in categories and subject to pre-set capital cost allowance rates that are applied on a declining-balance basis. The tax consequences of acquiring and disposing of capital assets is discussed in detail in Chapter Five.

Tax-Deductible Operating Expenses

Following are some specific examples of operating expenses that may be tax-deductible in your business.

ADVERTISING, ENTERTAINMENT AND PROMOTION

Advertising in Canadian publications is an allowable tax deduction. Canadian business will be allowed to deduct advertising expenses in Canadian magazines only if they are primarily owned by Canadians, typeset and printed either in Canada or the U.S., edited in Canada by a Canadian resident and published in Canada. Deductions for advertisements in foreign publications can be allowed if it can be demonstrated that the business was trying to attract customers from outside of Canada.

AUDITS, APPEALS AND APPRAISAL COSTS

The costs of preparing to challenge an appeal on the assessment or reassessment of taxes, interest or penalties under the Income Tax Act, any provincial tax act, any assessment of foreign taxes, decisions under the Employment Insurance Act or Canada Pension Plan will be tax-deductible. Generally this would be claimed either as a business expense or under "Other Deductions" on "Line 232". Should you pay for audit work or accounting fees in the business, such fees are tax-deductible, including costs of tax preparation or costs of issuing capital stock for the business.

Appraisal cost deductibility will depend on the purpose of the appraisal. Appraisals for fire insurance, for example, or other business insurance required would be fully deductible. Appraisals to determine the sale price of a business would be considered capital in nature.

BANKING FEES

Bank charges including service fees, electronic deposit fees, cheque writing fees, and so on, are all tax-deductible and should be supported by the entries on the returnable bank statements. Safety Deposit Boxes held for the company's important papers are also tax-deductible. Also deductible are stand-by fees, guarantee fees, fees of a registrar or agent, any filing fees, and such, which the financial institution may charge. Interest paid on business loans is fully tax-deductible. (Discussed in more detail below.)

Interest paid on business loans is fully tax-deductible . . .

BONUSES

Bonuses paid to employees are considered to be part of their taxable salary and wages, and are fully deductible by the employer. It is a requirement to take tax deductions from the bonus, however, amounts of tax withdrawals can be minimized by annualizing the deductions. (*See* Chapter Six.)

CONVENTION EXPENSES

Two conventions a year are all that can be claimed as a tax deduction for business owners. The conventions must be in connection with a business or profession carried on by the business owner and expenses claimed must be reasonable. If a vacation trip is added onto the journey, the expenses must be prorated according to the expenses that were for business purposes and those that were personal in nature. In general the full costs of the travel from the business to the convention location and back will be allowed, as will costs of accommodation for the convention. For a discussion of restrictions on claiming expenses of meals and entertainment, see "Maximizing Claims for Entertainment and Promotion," earlier in this chapter.

DEPRECIATION

Revenue Canada allows you to recognize the cost of the wear and tear on capital assets as they are used in your business. This is accomplished under the rules for Capital Cost Allowances. As previously discussed, the actual amounts claimed for the capital cost allowance deduction may differ from depreciation for accounting purposes, where the book value of an asset is generally determined on a straight-line basis according to a projection of its useful life.

On the tax return, assets are grouped into specific CCA classes with specific write off rates and can be used as a deduction from business income, up to those maximum rates. CCA is always taken at the taxpayer's option, so as to influence the size of a business' net income or net loss. For example, it may be better to use up home-office expenses before making a claim for CCA, as the book value of the depreciable asset can be "saved" for a future year. As well, this strategy may go a long way in reducing any recaptured deductions for CCA when all the assets of a class are sold. (*See* Chapter Five.)

DISABILITY-RELATED EQUIPMENT AND MODIFICATIONS

. . . a reduction in an employee's taxable employment benefits will be allowed if the employer provides transportation and parking to disabled persons . . .

A reduction in an employee's taxable employment benefits will be allowed if the employer provides transportation and parking to disabled persons who are blind or who have severe mobility problems.

Costs of an attendant hired to assist the disabled person in performing employment duties will also be provided tax free to the employee and modification to buildings used to earn income from a business (whether owned by employer or not) can be deducted rather than depreciated effective 1991. This includes installation of hand-activated power door openers, interior/exterior ramps, widening of doorways, and modifications to bathrooms to accommodate wheelchairs. Also deductible will be the installation or acquisition of elevator car position indicators, visual fire alarm indicators, telephone devices, listening devices for group meetings and disability-specific computer software and hardware attachments acquired and paid for after February 25, 1992.

DIRECTORS

Fees paid to a director of a corporation are tax-deductible.

EMPLOYEES' PROFIT SHARING PLANS

This is a type of deferred profit sharing whereby an employer makes payments to a trustee for the benefit of the employees, in relation to the size of the company's profits. A specific contract is set up under which the contributions are made based on a formula that revolves around the annual profits. A trustee will allocate amounts to each employee based on employer contributions or income earned in the trust. The plan does not have to be formally registered, but must meet certain statutory conditions, as described in subsection 144 (10) of the Income Tax Act. Contributions made by the employer during a tax year or within 120 days thereafter are a tax-deductible expense of the employer.

If the plan permits employee contributions, such contributions will not be tax-deductible to the employee, but any income earned on the deposits will in fact be taxable when allocated each year to the employee's account.

The trust holding the money on behalf of the employees is not subject to tax if it was governed by the Employee Profit Sharing Plan all year. A "T4PS" slip must be issued each year to report amounts allocated during the year, amounts forfeited and amounts paid to the members. The employees are generally taxed on amounts allocated in the year, and will not be taxed on the eventual withdrawals. An allocation is not taxable if it represents a payment by the employee. There is also special treatment for capital gains and dividends. (*See* IT 280R.)

FINES AND PENALTIES

. . . fines and penalties are not normally deductible in computing income from a business or property . . .

Fines and penalties are not normally deductible in computing income from a business or property. This is because they are generally not considered to be incurred for the purpose of earning income. However, there are certain exceptional circumstances under which fines and penalties are legitimately deductible; that is, when all the following tests are met:

- When the fine or penalty can be shown to have been laid out for the purpose of earning income.
- When the nature and circumstances of the conduct are such that allowing the deduction of the expense would not be contrary to public policy.
- Where incurring the type of fine or penalty is a normal risk of carrying on the business and even though due care is exercised, the violation was inevitable and beyond the control of the taxpayer and his or her employees. Fines for pollution and speeding offenses will not be allowed.
- Where the breach of law does not result from negligence, ignorance or deliberate disobedience of the law and does not endanger public safety.
- Where the deduction of the expenses is not otherwise prohibited (*i.e.,* it is not a capital outlay; not incurred to earned tax-exempt income or not in excess of a reasonable amount).

Examples of deductible fines and penalties are:

(a) Interest paid on late or deficient GST, sales tax or excise tax that relate to a business or property.

(b) Penalties imposed for default in payment of property or business taxes levied by a municipality will be deductible, provided the taxes themselves are deductible.

(c) Penalties imposed by trade organizations with common business interests, such as trade associations or farmers' associations.

(d) Penalties for failure to fulfill obligations under private contracts (*e.g.,* failure to complete a contract on schedule).

(e) Penalty or bonus payable because of the pre-maturity repayment of the principal of an outstanding debt obligation. Such amounts are considered to be "prepaid interest" and therefore deductible.

GUARANTEES AND WARRANTIES

If you are obligated by law to guarantee your work, as in the construction industry, any outlays and expenses incurred to carry out the terms of the guarantee or warranty will be deductible.

INTEREST EXPENSES AND CAPITALIZATION

Expenses of borrowing money will generally be deductible if incurred to earn income from the business. This can include money borrowed for working capital and/or acquisition of depreciable assets. If there is a partial personal use component, only the business portion of the expenses will be deductible.

The following costs of borrowing money will be deductible:

1. legal fees for preparation and approval of a prospectus,

2. accounting or auditing fees in the preparation or certification of financial statements,

3. costs of printing the prospectus,

4. commitment fees or standby interest paid to a lender if the lender is committed to making a specified amount of money available,

5. soft costs incurred in the construction of a building for the purposes of earning income including mortgage application, appraisal, processing and insurance fees,

6. mortgage guarantee fees,

7. mortgage brokerage and finders fees and legal fees related to mortgage financing,

8. a promoter's service fees relating to soft costs,

9. premiums on a term life insurance policy assigned to the lender as required collateral security on a loan, and

10. commissions charged by a bank in connection with the sale of bankers' acceptances.

PENALTIES OR BONUSES

A penalty or bonus paid by a borrower to a lender to retire a loan prior to its maturity may or may not deductible, as the amounts are considered to be incurred in the course of repaying the money, rather than in the course of borrowing the money. The facts in each case must be examined separately.

CAPITALIZATION OF INTEREST COSTS

A taxpayer may also elect, at his or her option, to capitalize the cost of money borrowed for the purposes of acquiring depreciable property. The election need not be made for all the depreciable property acquired, and it may be made for either a portion or all of the costs of the money borrowed at the taxpayer's discretion. The elected amount is then added to the capital cost of the depreciable property instead of being deducted as an expense. The amount can then be deducted annually under the CCA provisions, and may be subject to recapture. To make the election, all that is required is that the depreciable property be on hand at the end of the tax year for which the election is being made and a statement be filed with the return indicating this elected treatment. An election must be made for each year in which the treatment is desired or the process will be discontinued for future years.

Example

> *Phillip is a farmer whose operations are not yet profitable. One of the reasons is that he has borrowed a large sum of money to finance the purchase of farm machinery. The interest costs on the machinery are $25,000 each year, which contribute to his operating loss.*

In this case, Phillip can choose to add the interest to the capital cost of his equipment, thereby taking a reduced deduction under the CCA rules, instead of deducting the interest costs in full. This makes sense because the non-capital loss carry-back rules are limited, while CCA is taken at the taxpayer's option, for as long as he or she owns the assets. Because the election is made on an annual basis, Phillip can choose to write off the expense in full as his profitability position varies.

LOSS OF ASSET

When the asset upon which a loan is made is lost, or its value otherwise decreases, interest costs might continue to be tax-deductible under new rules introduced on August 30, 1993. These provisions give a tax break when the source to which the interest relates no longer exists. For example, where a taxpayer who has used borrowed money for the purpose of earning income from a capital property (other than real property or depreciable property) stops using the money for that purpose after 1993, and finds that a portion of the borrowed money has been lost because of a decline in the value of the property, the portion that has been lost is "deemed" to continue to be used for the purpose of earning income from property. That portion of the interest will still be tax-deductible.

Usually, it is considered that one has stopped using the principal for the purpose of earning income when the property is sold or otherwise disposed of. But if the taxpayer has used borrowed funds to acquire shares in a corporation that has subsequently become bankrupt, a continued interest deduction may also be available. To calculate the deduction, one must determine the total amount of borrowed money outstanding just before it stopped being used to earn income, less the amount of borrowed money that is not considered to be lost.

To make this determination, the amount considered not to have been lost is the amount of borrowed money traceable to the consideration received on disposition, if the property was disposed of at "fair market value". Otherwise, the amount considered not to have been lost is the amount that would be traceable to consideration received if the taxpayer had disposed of the property at "fair market value".

Where the property is acquired by a creditor for a reduction in the debt owing, the reduction is subtracted in determining the amounts of monies borrowed for the purposes of the interest deductibility calculations explained above.

LEGAL FEES

. . . legal fees incurred for the purposes of gaining or producing income from a business or property are deductible . . .

The type of legal fees that are deductible will depend on whether or not these fees are incurred in the operations of the business, or on account of capital. In general, legal fees incurred for the purposes of gaining or producing income from a business or property are deductible, including the legal expenses paid for assistance in filing an objection or appeal of tax, interest or penalties assessed under the Income Tax Act, a decision under the Employment Insurance Commission Act or the Canada Pension Plan. (*See* "Maximizing Claims for Entertainment and Promotion," earlier in this chapter, for a discussion of non-deductible legal fees.)

LISTS OF CLIENTS

If there is temporary value only, the amounts paid for the ledger lists will likely be held fully deductible; however, if the expenditure is for the acquisition of the business of the seller, the amounts paid are considered to be "eligible capital property".

MEMBERSHIP DUES

These are generally deductible in full and include fees for membership in professional associations, commercial associations, trade associations, service clubs, cultural organizations and learned societies. Initiation fees for use of any dining or recreational club are not allowed.

(Note: Admission fees that are paid once to obtain an enduring benefit are considered to be a capital outlay. This includes fees paid as a call to the bar or a professional accounting institute. They would be classified as eligible capital property. *See* Chapter Five.)

MOVING EXPENSES

You can claim the expenses of moving your business from one location to another, as well as the costs of moving an employee from one location to another.

PATENT COSTS AND LICENSING

Generally speaking outlays and expenses for acquiring or attempting to acquire a patent or license for use in a business will qualify as "eligible capital property," but not as a deductible business expense. License fees paid to a municipality or province are usually deductible, unless they are granted for a limited period, in which case they are again treated as eligible capital property in Class 14.

RENTS AND LEASING ARRANGEMENTS

Such amounts are normally tax-deductible, unless there is a personal use component. In the case of lease-option agreements it is important to determine if the payments are on account of rent, or on account of the purchase price of the property.

Under the following conditions, the transaction is considered to be a sale of depreciable property that must be scheduled for CCA purposes:

1. the lessee automatically acquires title after payment of a specified amount,

2. the lessee is required to buy the property from the lessor during or at the termination of the lease,

3. the lessee has the right to acquire the property at a price that is substantially less than the probable "fair market value" of the property, or

4. the lessee has a right to acquire the property at terms that no reasonable person would fail to exercise.

RESERVES

A reserve that is taken in one year for doubtful accounts, transitional reserves under the common year-end changes, amounts not yet due, livestock inventory provisions, and so on, are deducted from income in one year, and added back to income in the next.

SALARIES, WAGES AND DEFERRALS

These amounts are tax-deductible to the payor. An amount may be deducted for contribution to a retirement compensation arrangement for services of an existing or former employee. Amounts paid as retiring allowances or death benefits are deductible. If salary or wages payable to an employee remain unpaid 180 days after the end of the tax year in which they were accrued on the books, the amounts are deemed not to have been incurred and become deductible only when paid. A deduction may generally not be taken for salary deferral arrangements unless the arrangement is for the benefit of non-resident employees who render their services outside of the country.

TAXES

. . . Taxes on real property are tax-deductible if the property is used to earn income from a business . . .

Sales and excise taxes are tax-deductible less any amounts that are reimbursed (such as input tax credits under the GST). Taxes on real property are tax-deductible if the property is used to earn income from a business.

TELEPHONE AND COMMUNICATIONS

All air time, rental charges, long distance charges, hook up charges, and so on, will be tax-deductible. Equipment costs are depreciated.

TRAINING COSTS

In general, expenses of attending training courses outside the taxpayer's general geographic area are considered to be unreasonable, to the extent that they exceed what a similar course would have cost in the local area, if available. The costs of training will include costs for travel, food, beverages and lodging incurred in connection with attending a training course. The costs may not include tuition fees that otherwise qualify for a tuition tax credit.

In cases where the training course results in a lasting economic benefit to the taxpayer, the costs are considered to be capital in nature. These costs are then deducted as "eligible capital property". Training in connection with a course to obtain credit for a degree, diploma, professional qualification or similar certificate would be considered capital in nature.

Examples of capital expenditures of this type include:

1. a medical general practitioner training to become a specialist,

2. a lawyer who is taking an engineering course unrelated to the legal practice,

3. someone who is taking a university course other than that leading to a degree, and

4. a professor employed by a university taking a course during a sabbatical in order to earn a new skill needed for a sideline business.

Where courses are taken mainly to maintain, update or upgrade an already existing skill or qualification with respect to a business or profession, expenses incurred will be fully deductible.

This would include courses taken to enable a professional to learn the latest methods of carrying on his or her profession, specialization courses such as a tax course taken by an accountant qualified to do tax work, a course on modern building materials taken by an architect or a course on electronic ignitions taken by an auto repair shop owner.

TRAVELLING COSTS

Such costs are generally deductible if incurred to earn income from the business. A detailed accounting of expense accounts should be available. The general limitation on meals and entertainment costs (50%) will be enforced.

NON-DEDUCTIBLE EXPENDITURES

. . . the Income Tax Act is specific about what expenditures are not deductible to those who are self-employed . . .

It is just as important for you to know about specific expenditures that are not deductible under the Income Tax Act as it is to know about the deductible amounts. This will help you to make important spending decisions throughout the year and account for the possible real cost, after-tax consequences.

It's interesting in fact, to draw a comparison of tax treatment between employees and the self-employed at this point: the Income Tax Act is specific with regard to the tax-deductible expenses of employees; they are listed in Section 8. However, the Income Tax Act is specific about what expenditures are *not* deductible to those who are self-employed.

Advertising Costs

In a foreign media, these are not allowed unless it can be shown that the Canadian business is attempting to attract clients from outside the country.

Appraisal Fees

If for the purposes of sale of an asset, these are capitalized.

Artificial Transactions

Should the expenditures made within your business be a sham, exercised only for the purposes of tax avoidance, they can be ignored under the provisions of GAAR (the General Anti-Avoidance Rules) and treated as if they are not deductible. One must show that the expenditures were for bona fide business purposes to avoid the GAAR applications.

Capital Expenditures

The capital cost of an asset is not deductible; rather it must be scheduled for the purposes of claiming a deduction called Capital Cost Allowance. Major expenditures to improve upon the condition of the asset will always affect the adjusted cost base of the asset rather than be deductible in full as operating expenses.

Charitable Donations

These items are generally deducted as a personal charitable donation by the donor on the tax return on "Line 340" unless the amounts are made in the form of advertising.

Christmas Gifts

Gifts to employees of no more than $100 are received tax-free and not deductible by the employer ($200 in the year an employee marries).

Club Dues and Recreational Facilities

. . . membership fees for dues in dining, recreational or sporting clubs are not tax-deductible . . .

Membership fees for dues in dining, recreational or sporting clubs are not tax-deductible. Such fees paid for an employee where it is to the benefit of the employee to be a member will not be considered a taxable benefit to the employee. Also non-deductible are the costs of keeping a yacht, camp, lodge or gold course, except if any of these are run for profit.

Dividends Paid

The amounts paid to shareholders are not deductible by the corporation.

Entertainment

Fifty percent of costs are restricted.

Expenses incurred to Earn Exempt Income

Generally such amounts will be disallowed.

Fines and Penalties

The following amounts will not be tax-deductible:

(a) Penalties imposed for default in payment of excise and federal sales tax;

(b) Penalties paid for late or deficient payments of the Goods and Services Tax or provincial sales taxes (however interest is deductible);

(c) Penalties imposed under tax, customs, corporations acts or other legislation for failure to maintain books and records;

(d) Fines levied by provincial law societies, accounting institutes, colleges of physicians and stock exchanges or other governing bodies will not be deductible from income; and

(e) Fines or penalties for participating in illegal activities.

Insurance Payments

Amounts paid to cover personal injury or disability are not deductible and proceeds receivable are not taxable. Amounts paid to defer the cost of overhead in replacing an incapacitated employee will be deductible, however. Proceeds received will be treated as income from a business.

Premiums paid to insure the lives of officers, employees or shareholders are not allowed as a deduction in general, if the policy amounts are payable to the company — in which case such proceeds would be received tax free.

Interest Payments

If incurred to earn income, these will be tax-deductible, even if the source of the loan diminishes or disappears. However, if the source is converted to personal use, no further interest payments can be deducted. Interest paid on income tax bills will not be deductible either.

Lease Payments

Amounts paid under a conditional sales contract are not deductible, as explained above.

Legal Fees

The following situations describe cases where legal fees are not deductible:

(a) Legal expenses for outlays of a capital nature (included as part of the capital cost of the property) are not deductible.

(b) Legal expenses incurred for advice in preparing a tax return (unless incurred in connection with earning income from a business or property or by a taxpayer employed in selling property or negotiating contracts) are not deductible.

(c) Legal expenses incurred for costs in obtaining a divorce or separation agreement are not deductible, nor are costs in establishing or enforcing child custody.

(d) Legal expenses to protect a real estate license to earn commissions are not deductible.

(e) Legal fees attributable to an automobile accident that occurred while the vehicle was used for personal purposes are not deductible.

Personal Consumption

Any expense incurred for personal purposes will not be tax-deductible.

Political Contributions

These are generally claimed on page 4 of the tax return of the individual, but may not be claimed as business expenses on the "Income and Expense Statement".

Prepaid Expenses

. . . pre-production or start-up costs of a new business must be claimed in the year incurred . . .

In the case of farmers on the cash method, only expenses of the current and one additional year are deductible in the current year, the other prepaid amounts must be deducted in annual increments in accordance with the years to which they pertain. In general, for all other businesses, all costs incurred must be allocated for future periods and expensed in those periods. Pre-production or start-up costs of a new business must be claimed in the year incurred.

CHAPTER FIVE

Handling Assets

The evidence unmistakeably indicates that you have to spend money in order to make money.
— Srully Blotnick

CAPITAL EXPENSES

Under the Income Tax Act, a special tax deduction is allowed to account for the wear and tear that occurs in the course of business activities, on depreciable assets. This deduction is called Capital Cost Allowance (CCA).

> *. . . the cost of the acquisition of the asset itself will not be deductible from income in the year acquired . . .*

Many taxpayers who are unfamiliar with the Income Tax Act are unaware that the cost of the acquisition of the asset itself will not be deductible from income in the year acquired. Maxine, for example, put a tool box on her pick-up truck recently. This improvement cost $2,500, which Maxine was expecting to write off on her income tax return in full. She estimated that at her 27% tax rate, she'd see a reduction in her income taxes of about $675.

Unfortunately, the acquisition of the tool box is considered by Revenue Canada to be a capital addition rather than a fully deductible operating expense. This is because: (1) an improvement has been made to the original condition of an asset, (2) the asset has a useful life of more than a year, and (3) the amount spent on the improvement is over $200. These are the three basic guidelines that Revenue Canada uses to judge whether an expenditure is capital or operating in nature.

Maxine was able to write off significantly less from her transaction. The addition was placed in Class 10, with a depreciation rate of 30%. In the first year an addition is made, the deduction for capital cost allowances is calculated at only one-half the normal amounts. This is known as the "half-year-rule". So her actual deduction on the $2,500 expenditure would be only 30% of $1,250 (one-half the acquisition cost) for a total of $375. Her actual tax savings on the deduction, using her marginal tax rate of 27% would amount to slightly more than $100.

So you see, it pays to know the tax consequences of these decisions beforehand, so that you don't get a nasty surprise come tax time.

Classification of Assets

Income-producing assets with a useful life of more than one year can fall into two main classifications: tangible assets, which are items such as equipment, buildings, vehicles, signs or other assets with a physical presence. One can also acquire "intangible properties" such as goodwill, patents or other intellectual properties. For tax purposes, these are call "eligible capital properties" and an allowance on three-quarters of the value of such properties is allowed. These types of properties are covered in detail later in this chapter.

There are 41 different Classes and Rates of Capital Cost Allowances (as of time of writing). Only income-producing assets are eligible for CCAs. Taxpayers must be involved in a business enterprise, or in some cases can be investors in a revenue property. In some cases, an employee required to use an automobile, aircraft or musical instrument to pursue income from employment may claim capital cost allowance, but only on these specific asset types.

There are two ways to depreciate, or write off the declining value of an asset to arrive at its current or "book value".

THE STRAIGHT-LINE METHOD

> *. . . the straight-line method is not acceptable for income tax purposes . . .*

The straight-line method is generally used for accounting purposes, but is not acceptable for income tax purposes. This is why the statements your accountant may prepare for accounting purposes will have to be adjusted for tax purposes.

DECLINING-BALANCE METHOD

Under the declining-balance method, which is the method used for tax purposes, a certain percentage is applied to all the assets of the same class. Assets that are placed in the class will generally lose their identity and all values are "pooled together" as one "undepreciated capital cost," or balance. Whenever assets of the same class are acquired their "cost of addition" is added to the undepreciated balance in the class.

Example

Kevin bought a van for use in his plumbing business. The van is used 90% of the time or more on the business, so qualifies for addi-

tion into Class 10 with a declining-balance rate of 30%. It was acquired for $40,000. Taking the half-year rules into account in the year of acquisition, the deduction Kevin can take for this asset on his business statement is the following:

Cost of Addition		$40,000
Less Half the Value in Year 1		$20,000
Value for Depreciation in Year 1		$20,000
× rate (30%)	=	6,000 = the maximum CCA deduction for this year.
Undepreciated Capital Cost	=	$34,000

Next year, the undepreciated capital cost of $34,000 will be used to compute the deduction of up to $10,200 ($34,000 × 30%).

You will notice that we say "up to" $10,200 can be taken as a deduction on the income and expense statement in Year 2. That's because the CCA deduction is always taken at the taxpayer's option. If you don't need a deduction of this size to reduce your income, you can "save" the undepreciated balance for a future year, when your income may be higher.

> *. . . the CCA deduction is always taken at the taxpayer's option . . .*

Under this method, the assets will never be totally depreciated. Usually, the only time the assets can be taken off the books for tax purposes is if the taxpayer disposes of some or all the assets in the class.

Whenever assets are disposed of, the disposal value — not to exceed the original cost — is subtracted from the undepreciated balance left in the class. Should all the assets of the class be sold, and for more than its original cost plus major additions, a capital gain will result.

Example

Katlin and Patrick work as self-employed publishers' representatives in their city of Calgary. They recently bought a laptop computer for each of them and a printer for their home office. The total investment was $5,500, and the assets will be classed as Class 10 items with a declining-balance rate of 30%.

When the duo added a communications centre including modem and fax, an additional investment of $500 was made. This was added to their existing Class 10 pool as a capital addition.

Katlin and Patrick then received an offer they couldn't refuse: to start a new venture in San Francisco. They promptly sold all their assets and moved. They were lucky enough to sell their Class 10 assets for $6,200, which was $200 more than they originally paid.

The increase in value over the original cost of the assets, $200, is considered to be a capital gain.

In certain instances, special rules have been designed to modify these general principals. For example, in the first year of business, when the fiscal year is less than 12-months long, the normal capital cost allowance must be prorated to reflect only the period of time in which you were actually in business.

In the year a business ceases, assets are generally considered to be disposed of and therefore no CCA deduction is claimable. However, there may be a reconciliation of the account through the reporting of recapture or terminal losses, which are discussed in "Calculating Cost of Additions" later in this chapter.

There are also certain exclusions to the general rules:

1. Property with an enduring useful life, valued on acquisition, at less than $200. In general such expenditures can be written off in full as operating expenses. However, it is not unusual for certain tax auditors to apply the "useful life of more than one year" parameter strictly. This means that if you acquired two used sinks for use in your home-based hairdressing salon for $75 each at a local auction sale, you will likely be required to write this off as business assets subject to the CCA deduction, even though the combined cost was only $150.

2. Inventory, which is materials, supplies and the like, usually held for resale. Costs of inventory are reduced by the value of inventory on hand at the end of the year. These costs are considered to be a direct cost of doing business.

3. Personal use property, or any portion of assets used for personal use.

4. Certain works of art acquired after November 12, 1981 including prints or paintings worth more than $200 at cost.

5. Expenses for the maintenance of a yacht, camp, lodge or golf course if the maintenance costs are otherwise not deductible.

6. Farm property acquired prior to 1972 (which was depreciated on a straight-line method).

7. Land is not a depreciable asset and cannot be depreciated, although there is a special rule for Class 37 which includes the land and constructed waterways of an amusement park. Class 36 includes land "rented" under a lease-option agreement where the rent is later applied to the purchase of the property.

8. Property owned by non-residents who are taxable in Canada if the property is located outside of Canada.

9. Animals, trees, shrubs or other growing things

10. Gas wells, mines, oil wells, rights of way

In the case of condominiums, if more than one unit is owned in the complex, all units together are considered as one for the purposes of claiming CCA. Otherwise, buildings over $50,000 must be allocated to a separate class.

The schedule for claiming Capital Cost Allowance is found with the "Business Income and Expense Statements" in Revenue Canada's Business Guide books. The entries on the schedule should always be accompanied by a complete description of any additions or dispositions within the classes. The description should look something like this:

TABLE 5-1
CAPITAL COST ALLOWANCE SCHEDULE FOR HMS ENTERPRISES

Additions during the year:	1. 1996 Honda Civic	$25,000
	Taxes (7 + 7%)	3,500
	Total Cost	$28,500
	Maximum Capital Cost for CCA	
	($24,000 plus PST/GST)	$27,360
	2. Computer System	$ 3,500
	Taxes (7 + 7%)	490
	Total Cost	$ 3,990
Dispositions during the year:	Fax Machine	$ 250 private sale

1 Class number	2 Undepreciated capital cost (UCC) at the start of the year	3 Cost of additions in the year (see Areas B and C below)	4 Proceeds of dispositions in the year (see Areas D and E below)	5 * UCC after additions and dispositions (col. 2 **plus** 3 **minus** 4)	6 Adjustment for current year additions (1/2 x (col. 3 **minus** 4)) If negative, enter "0"	7 Base amount for capital cost allowance (col. 5 **minus** 6)	8 Rate %	9 CCA for the year (col. 7 x 8 or a lower amount)	10 UCC at the end of the year (col. 5 **minus** 9)
10.1	—	27,360	—	27,360	13,680	13,680	30	4,104	23,256
10	—	3,990	—	3,990	1,995	1,995	30	598.50	3,391.50
8	250	—	250	0	0	0	20	0	0

Total CCA claim for the year (enter this amount, minus any personal portion, on line 8207 on page 1 of this form) | 4702.50

* If you have a negative amount in this column, add it to income as a recapture under "Other income" on page 1 of this form. If there is no property left in the class and there is a positive amount in the column, deduct the amount from income as a terminal loss under "Other expenses" on page 1 of this form. Recapture and terminal loss do not apply to a Class 10.1 property.

COMMON CAPITAL COST ALLOWANCE CLASSES AND RATES

In previous chapters we have discussed the calculation of a deduction for the wear and tear on capital assets, called Capital Cost Allowance, or CCA, and you have become familiar with the concept that this deduction is based on a specified classification and rate structure described in the Income Tax Act.

The following is a brief overview of some of the common classes and rates into which your business assets may fall. It is important for you to know about this, so that you can take the appropriate rate structure into account in planning your annual tax affairs. Before we begin the discussion, here is a summary of how to make a deduction for the capital cost allowance you calculate.

Summary: How to Claim Depreciation on the Tax Return

The deduction for depreciation or Capital Cost Allowances will end up on the "Business Income and Expense Statement" and will reduce net income or increase a net loss. To do the actual calculations, go to the CCA schedule provided on the back of the forms by Revenue Canada, or on your computer program. The CCA schedules will generally have 10 columns:

Column 1: Class number

Column 2: Undepreciated Capital Cost at the start of the Year (UCC)

Column 3: Cost of Additions in the Year (Itemized elsewhere on the schedule)

Column 4: Proceeds of Dispositions in the Year (Itemized elsewhere on the schedule)

Column 5: UCC after Additions and Dispositions

Column 6: Adjustment for current year additions (1/2 of column 3 less column 4)

Column 7: Base amount for CCA purposes

Column 8: CCA Rate

Column 9: CCA for the Year (This is the amount claimed as a deduction)

Column 10: UCC at the end of the year (Column 5 less Column 9)

A blank sample follows; see completed example, prior page.

1 Class number	2 Undepreciated capital cost (UCC) at the start of the year	3 Cost of additions in the year (see Areas B and C below)	4 Proceeds of dispositions in the year (see Areas D and E below)	5 * UCC after additions and dispositions (col. 2 **plus** 3 **minus** 4)	6 Adjustment for current year additions (1/2 x (col. 3 **minus** 4)) If negative, enter "0"	7 Base amount for capital cost allowance (col. 5 minus 6)	8 Rate %	9 CCA for the year (col. 7 x 8 or a lower amount)	10 UCC at the end of the year (col. 5 **minus** 9)

Total CCA claim for the year (enter this amount, minus any personal portion, on line 8207 on page 1 of this form)

* If you have a negative amount in this column, add it to income as a recapture under "Other income" on page 1 of this form. If there is no property left in the class and there is a positive amount in the column, deduct the amount from income as a terminal loss under "Other expenses" on page 1 of this form. Recapture and terminal loss do not apply to a Class 10.1 property.

Summary of Classes Falling Under General Regulations Under Schedule II

CLASS 1: BUILDINGS

The CCA Rate in this Class is 4% and includes property that is a bridge, canal, culvert, dam, and a building or other structure that includes component parts such as electric wiring, plumbing, sprinkler systems, air-conditioning equipment, heating equipment, lighting fixtures, elevators, and so on. Remember to put each building valued at $50,000 or more into a separate Class 1 (exception: two or more condominiums in the same complex).

CLASS 2: ELECTRICAL GENERATING EQUIPMENT

The CCA Rate is in this Class is 6% and it generally includes electrical generating equipment, a pipeline, generally acquired before 1988 or 1990.

CLASS 3: BUILDINGS, DOCKS, WHARVES, TELECOMMUNICATIONS WIRING

The CCA Rate in this Class is 5% and includes a building acquired before 1988 or 1990 in the case of certain agreements, docks, breakwaters, wharves, windmills, telecommunications wiring acquired after May 25, 1976.

CLASS 6: BUILDINGS, FENCES, GREENHOUSES, STORAGE TANKS

The CCA Rate in this Class is 10%. Buildings and their component parts used for the purposes of gaining or producing income from farming or fishing that have no footings or any other base support below ground level, acquired before 1979 or in some instances after 1978 if construction had commenced beforehand. Included in this class: a wooden breakwater, a fence, a greenhouse, an oil or water storage tank.

CLASS 7: VESSELS

The CCA Rate in this Class is 15%. This can include a canoe, rowboat, scow, vessel, furniture or equipment attached except for radiocommunication equipment, and so on.

CLASS 8: EQUIPMENT

The CCA Rate in this Class is 20%. It includes most properties that are tangible properties used in a business, such as equipment, furniture, and so on;

a building acquired after February 19, 1973 that is used to store fresh fruits or vegetables at a controlled environment, radio communication equipment not included in another class, outdoor advertising poster panels or bulletin boards, greenhouses, and so on.

CLASS 9: AIRCRAFT AND INTERIORS

The CCA Rate in this Class is 25% and generally includes property acquired before May 26, 1976 that is electrical generating equipment, radar equipment, and so on; and property acquired after this date that is an aircraft, furniture, fittings or equipment attached to the aircraft, and so on.

CLASS 10: AUTOMOTIVE EQUIPMENT, CERTAIN FILMS, COMPUTER EQUIPMENT

The CCA Rate in the Class is 30%. It includes automotive equipment, a portable tool acquired for the purpose of earning rental income for short terms, such as hourly, daily, weekly, and so on; a harness, sleigh, wagon, trailer, general purpose electronic data processing equipment and systems software acquired after May 25, 1976, contractors' movable equipment including portable camp buildings, a roller skating rink, property acquired for a motion picture drive-in theatre, a motion picture film or video tape acquired after May 25, 1976 except if included in Class 12, and so on.

(Note: Class 10.1 is any property that would have been included in Class 10 that is a passenger vehicle whose cost exceeded $24,000 if acquired after August 31, 1989. The CCA rate is the same but Class 10.1 assets are not pooled; rather each asset must be listed in a separate Class 10.1.)

CLASS 12: COMPUTER SOFTWARE, BOOKS, MEDICAL INSTRUMENTS UNDER $200

The CCA Rate in this Class is 100%. This includes property that is a book that is part of a lending library, china, cutlery, kitchen utensils costing less than $200, medical or dental instruments that cost less than $200, linen, tools costing less than $200, rental costumes, television commercials on video, computer software that is not systems software, videos acquired after February 15, 1984 for the purposes of rentals and property acquired after August 8, 1989 and before 1993 that is used in business as a cash register, electronic bar code scanning equipment, and so on.

(Note: A taxpayer may make an election to have all properties owned and acquired for the purpose of gaining or producing income, that fall into Classes 2 to 12, to be included in Class 1 (4% Rate). This election applies to all properties on hand at the beginning of the year, and would be effective for all subsequent years. New assets acquired in the future could be placed into their normal classes even if this election was made for previously-acquired assets.)

This may be a tax-planning alternative for those who wish to limit the CCA deduction for their assets to 4% a year.

Classes With Special and Unique Calculation Methods

Class 13 and Class 14 have unique methods of calculation.

CLASS 13: LEASEHOLD INTERESTS

. . . the rights to the assets are generally referred to as "leasehold interests" . . .

When a taxpayer rents certain assets, such as office premises, the rights to the assets are generally referred to as "leasehold interests" under a leasehold agreement. If a leasehold interest is acquired from a third party, the amount paid is amortized in this Class 13. The same rules will hold if the tenant expends his or her own money to improve the property. These costs again will be amortized in Class 13. Generally the costs will be amortized over the remaining life of the lease provided that the annual write-off does not exceed 20% of the cost. If the leasehold expires before the end of five years, the remaining costs can be deducted in the last year. If there is a renewable option, the costs are amortized of the remaining life of the current term of the lease plus one term of renewal. The maximum period of amortization is 40 years.

Example

Wally decided to move a portion of his business out of his home office and into a rented premises. He agreed to pay $10,000 in leasehold improvements when he signed his five-year lease, which does not have a renewable term. The costs will be amortized and written off over the five-year period in the amount of $2,000 per year. This meets the 20% rule as well.

CLASS 14: PATENTS, FRANCHISES, LICENCES

A taxpayer who acquires a patent, franchise, concession, licence or other intangible property that is income-producing will receive special tax write offs amounting to an amortization over the life of the patent, franchise or licence. Patents costs are generally amortized over the life of the patent, (generally 17 to 20 years) using equal amounts each year. If the costs in later years are variable, they can be written off in the years to which they apply.

Example

Taylor has invented a unique home care product. The cost of making the product, registering it and obtaining the patent has been

$5,000. Taylor received a patent for 17 years. She may claim a CCA deduction of $294.12 ($5000 ÷ 17).

There is also an alternative 25% write-off for patents acquired after April 26, 1993. See detailed discussion later this chapter.

Separate Classes of the Same Type

In certain cases, you must open separate Classes of the same type to write off your assets at tax time. This can happen in the following instances.

ASSETS OF DIFFERING BUSINESSES

This will happen when the same types of assets were acquired for use in different businesses. In other words, if you buy one computer for Business A and one computer for Business B, each would be set up in a separate Class 10 and written off under the "Income and Expenses Statement" that pertained to each separate business.

PARTNERSHIP ASSETS

After 1971, all depreciable property of the business is considered to be held by the partnership itself, however, individual partners will generally depreciate their personal vehicles used in business, as separate individuals, as an adjustment on their personal tax returns.

RENTAL PROPERTIES WORTH OVER $50,000

Each building you own must be classified in a separate class. That is, if you owned three buildings each valued at $100,000, you would set up three Classes in which to schedule the buildings. There is an exception to this rule: condos owned in the same complex can all be grouped together in the same class.

. . . if a taxpayer has erred in allocating assets . . . the assets may be transferred to the correct class . . .

PASSENGER VEHICLES

As previously mentioned, luxury vehicles must be classed in Class 10.1.

Misclassified Properties

If a taxpayer has erred in allocating assets to their proper class, the assets may be transferred to the correct class at the start of the year. The amounts previously claimed as CCA are added back into the first class. The UCC of the proper class is adjusted by adding the capital cost of the transferred property and deducting any CCA previously allowed.

Example

> *Last year Marcia acquired a computer which she erroneously classified into Class 8, which has a 20% rate. Its cost was $3,000 and she claimed depreciation on the half-year basis of 20% of $1,500 or $300. It should have been put into Class 10, which has a 30% rate.*

1 Class number	2 Undepreciated capital cost (UCC) at the start of the year	3 Cost of additions in the year (see Areas B and C below)	4 Proceeds of dispositions in the year (see Areas D and E below)	5 * UCC after additions and dispositions (col. 2 **plus** 3 **minus** 4)	6 Adjustment for current year additions (1/2 x (col. 3 **minus** 4)) If negative, enter "0"	7 Base amount for capital cost allowance (col. 5 **minus** 6)	8 Rate %	9 CCA for the year (col. 7 x 8 or a lower amount)	10 UCC at the end of the year (col. 5 **minus** 9)
8	3000		3000	0					0
10	2700			2700		2700	30	810	1890

Total CCA claim for the year (enter this amount, minus any personal portion, on line 8207 on page 1 of this form) | 810

* If you have a negative amount in this column, add it to income as a recapture under "Other income" on page 1 of this form. If there is no property left in the class and there is a positive amount in the column, deduct the amount from income as a terminal loss under "Other expenses" on page 1 of this form. Recapture and terminal loss do not apply to a Class 10.1 property.

> Class 8   *UCC $2,700 plus previous reported CCA deduction, $300 = $3,000.*
>
> *Show a disposal of $3,000 in Class 8. There is no tax consequence.*
>
> Class 10   *Add to the UCC of Class 10: $3,000 less $300 = $2700*

Statute of Limitations on Adjustments to Prior-Filed Returns

In general, Revenue Canada will not allow adjustment to claim additional CCA after 90 days have lapsed from the date of the Notice of Assessment, or Reassessment, unless no other change occurs in the assessed tax for the year. In the case of a non-taxable year, Revenue Canada will generally allow the taxpayer to change the CCA deduction even after the 90-day period has expired, again providing there is no change in the tax payable. It is common that where a capital expense was deducted in full by the taxpayer but capitalized on audit by Revenue Canada, the CCA deduction will be allowed by Revenue Canada. Also if Revenue Canada has increased the income but the taxpayer has not claimed the maximum CCA, a retroactive claim for CCA will generally be allowed.

Remember — Depreciation Is Taken at Taxpayer's Option

The CCA rates discussed earlier are maximums, however, the taxpayer may choose to take some or all of the allowable amounts, depending on what is best for the particular tax year. For example, if net income is already below the basic personal amount ($6,456), the taxpayer is not taxable and generally will not need the CCA deduction (except, perhaps to reduce amounts payable to the Canada Pension Plan or increase refundable tax credits). The CCA deduction can, however, be saved by way of an intact UCC balance, for next year.

CALCULATING COST OF ADDITIONS

Now that you know the basics about capital cost allowances, classes and rates, let's zero in on the fine points of calculating the capital cost of your assets, before you buy them.

The capital cost includes the purchase price of the asset (excluding the cost of land), legal, accounting, engineering, installation and other fees that relate to the purchase or construction of the asset, the cost of any additions or improvements made to the property after it is acquired and in the case of a building, certain soft costs such as interest, legal and accounting fees, and property taxes.

Transfers to Business

. . . the "fair market value" is the highest dollar value you could get . . . in an open and unrestricted market . . .

Where the asset is acquired by way of gift or transfer, the "fair market value" of the asset is used as its cost of addition. This can also occur if a personal use asset is transferred to business use. The "fair market value" is the highest dollar value you could get for the property in an open and unrestricted market between a willing buyer and a willing seller who are dealing at arm's length.

Example

Terri just started selling real estate as a self-employed agent. Her car is valued at $15,678 as of the date her business started. She bought it a year ago for $22,500. Her cost of additions for purposes of the CCA schedule will be $15,678.

Non-Arm's Length Transactions

In the case of non-arm's length transactions, such as between family members, different rules apply. Generally the "fair market value" of the asset transferred will be used, except in the case of husband and wife. If assets are transferred during the spouse's lifetime, they can be transferred at the adjusted cost base (or UCC in the case of depreciable property), but subsequent gains on sales are taxed back to the transferor. Or they can be transferred at "fair market value" with all the resulting tax consequences, if you elect such treatment. If the transfer occurs due to the death of the spouse, any amount between the adjusted cost base (or UCC) and the "fair market value" may be used to transfer the assets to the spouse.

Example

Terri's husband, Stan, has also just started selling real estate. Terri has a desk she sells to him for use in his business. Its current resale value is $2,500. She previously acquired it for $3,000. The undepreciated capital cost is $2,000.

Terri could transfer the asset at its FMV ($2,500). Or she can transfer the asset at its UCC of $2,000 and show no tax consequences.

(Note: New "stop-loss rules" re-introduced on June 20, 1996, put into place restrictions on the writing off of losses arising from the transfer of assets between parties until the earliest of:

1. a subsequent disposition of property to someone who is neither the transferor nor someone affiliated to the transferor,

2. a change in the property's use from income-producing to non-income producing, or

3. a "deemed disposition" due to the change of taxable status. See later discussion.)

Finally, if you sell property to others you do not deal with at arm's length, you must follow these rules:

(a) selling price is less than FMV; selling price is considered for tax purposes to be FMV.

(b) selling price is more than FMV; selling price is considered to be FMV.

Half-Year-Rules

As discussed earlier, in the first year an asset is acquired, only one-half the normal depreciation is allowed. This is called the "half-year-rule". The half-year rules will not apply in the following cases:

1. Certified feature films and short productions in Class 12, or

2. Property included in Class 13, 14, 15, 23, 24, 27, 29 and 34.

Some Tax Planning Techniques

Try to claim only the proper amount of CCA to take into account the following options:

1. When to buy an asset can often be influenced by your tax affairs. For example, Holly is thinking of buying a new car to use in her network marketing business, which she has been running for two years. Should she do this in January or in November?

> ► *. . . be aware that you'll be able to claim a capital cost allowance on only half its value . . .*

If you acquire the car in January, be aware that you'll be able to claim a capital cost allowance on only half its value in the first year. So, while your money is out for 12 months, your tax recognition on the depreciation is for six months only. Instead, if you buy the car in November, you will have tax recognition for six months of the current year even though you only owned it for two months.

2. In the year you start your business, your CCA will be prorated both for the half-year-rule and for the number of days you've actually been in business.

Example

Kerry opened his Taxidermy Shop out of the main floor of his two-story house on July 2 of the current tax year. He lives upstairs. His total acquisitions of assets in Class 8 (20%) were $4,500 during the year. He has no other assets at this time.

In this case, the maximum allowable claim for Kerry on his Class 8 assets is:

$4,500 × 20% = $900 × 50% for the half-year rule = $450

$450 × 183/365 for the number of days he was in business = maximum deduction $ 225.62

Generally speaking, in the year a business starts, the maximum CCA that is claimable is prorated according to the number of days in the period over 365. The proration requirements in the case of short fiscal years will not apply in cases where a franchise is acquired in Class 14.

(Note: No CCA deduction is claimable in the year of death, as the property must be owned as of the end of the year for a claim to occur.)

3. When determining the size of your net business income, which can be influenced by your optional CCA deduction, take into account the level of RRSP contribution room you will want to make next year, as this is based on the net income of the business from this year. You may wish to claim less CCA to bolster RRSP room in some cases.

> ► *. . . the lower your net income . . ., the lower your contributions to the Canada Pension Plan . . .*

4. The lower your net income from the business, the lower your contributions to the Canada Pension Plan on net self-employed earnings. You can use your CCA deduction to influence this liability.

5. In determining whether to increase net income for RRSP purposes, which will also have the effect of increasing the CPP contributions, take into account your cash flow availability for the purposes of paying your resulting income tax balance, and, if possible, to stay out of the profile for making instalment remittances to Revenue Canada during the year.

6. Keep in mind that if you are maximizing the CCA deduction in a period of time when the value of the asset is actually increasing, there is the potential for recapture of depreciation. In this case, you might want to look at not only your cash flow availability but at other ways to reduce your personal net income: RRSP contributions, carrying charges, and so on.

7. Where a principal residence is used for business purposes, as in most home-based businesses, the effect of claiming CCA on the principal residence exemption should be taken into account. That is, the tax-exempt status on that portion of the residence will be removed if CCA is claimed.

Restrictions

In the case of revenue properties, CCA on the building, or fixtures, cannot be claimed if it increases or creates a rental loss.

Carrying Forward the UCC

The Undepreciated Capital Cost balances of each class must be carried forward from year to year. For this reason it is always necessary to refer to the records of the prior year before starting this year's filing process.

DISPOSING OF YOUR ASSETS

Tax consequences occur with the disposition of a depreciable asset, as is illustrated by the following examples:

Some Typical Dispositions

Example 1

The asset is sold or transferred to someone else:

> *Judith sold her fax machine, whose undepreciated capital cost was $450, to her friend Tannis, for $200.*

Example 2

The taxpayer receives compensation for property that was stolen:

> *Cora's home-based tailor shop was vandalized. The thieves took her sewing machines. The damage was estimated at $1,200. Her insurance company reimbursed her for the losses.*

Example 3

The taxpayer receives compensation for destruction of property (where compensation is used to repair damaged assets, no disposition is considered to have taken place):

> *Cora also suffered damages to her pattern-making tables and antique oak desk. The insurance company repaired these assets for her. There was no disposition to report. Had the insurance company paid her for the damages, so that she could replace the property, a disposition of the old assets would have been reported.*

Example 4

▶ *. . . the taxpayer receives compensation for assets taken or sold under statutory authority . . .*

The taxpayer receives compensation for assets taken or sold under statutory authority (*e.g.*, expropriation, bankruptcy):

> *Marvin received $15,000 for buildings that were expropriated by the city.*

Example 5

When there is a "deemed disposition" (*i.e.*, when the taxpayer dies, emigrates, gives the property away, or changes the asset's business use):

> *When Tanya died, her income-producing assets were deemed to have disposed of at their "fair market value" at the time of her death.*

Where there is a disposition without the benefit of dollars changing hands, as described in the examples above, the disposal value can be determined under a variety of different rules depending on the circumstances. However, it is usually determined to be the "fair market value," which must be recorded on the Capital Cost Allowance (CCA) schedule in the fiscal year of its occurrence.

Dispositions of assets will affect the Undepreciated Capital Cost (UCC) in the pool of assets. What will result is either a tax deduction or income inclusion on the business statement which will reconcile the amount of CCA previously taken with the actual value of the asset when it is eventually disposed of.

Example

> *Maggie has a number of Class 10 assets that includes some computer equipment she acquired for her home-based bookkeeping service. When she acquired these assets their original cost was $7,500. The UCC in the Class currently sits at $4,300. This means she has previously claimed CCA deductions of $3,200 on prior tax returns. During this tax year she converts her laptop computer to personal use by giving it to her university-bound son. The value of*

the computer is $750 at the time of conversion to personal use. This would be reported on the CCA schedule as follows:

1 Class number	2 Undepreciated capital cost (UCC) at the start of the year	3 Cost of additions in the year (see Areas B and C below)	4 Proceeds of dispositions in the year (see Areas D and E below)	5 * UCC after additions and dispositions (col. 2 **plus** 3 **minus** 4)	6 Adjustment for current year additions (1/2 x (col. 3 **minus** 4)) If negative, enter "0"	7 Base amount for capital cost allowance (col. 5 **minus** 6)	8 Rate %	9 CCA for the year (col. 7 x 8 or a lower amount)	10 UCC at the end of the year (col. 5 **minus** 9)
10	4300		750	3550		3550	30	1065	2485

Total CCA claim for the year (enter this amount, minus any personal portion, on line 8207 on page 1 of this form) **1065**

* If you have a negative amount in this column, add it to income as a recapture under "Other income" on page 1 of this form. If there is no property left in the class and there is a positive amount in the column, deduct the amount from income as a terminal loss under "Other expenses" on page 1 of this form. Recapture and terminal loss do not apply to a Class 10.1 property.

This example shows what will happen when only one of the assets in the class is disposed of. You will see that the UCC in the "pool" of assets in the class is decreased, which reduces the CCA deduction for the year, as it is calculated on a lower value.

There are different consequences when all the assets of a class are disposed of.

Example

Maggie decides to transfer her bookkeeping business and all its assets to her son. Her Class 10 assets have a "fair market value" of $3,200 at the time of conversion.

1 Class number	2 Undepreciated capital cost (UCC) at the start of the year	3 Cost of additions in the year (see Areas B and C below)	4 Proceeds of dispositions in the year (see Areas D and E below)	5 * UCC after additions and dispositions (col. 2 **plus** 3 **minus** 4)	6 Adjustment for current year additions (1/2 x (col. 3 **minus** 4)) If negative, enter "0"	7 Base amount for capital cost allowance (col. 5 **minus** 6)	8 Rate %	9 CCA for the year (col. 7 x 8 or a lower amount)	10 UCC at the end of the year (col. 5 **minus** 9)
10	4300		3200	1100	Terminal loss		—	1100	0

Total CCA claim for the year (enter this amount, minus any personal portion, on line 8207 on page 1 of this form) **1100**

* If you have a negative amount in this column, add it to income as a recapture under "Other income" on page 1 of this form. If there is no property left in the class and there is a positive amount in the column, deduct the amount from income as a terminal loss under "Other expenses" on page 1 of this form. Recapture and terminal loss do not apply to a Class 10.1 property.

. . . the terminal loss will reflect . . . that not enough depreciation was taken over the years . . .

In this example, Maggie has suffered a "terminal loss". A terminal loss occurs where the value on disposal is less than the undepreciated capital cost in the pool. Generally this will happen when all the assets of a class are disposed of, as in the case of a business closure, or deemed disposition upon death. The terminal loss will reflect the fact that not enough depreciation was taken over the years to show the true value of the assets. Therefore, the difference between UCC and the disposal value can be taken as a deduction on the "Business Income and Expense Statement" for tax purposes. This amount is fully deductible from business income.

(Note: Employees who claim CCA on their Class 10 vehicles used for employment may not deduct terminal losses. However, they may be subject to "recapture" provisions described below.)

Let's assume now that Maggie finds a buyer for her bookkeeping business. She receives a total of $4,500 for her Class 10 assets. This would be recorded for tax purposes as follows:

1 Class number	2 Undepreciated capital cost (UCC) at the start of the year	3 Cost of additions in the year (see Areas B and C below)	4 Proceeds of dispositions in the year (see Areas D and E below)	5 * UCC after additions and dispositions (col. 2 **plus** 3 **minus** 4)	6 Adjustment for current year additions (1/2 x (col. 3 **minus** 4)) If negative, enter "0"	7 Base amount for capital cost allowance (col. 5 **minus** 6)	8 Rate %	9 CCA for the year (col. 7 x 8 or a lower amount)	10 UCC at the end of the year (col. 5 **minus** 9)
10	4300		4500	(200)		Recapture		(200)	0

Total CCA claim for the year (enter this amount, minus any personal portion, on line 8207 on page 1 of this form) **(200)**

* If you have a negative amount in this column, add it to income as a recapture under "Other income" on page 1 of this form. If there is no property left in the class and there is a positive amount in the column, deduct the amount from income as a terminal loss under "Other expenses" on page 1 of this form. Recapture and terminal loss do not apply to a Class 10.1 property.

When the proceeds of disposal are higher than the undepreciated capital cost in the class, it means that the taxpayer has taken too much of a deduction for CCA over the years. The asset has depreciated on a slower scale that the rate used in the Class. Here the difference between the disposal value, and the UCC is "recapture," an amount that must be added to income in full.

(Note: For the purposes of reconciling the CCA schedule, the disposition value of the assets in the class cannot exceed the original cost (plus capital additions and improvements) when they were originally scheduled upon acquisition. If an asset is disposed of at a value above its adjusted cost base, a capital gain will occur.)

Example

> *Maggie, who originally paid $7,500 for her Class 10 assets, sells them for $8,000. The UCC in her CCA schedule is $4,300.*

1 Class number	2 Undepreciated capital cost (UCC) at the start of the year	3 Cost of additions in the year (see Areas B and C below)	4 Proceeds of dispositions in the year (see Areas D and E below)	5 * UCC after additions and dispositions (col. 2 **plus** 3 **minus** 4)	6 Adjustment for current year additions (1/2 x (col. 3 **minus** 4)) If negative, enter "0"	7 Base amount for capital cost allowance (col. 5 **minus** 6)	8 Rate %	9 CCA for the year (col. 7 x 8 or a lower amount)	10 UCC at the end of the year (col. 5 **minus** 9)
10	4300		7500	(3200)		Recapture	—	(3200)	0

Total CCA claim for the year (enter this amount, minus any personal portion, on line 8207 on page 1 of this form) **(3200)**

* If you have a negative amount in this column, add it to income as a recapture under "Other income" on page 1 of this form. If there is no property left in the class and there is a positive amount in the column, deduct the amount from income as a terminal loss under "Other expenses" on page 1 of this form. Recapture and terminal loss do not apply to a Class 10.1 property.

This entry clears the assets out of Class 10, and shows that over the years, the assets' values have increased, while on the tax returns, the taxpayer claimed CCA deductions. These deductions must now be paid back to reflect the true change in value in the assets. The $3,200 is added to business income in full. But there is yet another part of this transaction to record; on Schedule 3, Capital Gains and Losses:

Real estate and depreciable property (do not include losses on depreciable property)

Address or legal description							
CLASS 10 DISPOSITION		8000	—	7500	—	—	500	—
	Total 023	8000	—	Gain (or loss) 024 +			500	—

If you dispose of an asset for more than its original cost, the resulting capital gain is recorded on Schedule 3. The capital gain is the increase in value over the original cost. In the example above, $500 ($8,000 − $7,500) is reported as a capital gain. Here's another example.

Example

Asset A was acquired for $5,000 and Capital Cost Allowances of $2,000 were claimed during the year, leaving a UCC of $3,000. Asset A was the only asset in the class when it was sold during the tax year for $6,000. What are the tax consequences? (The answer is at the bottom of this page.)

From this discussion it is easy to see why detailed records of all acquisitions and dispositions of assets over the years are important. You may be called upon to retrieve these records from prior filed returns many years later, when you dispose of these assets.

Replacement Properties

It is possible to defer paying tax on a capital gain, if you acquire a "replacement property" for a "former business property," or a property that was stolen, expropriated or destroyed. Recapture may also be deferred when a depreciable property is replaced.

The tax consequences are the following:

1. Recapture of $2,000 (Original cost less deductions of $2,000). This is added to business income in the year of disposition.

2. Capital gain of $1,000 (Proceeds of disposition less original cost). Three-quarters of this will be taxable on "Line 127" of the return.

A "former business property" generally means real property or an interest in real property that is used in earning business income. It specifically excludes rental properties and their adjoining areas, unless the property is leased by the owner to another related party who uses the property in a rental operation. It is Revenue Canada's position that hotel and motel businesses generate business income and not rent. Therefore the replacement rules would apply to those who own such businesses. For the election to work, the "replacement property" must be used in the same or similar business and reacquired in certain specific time frames.

The opportunity to elect to defer recapture and capital gains, will arise when there is either an involuntary disposition or a voluntary disposition. Under an involuntary disposition, property is stolen, expropriated, or destroyed, for example. Where the disposition was involuntary, the replacement property must be acquired before the end of the second tax year following the year in which proceeds of disposition became receivable.

A voluntary disposition occurs when you actually sell or transfer the former business property to someone else. In such cases, the replacement property must be acquired before the end of the tax year following the year that proceeds of disposition became receivable.

Filing Tip

On disposition of the asset, either involuntarily or voluntarily, report the capital gains or recapture in the normal manner. Then, when the replacement property is acquired within the time limits set out above, request an adjustment to remove the recapture or capital gains from income in the previous year.

Example

> Thomas and Dorothy sold their motel at Grand Marais, a resort on beautiful Lake Winnipeg, for $250,000. They acquired it for $200,000 three years ago. They reported their $50,000 capital gain on "Schedule 3" in the current tax year. The following spring, they bought a motel at the resort of Gimli for the bargain price of $295,000. Because this was a replacement property within the time limits set out by Revenue Canada, Thomas and Dorothy could request that their capital gain of the prior year be removed.

The cost of addition of the new property would be $250,000 (the original cost of the first property plus the capital gain).

Uncollectible Proceeds of Disposition

If you have sold a capital asset and its proceeds become uncollectible, you can write off the bad debt against other business income of the year. The

▶ . . . *if* . . .
proceeds
become
uncollectible,
you can write
off the bad
debt . . .

deductible amount must not exceed the capital cost of the property less the amount of proceeds collected. This rule will not apply to uncollectible proceeds of a passenger vehicle (Class 10.1), as these properties are not subject to the normal recapture and terminal loss rules.

Example

Claude sold his prize 1989 Corvette for $28,000. He had used this car, which he acquired for $32,000 in his business driving as a self-employed commissioned salesman. Unfortunately, he did not ask for a certified cheque when he sold the auto privately. It bounced, the amounts became uncollectible as the buyer fled the province, and Claude wished to write off this bad experience both in his mind and on his return. While he succeeded emotionally in chalking his bad luck up to experience, he was out of luck with the proposed tax write off, because this was a Class 10.1 asset — a luxury vehicle — where terminal loss and recapture rules are ignored.

Tim, on the other hand, sold his tractor to his neighbor, Samuel for $8,000. He received post-dated cheques which he cashed every month for three years, until Samuel declared bankruptcy. The original capital cost of the tractor was $18,000 when Tim bought it, and he was able to collect from Samuel all but $1,500.

As the uncollectible amount of $1,500 does not exceed the capital cost of $18,000, Tim is justified in taking a tax deduction on his business statement for the bad debt.

TRANSFERRING PROPERTY

Torie was so excited. After building up her veterinary practice out of her home office over the past three years, she was asked to join a new firm, as a partner in The WinWest Clinic. The partnership would begin on October 1 of this year, and Torie agreed to transfer her existing computer system and medical equipment to the partnership.

Property that is transferred from an individual proprietorship to a partnership may be transferred at "fair market value" at the time of transfer, or at certain agreed upon amounts, by special election on "Form T2059" — "Election on Acquisition of Property by a Canadian Partnership".

Example

The value of Torie's computer system was $4,000 at the time she acquired it, used, from another doctor. Her UCC was $2,300. Her medical equipment was acquired new last year for $2,500; the

UCC is $1,250. The partnership will acquire the assets at their Undepreciated Capital Cost.

In this case, the CCA schedule is simply closed out on Torie's personal return, and there are no tax consequences of the rollover. (Also see below)

Stop-Loss Rules

. . . be aware of new rules that "stop losses" on transfers of property between "affiliated parties" . . .

You should also be aware of new rules that "stop losses" on transfers of property between "affiliated parties".

In the context of an individual, two individuals are considered to affiliated only where they are spouses of one another.

In the context of a corporation, persons are considered to be affiliated with themselves, and that person includes a partnership. To clarify, a corporation is considered to be affiliated with three different categories of "person":

(a) a person by whom the corporation is controlled,

(b) members of an affiliated group of persons by which the corporation is controlled (*i.e.,* each member is affiliated with every other member), and

(c) spouses of any of the other persons in either of the first two categories.

The new rules apply to corporations, trusts or partnerships when a depreciable property is transferred to an affiliated party, or on transfers of property between individuals who are spouses. If the tax cost (the proportion of the UCC in the class that the value of the property being transferred out represents) is greater than the amount that is received on transfer, a terminal loss would normally occur.

Example

UCC of a class of assets is $5,000. The tax cost of the property being transferred out is $5,000. Proceeds that would be received upon transfer of assets into a partnership: $2,000. The amount by which the tax cost exceeds the proceeds ($5,000 − $2,000 = $3,000) will be the new capital cost of the property. The property is treated as having been owned by the transferor until the earliest of three dates, described below.

As a result, the transferor can claim CCA after the transfer on $3,000: the difference between the transferred property's tax cost ($5,000) and the proceeds of disposition ($2,000).

Any portion of the difference ($3,000) can be claimed as a terminal loss when one of three events occurs:

1. there is a subsequent disposition of property to a person that is neither the transferor or a person affiliated with the transferor,

2. there is a change in the property's use from income-producing to non-income producing, or

3. there is a "deemed disposition" due to a change of residence or change of taxable status.

Remember that under the new rules, where the transferor or someone affiliated with the transferor holds the right to acquire the property 30 days after the disposition, no loss can be recognized upon transfer by the transferor.

The rules above were introduced with the April 26, 1995 and again on June 20, 1996 by the Department of Finance, not passed into law at the time of writing, and as you can see, are extremely complicated. Be sure to see a tax professional before any such transfers are contemplated or recorded.

GST TAX CREDITS AND OTHER GOVERNMENT ASSISTANCE

If you are a GST registrant (*See* Chapter Three for details), you may be eligible to recover the GST you have paid on your income-producing assets through your GST return. If you do, this will have consequences on your personal income tax return.

Example

Hollis acquires a refrigeration unit for his home-based florist shop. This costs $5,000 plus GST of $350 and PST of $350, for a total of $5,700. On his tax return Hollis enters the full cost of the acquisition on the CCA schedule:

1 Class number	2 Undepreciated capital cost (UCC) at the start of the year	3 Cost of additions in the year (see Areas B and C below)	4 Proceeds of dispositions in the year (see Areas D and E below)	5 * UCC after additions and dispositions (col. 2 plus 3 minus 4)	6 Adjustment for current year additions (1/2 x (col. 3 minus 4)) If negative, enter "0"	7 Base amount for capital cost allowance (col. 5 minus 6)	8 Rate %	9 CCA for the year (col. 7 x 8 or a lower amount)	10 UCC at the end of the year (col. 5 minus 9)
8		5700		5700	2850	2850	20	570	5130

Total CCA claim for the year (enter this amount, minus any personal portion, on line 8207 on page 1 of this form) **570**

* If you have a negative amount in this column, add it to income as a recapture under "Other income" on page 1 of this form. If there is no property left in the class and there is a positive amount in the column, deduct the amount from income as a terminal loss under "Other expenses" on page 1 of this form. Recapture and terminal loss do not apply to a Class 10.1 property.

In January of the next year, he applies for and receives a GST rebate of $350, when he files his GST return. Now an adjustment is necessary on his income tax return:

1 Class number	2 Undepreciated capital cost (UCC) at the start of the year	3 Cost of additions in the year (see Areas B and C below)	4 Proceeds of dispositions in the year (see Areas D and E below)	5 * UCC after additions and dispositions (col. 2 **plus** 3 **minus** 4)	6 Adjustment for current year additions (1/2 x (col. 3 **minus** 4)) If negative, enter "0"	7 Base amount for capital cost allowance (col. 5 **minus** 6)	8 Rate %	9 CCA for the year (col. 7 x 8 or a lower amount)	10 UCC at the end of the year (col. 5 **minus** 9)
8	5130		350	4780		4780	20	956	3824
			GST rebate						

Total CCA claim for the year (enter this amount, minus any personal portion, on line 8207 on page 1 of this form) **956**

* If you have a negative amount in this column, add it to income as a recapture under "Other income" on page 1 of this form. If there is no property left in the class and there is a positive amount in the column, deduct the amount from income as a terminal loss under "Other expenses" on page 1 of this form. Recapture and terminal loss do not apply to a Class 10.1 property.

▶ . . *. assets that are used partially for business and partially for personal use can be tricky . . .*

In short, the government assistance he received through the GST rebate must reduce the undepreciated capital cost of the asset.

Claiming the GST Input Tax Credit (ITC) on assets that are used partially for business and partially for personal use can be tricky. Let's look at the basic rules.

ITCs on Individual Partners' Vehicles Used for Business Purposes

Where business use is more than 10% and up to 90%, claim 7/107 of the CCA deduction as a GST Rebate on "Form GST-370". (*See* Appendix 9.) Next year this amount is used to decrease the capital cost on the CCA statement.

Example

Mitch uses his 1992 Ford Taurus in pursuing his activities as a partner in M & G Meats, which he operates with his wife Gina. The partnership is a GST registrant, but the auto Mitch uses in the business must be written off separately on his individual income and expense statement for the partnership. He acquired the vehicle for $15,000 plus 7% PST and 7% GST for a total of $17,100. His auto log shows that he drove 12,000 kilometers for business purposes and 18,000 kilometers in total during the year or 2/3 of the time for the purposes of the business. The UCC on the car is $11,500.

In this example, Mitch can recover a portion of the GST he paid on the acquisition of this vehicle, but through a special GST Rebate on the "GST-370". This rebate would be calculated as 7/107 of the CCA deduction:

1 Class number	2 Undepreciated capital cost (UCC) at the start of the year	3 Cost of additions in the year (see Areas B and C below)	4 Proceeds of dispositions in the year (see Areas D and E below)	5 * UCC after additions and dispositions (col. 2 plus 3 minus 4)	6 Adjustment for current year additions (1/2 x (col. 3 minus 4)) If negative, enter "0"	7 Base amount for capital cost allowance (col. 5 minus 6)	8 Rate %	9 CCA for the year (col. 7 x 8 or a lower amount)	10 UCC at the end of the year (col. 5 minus 9)
	11500			11500		11500	30	3450	8050

Total CCA claim for the year (enter this amount, minus any personal portion, on line 8207 on page 1 of this form) | 3450

* If you have a negative amount in this column, add it to income as a recapture under "Other income" on page 1 of this form. If there is no property left in the class and there is a positive amount in the column, deduct the amount from income as a terminal loss under "Other expenses" on page 1 of this form. Recapture and terminal loss do not apply to a Class 10.1 property.

The CCA deduction of $3,450 is now used in the GST Rebate Calculation. Here, one must take into account the personal use component of the vehicle's use, and then claim the rebate. (See illustration on following page)

This GST Rebate is claimed on "Line 457" on the "T1 General Return" and is refundable if tax credits exceed taxes payable. Next year, reduce the capital cost of the vehicle by the rebate received.

Vehicles of Proprietorships

If the vehicle you use is driven more than 10% and less than 90% for business use, claim 7/107 of the CCA deduction as the ITC for the GST paid on your GST Return. In the year you receive the ITC back, use the refund to reduce capital cost of the asset on your personal income tax return.

Example

> Mandy uses her 1995 Honda, bought this year from a car dealership for $14,300 plus PST of 7% and GST of 7% for a total of $16,302, in her home-based catering business. Her total business driving in the year, according to her auto log is 18,345 kilometers and of this 14,997 was for business use. Therefore she uses her vehicle 82% of the time for business use.

On her GST Return, Mandy can claim 7/107 of her CCA deduction less her personal use component. She files her GST return once a year, so the refund for the GST paid comes to her in June of the new year. She will reduce the capital cost of the vehicle on her income tax return when she files it next spring.

> ... If the vehicle you use is driven 90% or more for business use, claim the full ITC ...

If the value of the vehicle had exceeded $24,000* plus PST and GST, Mandy would have been limited to claim 7% of $27,360 only as the Input Tax Credit. Then she would reduce the capital cost by the same amount on her personal income tax return in the year the ITC is received.

*25,000 for 1997 and future years.

Revenue Revenu
Canada Canada

EMPLOYEE AND PARTNER GOODS AND SERVICES TAX REBATE

This form is authorized for use pursuant to section 253 of the *Excise Tax Act.*
PLEASE COMPLETE AREAS A, B (If applicable), C and D ON THIS FORM AND ATTACH TO YOUR COMPLETED INCOME TAX RETURN.

- Instructions for completion of this form are outlined on the reverse side.
- The Employee and Partner Goods and Services Tax Rebate Guide contains information to help you complete this form.
- Please print or type.

AREA A — CLAIMANT IDENTIFICATION (To be completed by Claimant)

Claimant's Last Name

First Name and Initials

Taxation Year of Claim **19** _____

Employer's/Partnership's GST Registration No.

Social Insurance Number

Provision of the SIN is voluntary and if not provided, no right, benefit or privilege will be withheld and no penalty imposed.
The SIN will be used as an identifier to facilitate the matching of this application with your T-1 General income tax return.

AREA B — DECLARATION BY CLAIMANT'S EMPLOYER OR PARTNERSHIP   (Your employer or partnership must complete this section if you wish to claim a rebate for expenses for which you were paid an allowance which was included in your income for the

I hereby certify that for the Taxation Year stated above, the above-named claimant was paid the following allowance which at the time it was paid, I did not consider to be reasonable for the purposes of subparagraph 6(1) (b) (v), (vi), (vii), or (vii.1) of the *Income Tax Act* (e.g., which I may not include in determining an input tax credit pursuant to section 174 of the *Excise Tax Act).*

Amount Received $

Reason for Allowance(s) (List Activities)

Name of Employer/Partnership

Signature of Employer or Authorized Officer

Position of Authorized Officer

Date   Y   M   D

AREA C — REBATE COMPUTATION (To be completed by Claimant)

Use the amounts reported on your income tax return for the Taxation Year stated above to complete the following.

I) Rebate on Expenses

Total expenses (all employee/partnership expenses other than Capital Cost Allowance [CCA])	Line 1	

Deduct:

Zero-rated and exempt purchases	Line 2	
Non-eligible expenses (Include all expenses for which you received an allowance from your employer or partnership except expenses that relate to the allowance reported in area B above)	Line 3	
Non-eligible expenses of a partner	Line 4	
Total deductions (Add lines 2 to 4 inclusive)	Line 5	▶
Net expenses (Subtract line 5 from line 1)	Line 6	
Personal use included in net expenses	Line 7	
Expenses eligible for rebate (Subtract line 7 from line 6)	Line 8	▶

II) Rebate on Capital Cost Allowance (CCA)

CCA on motor vehicles, musical instruments and aircraft (Do not include CCA with respect to which you received an allowance from your employer or partnership unless it	Line 9	3 4 5 0 —
Personal use included in line 9	Line 10	1 1 5 0 —
CCA eligible for rebate (Subtract line 10 from line 9)	Line 11	2 3 0 0 00 ▶ 2 3 0 0 00
Total for rebate calculation (Add lines 8 and 11)	Line 12	**051** 2 3 0 0 00

Multiply the amount on Line 12 by 7/107

X 7/107

GST rebate (Enter this amount on line 457 of your income tax return)	Line 13 ▶	1 5 0 4 7

AREA D — CERTIFICATION (To be completed by Claimant)

I hereby certify that the information in this document is true and correct to the best of my knowledge and that I am eligible for the Employee and Partner Goods and Services Tax Rebate for the Taxation Year.

Signature

Date   Y   M   D

Canadä

GST 370 E (95/01) Cette formule est disponible en français(GST 370 F)

Example

> *Mandy buys a BMW in 1996 for $95,000 for use in her business.*
> *On her GST return, calculate the ITCs based on a value of $27,360 less any personal use component; the ITC is received in the next tax year.*
> *On her personal income tax return, calculate the cost of additions as $27,360, and claim the CCA according to the normal rules. Next year, remember to reduce the cost of additions by any ITCs received.*

1 Class number	2 Undepreciated capital cost (UCC) at the start of the year	3 Cost of additions in the year (see Areas B and C below)	4 Proceeds of dispositions in the year (see Areas D and E below)	5 * UCC after additions and dispositions (col. 2 **plus** 3 **minus** 4)	6 Adjustment for current year additions (1/2 x (col. 3 **minus** 4)) If negative, enter "0"	7 Base amount for capital cost allowance (col. 5 **minus** 6)	8 Rate %	9 CCA for the year (col. 7 x 8 or a lower amount)	10 UCC at the end of the year (col. 5 **minus** 9)
10.1		27360.00		27360.00	13680	13680	30	4104	23256

Total CCA claim for the year (enter this amount, minus any personal portion, on line 8207 on page 1 of this form)   **4104**

* If you have a negative amount in this column, add it to income as a recapture under "Other income" on page 1 of this form. If there is no property left in the class and there is a positive amount in the column, deduct the amount from income as a terminal loss under "Other expenses" on page 1 of this form. Recapture and terminal loss do not apply to a Class 10.1 property. Note for 1997 and subsequent years, maximum CCA ceiling is $25,000.

All Other Assets Other Than Real Property

When a GST registrant claims Input Tax Credits on the GST return for any assets other than real property and the special auto rules described above, claim the ITC for the full GST paid and reduce the capital cost by the ITC received, if commercial use is more than 50%. If commercial use is less than 50%, no ITC can be claimed as a refund on the GST return. However, you will still be able to use the full GST-included value for the purposes of the CCA deduction on your personal income tax return.

Example

> *Mandy owns a stereo system which she uses 25% of the time in her home-based business. This is usually on days when she has clients visit her home office. She can support this with her appointment log. Her stereo system cost $1,000 and GST and PST brought the cost up to $1,140.*
> *While Mandy can claim a cost of addition of $1,140 in Class 8 (20%) on her CCA schedule, she cannot claim an input tax credit for the stereo on her GST return, as it is not used at least 50% of the time for business purposes.*

Real Property Where Commercial Use Is More Than 10%

Claim ITCs on the GST return in proportion to the actual commercial use and reduce the capital cost by any such ITCs received.

Example

Todd uses a small barn located on his personal property in his business enterprise, Riding Gear Enterprises. He designs and sews leather riding pants for the stable located across the street from him. The stable's pro shop sells these pants to the riders for $250 a piece. Todd makes $125 each.

The "fair market value" of the barn plus all improvements Todd made to it at the time it was converted to business use, was $45,000. GST paid on the improvements was $1,500. The barn is used 100% for business use. Todd can claim an input tax credit of $1,500 on his GST return.

Other Government Assistance and Reimbursements

The capital cost of any asset for which assistance is received will be reduced on the CCA schedule filed with the personal income tax return.

Example

Todd received a grant of $5,000 from the provincial government to acquire new sewing machines in his business for the purposes of putting people to work. This grant was not repayable. It is used to reduce the capital cost of the value of the sewing machines listed in Class 8 of the CCA schedule on his personal income tax return.

In conclusion, when it comes to accounting for capital assets under our current tax systems, the integration of input tax credits under the GST rules does have an effect on the CCA deduction you can claim on your personal income tax return. Therefore, it will be necessary to dig out the GST Remittance forms for income tax preparation purposes.

GOODWILL AND OTHER INTANGIBLE ASSETS

Brock is a writer who works out of his home office. He owns a computer, with a complete communications system. He also owns the copyrights to numerous books and newsletters. Recently he acquired the copyrights to the newsletter of another company, at a cost of $15,000.

As a business owner, it is possible that you might own assets that are tangible, such as a building, furniture or equipment, or in Brock's case, a computer. These are depreciable assets upon which a Capital Cost Allowance deduction is allowed, at the taxpayer's option, for tax purposes.

It is also possible, however, to own "intangible assets," that is, assets that do not have a physical existence, but whose ownership gives to you a lasting economic benefit that generally will produce income. For Brock, this includes his copyrights to his own publications and the copyrights he acquired for $15,000.

Eligible Capital Expenditures

Properties that have no physical existence but a lasting economic benefit for an indefinite period of time are considered to be eligible capital properties. A deduction based on the eligible capital expenditure, or the price the taxpayer paid for the property, is available. This deduction takes the form of an annual allowance.

Types of Eligible Capital Expenditures

This is any expenditure made for the purpose of gaining or producing income from a business, including incorporation costs; the cost of acquiring goodwill in a business; customers lists and ledger accounts; trademarks; patents; franchises; licences; milk quotas and other government rights or licences; stock exchange seats; initiation fees and memberships; amounts paid for the right of way over or through land owned by another taxpayer; and an amount paid to obtain another person's covenant not to engage in competition during a defined period of time.

Expenditures That Will Not Qualify

The following expenditures do not qualify as eligible capital properties:

1. a depreciable property: any tangible property;

2. land;

3. dividend payments;

4. any expenditure made to produce "exempt" income;

5. patents that belong to Class 44 (after April 26, 1993);

6. patents, franchises, concessions or licences in Class 14; and

7. a forfeited deposit.

Assets will generally be considered "eligible capital properties" that qualify for a declining-balance write-down on 75% of their acquisition cost, unless there is a definite useful life to the asset. In this latter case, a straight-line method (annualized equal deductions based on the cost divided by the useful life of the asset) can be used. To use the straight-line method, the assets are generally placed in Class 14.

Goodwill

. . . A good example of eligible capital property is goodwill . . .

A good example of eligible capital property is goodwill. Goodwill has been defined in a number of different court cases in the past. Revenue Canada's IT 143R2 lists two definitions:

1. Goodwill is the whole advantage, whatever it may be, of the reputation and connection of the firm which may have been built up by years of honest work or gained by lavish expenditures of money.

2. Goodwill is the privilege, granted by the seller of a business to the purchaser, of trading as his recognized successor; the possession of a ready-formed "connection" of customers, considered as an element in the saleable value of a business, additional to the value of the plant, stock-in-trade, book debts, and so on.

Goodwill will only arise when a business is acquired at a price that exceeds the value of its net tangible assets. The amount received for goodwill, including any legal and accounting fees directly associated with the purchase of the goodwill, will qualify as an eligible capital expenditure.

Sometimes, the value of goodwill is not specified by the buyer and seller. In such cases, Revenue Canada will apply the provisions of Section 68 of the Income Tax Act. Under this section, a reasonable amount of the consideration paid can be *deemed* to be goodwill, based on all facts including relative fair market values of all the assets of the business.

In the case of customer lists, if that list brings an enduring benefit to the business, it is considered to be an eligible capital expenditure. If there is not enduring value, it could be considered an expense.

Operation of the Cumulative Eligible Capital Account

Just how does the write off for intangible asset acquisitions work? Let's have a look at the steps.

ACQUIRING ASSETS

To compute the annual allowance that is a deduction for eligible capital properties, one must establish a tax account called the Cumulative Eligible Capital (CEC) account. To this account will be added three-quarters of the eligible capital expenditure.

Example

Tom acquires goodwill in a business for $35,000 in 1995. He adds to his CEC 3/4 of $35,000 or $26,250.

CALCULATING AND CLAIMING THE ANNUAL REDUCTION

The annual allowance that Tom can use as a deduction against other business income is 7%:

Annual allowance	= $26,250 × 7%	= $1837.50*
Cumulative Eligible Capital Account Balance	= $26,250 − $1837.50 = $24,412.50	

*This amount is claimed as a deduction on Tom's "Business Income and Expense Statement".

The following tax year, Tom would take a 7% allowance on the CEC Balance of $24,412.50, and so on. As long as there is a positive balance in the Cumulative Eligible Capital Account balance, a deduction can be made for the annual allowance up to the maximum of 7%.

DISPOSING OF THE ASSETS

Should there be a negative balance in the account, perhaps due to the sale or other disposition in the CEC account, an income inclusion will result.

Example

Tom sells the goodwill in his business for $55,000.

CEC Account Balance at the start of the year	= $24,412.50
Proceeds of Disposition $55,000 × 3/4	= $41,250.00
Negative Balance in CEC Account	= ($16,837.50)

For all eligible capital properties other than qualifying farm properties, this negative balance will be included in business income, for transactions that occur after February 22, 1994. This was the date that the $100,000 Capital Gains Exemption was eliminated.

ACQUISITION OF REPLACEMENT PROPERTIES

If eligible capital property is sold and replaced with another similar property, all or part of the recapture or capital gains or recognition of the negative balance in the cumulative eligible capital account of the taxpayer, resulting from the sale can be postponed.

To be eligible for this tax deferral, the replacement property must be acquired no later than one year after the end of the tax year in which the property is sold. The replacement property must be for the same or similar use and for the same or similar business, and under new rules effective for 1993 and the subsequent years must have been acquired to replace the former property and for the same or similar uses.

Dispositions of Eligible Capital Property Acquired After Feb. 22, 1994

PROPERTIES OTHER THAN QUALIFYING FARM PROPERTY

In the future, any negative balances resulting in the CEC of eligible capital properties acquired after February 22, 1994, will simply be added to business income.

Example

> John acquired a new business in 1996; goodwill was valued
> at $50,000
> (a) to CEC Account: 3/4 of $50,000   = $37,500
>
> During ownership, 7% of the balance may be claimed as a
> deduction:
> (a) Year 1: Deduction of 7% × $37,500   = $ 2,625 is taken.
> (b) Ending Balance in CEC Account   = $34,875
>
> Value of Goodwill on Actual Disposition (1997) = $75,000
>
> CEC account is adjusted:
> (a) Balance in the account   = $34,875
> (b) 3/4 of designated proceeds   = $56,250
> (c) Difference (Report as Business Income)   = ($21,375)

DISPOSITION OF QUALIFYING FARM PROPERTY

Will continue to be eligible for the $500,000 Capital Gains Exemption.

Example

> Tom sells the goodwill in his business for $55,000. This is qualifying
> farm property. To record this transaction:
> CEC Account Balance at the start of the year = $24,412.50
> Proceeds of Disposition $55,000 × 3/4   = $41,250.00
> Negative Balance in CEC Account   = ($16,837.50) (a)
>
> Deductions previously taken as allowances   = $ 1,837.50 (b)
> Add to business income (lesser of (a) or (b)) = $ 1,837.50

$$Gain\ (\$16,837.50 - \$1837.50) \qquad\qquad = \$ \quad 15,000$$
$$to\ Schedule\ 3$$

Calculation of Capital Gains Deduction   *To T657*

CESSATION OF BUSINESS

The remaining balance of cumulative eligible capital is deductible in the year in which a business has ceased. This deduction will not be available if the taxpayer's spouse takes over the company or the company is taken over by a corporation controlled by the taxpayer.

Where the owner of the eligible capital property dies, the remaining balance of the CEC account may be transferred to the spouse on a tax-free basis, or a deduction for the balance is allowed on the final return.

Note that the dispositions of eligible capital property are subject to the "stop-loss" rules that affect "affiliated individuals," as previously discussed.

PATENTS AND OTHER PROPERTIES WITH A SPECIFIC LIFESPAN

Charlie is an avid inventor. His most recent discovery: a dog whistle that is 100% silent . . . and emits a desirable scent.

He has developed this product over the past several years. When it was perfect, Charlie decided to seek a patent for it from the Patent Office. Here is how Charlie would write off the costs of his endeavors.

Trademarks, Patents, Franchises and Licences

The costs of obtaining a trademark registration to protect a trade name, design or product may include the designing, legal and registration costs and also any payment made to some other person to stop contesting an attempt at registration. These expenditures can be subject to a variety of interesting tax consequences.

Where one taxpayer buys a trademark from another, the amount paid is considered to be an eligible capital expense. (*See* "Goodwill and Other Intangible Assets," earlier in this chapter.)

Any other outlay or expense made or incurred to acquire a patent, franchise, concession or licence for use in a business will usually be considered an eligible capital property, unless it is placed in Class 14. A Class 14 asset has a definite useful life. Class 14 will generally not include a trademark, leasehold interest, or a licence to use computer software, or Class 44 properties, described below.

Commonly held in Class 14 are franchises that have a specific term or industrial designs that are protected for a period of 5 or 10 years, and so on.

Class 44 assets are patents acquired after April 23, 1993, which qualify for a 25% declining-balance rate, allowing for faster write-downs of such qualifying property. These assets are, however, subject to the half-year rule. It may be more beneficial to place the patent in Class 14 if the patent is acquired late in its life, or to have the amount treated as an eligible capital property in the case of an indefinite life, at the taxpayer's option.

(Note: On Class 14 assets, the half-year rule for acquisitions will not apply, nor will the rules for short tax years be implemented.)

In addition, if a person only acquires a right to stand in place of another in applying for a property, this right cannot be considered a Class 14 asset, but might be considered to be an eligible capital property. This could happen, for example, if a taxpayer pays an amount of money to another for a licensed taxicab where the licence is not transferable but where the purchaser expects that the licensing authority will issue a new licence. In other words, what is being paid for is the expectation of being granted a license.

> *. . . Only intangible assets that have a "limited life" can be placed in Class 14 . . .*

Class 14 apportions the capital costs of the property over its remaining useful life on a straight-line method of depreciation. Only intangible assets that have a "limited life" can be placed in Class 14. For example, copyright in a literary work is usually in effect for the life of the author plus 50 years after the author's death. Certain patents are granted for a period of 18 years, and other licences may be granted for a period of 5 years, and so on. A patent is generally issued for a period of 17 years from the date the letters patent are granted.

The capital cost of a Class 14 asset includes the purchase price, if any, any legal fees and disbursements, registration fees and representation expenses paid to acquire the property. Any expenses paid in a year in making a representation for the purposes of obtaining a licence, permit, franchise or patent are tax deductible as business expenses. If the amounts were laid out specifically to acquire a Class 14 property, however, they will be added to the capital cost.

In the case of acquiring a franchise, concession or license, the life of the property is determined by including renewals or extensions that are automatic or in the control of the taxpayer because they do not include any further negotiation. An example of this is a franchise with an initial term of 5 years that has one further renewable option for a further 5 years. In this case, the life of the franchise for the purpose of Class 14 is 10 years. If the concurrence of the franchisor were required after the first 5-year period had elapsed, then the life of the franchise would only be 5 years. If the renewal periods are indefinite, the property does not belong in Class 14, and should instead form a part of the Cumulative Eligible Capital account.

Should a franchise, concession or license contain a clause which allows for early termination, there will be no effect on the computation of the useful life of the asset for Class 14 purposes.

If expenses related to a Class 14 asset are incurred prior to the year in which the property is actually acquired, they are added to the capital cost of the property in the year of acquisition. The capital cost to the original owner of a patent or industrial design includes research and development expenses incurred in discovering, designing or developing the property, if these amounts have not already been deducted as ordinary operating expenses. Once the invention or design is at the point where a patent or industrial design registration can be obtained, future expenditures will be deductible as operating expenses. (IT 477)

Optional Computation for Patents

Where all or a part of the cost of a patent is determined by reference to the use of the patent, a taxpayer may claim as a deduction the lesser of

(a) that part of the capital cost determined by reference to the use of the patent in the year and 25% of the Undepreciated Capital Cost Allowance in Class 44, or

(b) the UCC at the end of the tax year in Class 44.

Similar optional rules are in place for patents in Class 14. Check these out with your tax professional.

Be aware that once activities change — that is, the taxpayer goes from the business of obtaining a patent into the business of marketing and selling the product, one business is considered to have ceased and the other to have begun, with all the resulting tax consequences.

CHAPTER
SIX

Time to Grow

Money never starts an idea: it is the idea that starts the money.

— W. J. Cameron

TAX OBLIGATIONS FOR HUMAN RESOURCES

Gina runs a home-based beauty salon. Her clients enter the establishment through the side entrance, which leads right into the den. The den has been completely converted into a salon. She started with one sink and one dryer. Now she can do three clients at one time. Gina's daughter, Marion is 15 and loves to help her mom. From washing, drying and folding the towels for the client's hair to sweeping the floors and distributing flyers throughout the neigborhood, Marion is truly a blessing.

During tax time, Gina's tax accountant asked her whether she was paying Gina anything for the work she does around the salon. "No," replied Gina. She was not aware that she could pay her own daughter for this work. Fortunately, Gina's accountant set her straight.

. . . it is entirely permissible to pay your family members . . . provided certain criteria are met . . .

It is entirely permissible to pay your family members for work done in your home-based business, provided certain criteria are met:

1. The work was actually done by the family member and it was necessary in earning income from the business.

2. A stranger would have been hired to do the work, if the relative was not doing it.

3. The amount paid was comparable to what a stranger would have been paid and reasonable based on the relative's age.

4. Documentation is provided to justify the time spent at work (*i.e*, time cards or employment contracts) and the amounts paid in cash or in kind.

183

Example

Perry works on his dad's farm in Saskatchewan. He feeds the chickens, milks the cows and tends to the weeding in his father's commercial garden. His father pays him $5.50 an hour, and gives him two cows every year to raise on his own.

In this instance, the cash remuneration is deductible, as are all required source deductions such as Employment Insurance and Income Tax. The two cows are taken out of inventory, the expenses of which his father has already written off. The "fair market value" of the cows must be added to his father's income as sales, and also to Perry's to record this "in kind" transaction.

Obligations to Make Source Deductions

As a home-based business owner, it is important for you to understand which income sources are taxable and subject to withholding taxes, which sources are subject to special calculations, and which may be exempt altogether, in order to remunerate the people who work for you.

For tax purposes, "income" of a taxpayer includes all sources from inside or outside of Canada including the taxpayer's income from each office, employment, business and property. "Income from an office or employment" usually refers to employment status; while "income from business or property" generally refers to the status of a self-employed person or an investor.

Income from office or employment is defined as income for a taxation year (January 1 to December 31) that is salary, wages and "other remuneration," including gratuities, overtime, premium hours, banked time, retroactive earnings, salary, bonuses, commissions, advances or draws, gifts, severance pay, sick pay, vacation pay, wages in lieu of notice, or a whole series of taxable benefits received by the taxpayer in the year.

> *. . . for employees, income is reported for tax purposes in the year it is paid . . .*

For employees, income is reported for tax purposes in the year it is paid, which is not necessarily in the year it was earned. Therefore advances are taxed when taken.

"Other remuneration" includes the value of taxable benefits. This is defined as the value of board, lodging and any other benefits of any kind whatever, received or enjoyed by the taxpayer, by virtue of his or her employment with your business. This will be discussed in greater detail in "Tax-Free and Taxable Benefits," later in this chapter.

It is also important to note that your business may have both employer-employee relationships, and sub-contracting relationships. In the former case, source deductions, such as income tax, Canada Pension Plan (CPP) and

Employment Insurance (formerly Unemployment Insurance) premiums must be deducted. In the latter, the services provided to the company are considered to be on a self-employment basis on the part of the sub-contractor, and no source deductions are required.

Employer-Employee Relationships

An employer-employee relationship exists when someone (the employer) controls and directs another person (the employee). The employee will be considered to have earned "income from an office of employment," from which deductions of Canada Pension Plan (CPP) premiums, Employment Insurance Premiums (EI) and Income Tax Deductions (IT) are made by the employer. These are known as "Statutory Deductions".

▶ *. . . have the employee complete . . . the "Personal Tax Deduction" return . . .*

To determine the amount of tax to be deducted, have the employee complete "Form TD1," the "Personal Tax Deduction" return, available from Revenue Canada.

Employee or Sub-Contractor?

Whether the individual is an employee or an independent contractor will depend on different circumstances in each situation. The central issue is whether the person working for the company has a "contract of service" or a "contract for service". The "tests" that determine the worker's status are applied on an individual basis, but are summarized in general terms below.

THE "NATURE AND DEGREE OF CONTROL" TEST

▶ *. . . the general test is the "nature and degree of control" over the person . . .*

The general test is the "nature and degree of control" over the person in your service. A "servant" will generally act under the control and supervision of his "master" and must perform all reasonable requests or "orders" given. By contrast, an "independent contractor" is entirely independent of the "master"; this person simply undertakes an agreed upon task, and uses his or her own resources to produce results.

THE INTEGRATION TEST

This test looks at the service contract itself. If the work done is an integral part of the business, the person who performs it is generally considered to be employed by the firm. However, if the work is only an accessory to the main business of the company, the contract may be considered that of a sub-contracting arrangement.

THE ECONOMIC REALITY TEST

This test revolves around the issue of risk. Who has the risk for buying capital assets, repaying business loans, and making a profit? If that is the worker, likely that person is an independent contractor.

THE SPECIFIC RESULT TEST

This tests asks that question: are you working until a specific result is accomplished? In this case you are likely an independent. Or, are you working for a period of time or indefinitely for a specific person? In other words, as an employee, you are making yourself available to your "master" for a period of time; while the independent contractor is free to work elsewhere when the contract for work is finished, and does not necessarily have to do the work personally.

No source deductions are made for a subcontractor. This person must remit his or her own income taxes, either by quarterly instalment, or once a year when filing the income tax return as a self-employed individual.

Obligations to Remit Source Deductions Taken

Payroll deductions are usually sent in to Revenue Canada on the 15th day of the month following the one in which the deductions are made. If the 15th day falls on a Saturday, Sunday or holiday, the remittance is due on the next working day.

Larger companies can be considered "Accelerated Remitters". There are two thresholds for these situations: monthly payrolls of $15,000 to $49,999 and payrolls over $50,000.

Fines and Penalties

. . . late remittances . . ., or incorrect accounting . . . can result in costly tax audits and penalties . . .

Late remittances of source deductions, or incorrect accounting of taxable benefits can result in costly tax audits and penalties, as listed in Table 6-1 and Table 6-2.

If the failure to deduct or withhold source deductions happens more than once in a calendar year, the penalty increases to 20% of the amount deficient, if the employer knowingly or through gross negligence failed to remit the required amounts. This enhanced penalty will apply in amounts over $500 in most cases.

Companies that fail to comply with these rules can be prosecuted and fined from $1,000 to $25,000 and/or imprisonment for up to 12 months may result.

In addition, interest is charged from the day the payment is due. However, interest or penalties may be waived or cancelled under extraordinary circumstances.

TABLE 6-1
SOURCE DEDUCTIONS AND TAXABLE BENEFITS:
REQUIREMENTS UNDER THE INCOME TAX ACT

RESPONSIBILITY	REQUIRED ACTION	ITA
Director's Liability	Every person who deducts or withholds an amount under this Act shall be deemed to hold the amount so deducted or withheld in trust, separate and apart from the person's own moneys . . . and Her Majesty has a lien and charge on the property and assets of the person whether or not the person has kept the amount separate and apart, or is in receivership, bankruptcy or liquidation or has made an assignment. An action may be made against a director for a corporation's failure to deduct, withhold or remit tax within 2 years of ceasing to be a director.	227.1(4)
Keeping Books	Every person carrying on business and every person who is required to pay or collect taxes or other amounts shall keep records and books of account (including an annual inventory kept in prescribed manner) at the person's place of business or residence in Canada . . . in such form and containing such information as will enable the taxes payable under this Act, deducted, withheld or collected, to be determined.	230 (1)
Record Retention	Every person required by this section to keep records and books of accounts shall retain . . . every account and voucher necessary to verify the information . . . until the expiration of six years from the end of the last taxation year to which the records and books of account relate.	230 (4)
Permission for Early Disposal	A person required to keep books and books of account may disposed of these records before the end of the six-year period if written permission for their disposal is given by the Minister	230 (8)

New for July 1, 1996 and Subsequent Years

The newly revamped Employment Commission may now impose penalties for any acts of the employer, or anyone acting for the employer that were knowingly false. There can be penalties as high as $12,000 for falsifying or selling a Record of Employment, for instance. Where fraud involves employer/employee collusion, employer penalties may be imposed equal to

TABLE 6-2
SOURCE DEDUCTIONS AND TAXABLE BENEFITS:
VIOLATIONS AND PENALTIES UNDER THE INCOME TAX ACT

VIOLATION	PENALTY	ITA
Failures to deduct, withhold or remit tax	First occurrence, 10% of amount not withheld, Subsequent occurrence in same year 20% of amount not withheld if failures was made knowingly or under gross negligence	227 (8), (9)
Upon successful prosecution	$1,000 to $25,000 and/or up to 12 months in prison	238 (1)
Failures to File T-Slips	$25 per day to a maximum of $2,500/ minimum $100	162 (7)
Failure to provide SIN by individual	$100 for each failure	162 (6)

the dollar value of all claimant penalties. As well, corporate directors, officers or agents may be penalized for fraud. Contact Human Resource Development Canada for more information.

Year-End Reporting Requirements

As mentioned earlier, "T4 Slips" must be prepared for employees of the business before the last day of February of the new year.

Source Deductions for Family Members

The parameters for paying family members were discussed earlier in this chapter. To make source deductions, follow these rules:

1. The business owner must contribute a portion of required premiums payable for CPP and Employment Insurance. As in all other cases, the employer's portion in such cases is a tax deductible expense on the business statement.

2. If the child of the owner is under 18, no CPP deductions are made.

Can Family Members Collect Employment Insurance?

It is particularly important to have an employment or partnership agreement between spouses. Human Resources Canada will consult Revenue Canada on the status of the relationship, which may stall the payment of benefits if such

. . . have an
employment or
partnership
agreement
between
spouses . . .

an agreement is not in place. Employment Insurance is not deductible for any person who owns more than 40% of the shares in a company.

For more information see "How to Make Source Deductions," later in this chapter.

TAX-FREE AND TAXABLE BENEFITS

Katja and Joseph Stravinski work together in their family business, a European import business they run from their home. They earn $125,000 in sales from the business, and net $50,000, which they split between themselves on a 50-50 basis. A partnership agreement is drawn up.

The Stravinskis will be expanding their sales this year, as they just landed a contract with a local department store for some of their import lines. They will be hiring a bookkeeper and subcontracting to a delivery service. They want to explore remuneration methods before offering employment to their new staff member.

. . . there are
numerous forms
of remuneration
for employees . . .

There are numerous forms of remuneration for employees, besides the money they receive as their regular salaries or hourly wages. This can include both taxable and non-taxable benefits, or "perks," that enhance an employee's living standards, with real economic returns on an after-tax basis. Remember too, that an "employee" can be a family member.

When negotiating an employment contract with an employee, it may not always be possible to meet wage demands. For this reason, it is good to have at hand the following lists of commonly used tax-free and taxable benefits that can be offered to an employee. See Table 6-3 and Table 6-4.

Tax-Free Benefits

TABLE 6-3
COMMON TAX-FREE BENEFITS

TAX-FREE BENEFITS	DESCRIPTION
1. Wedding or Christmas gifts that do not exceed $100; $200 in year employee marries	While these perks are not taxable, the amount of the gift is also not deductible by the employer.
2. Discounts on Merchandise	This status will not extend to cases where the merchandise is purchased below the merchant's cost. A commission received by a sales employee on merchandise acquired for the employee's personal use is not taxable, nor is a commission received by a life insurance salesman for the acquisition of his/her own policy.

(continues)

TABLE 6-3
(continued)

TAX-FREE BENEFITS	DESCRIPTION
3. Subsidized Meals	Not taxable if the employee is charged a reasonable amount that covers the cost of food, its preparation and service.
4. Uniforms and Special Clothing (including safety footwear)	These are not taxable benefits. Payments made by an employer for laundering special uniforms or for reimbursement of the employee's expenses in laundering uniforms will not be taxable.
5. Recreational facilities, including memberships to social or athletic clubs	No taxable amount is included in the employee's income for memberships to pools, gyms, or exercise rooms, or where the employer pays the fees for membership in a social or athletic club. The amounts are not tax deductible to the employer.
6. Premiums paid under private health services plans	This includes a contract of insurance for hospital expenses, medical expenses, such as Blue Cross, paid by the employer.
7. Employer's required contribution to provincial health and medical plans	Remittances to certain Health Insurance Plans in Quebec, Manitoba, Ontario, Newfoundland are considered to be employer levies, and so are not taxable to the employee.
8. Transportation to and from work, disabled	Not taxable to the employee.
9. Employee counselling services	Not taxable if for re-employment or retirement; or for mental or physical health counselling.

Moving Expenses

If the employer pays for the following moving expenses, they will not be considered to be taxable benefits to the employee, but rather reimbursements:

1. Cost of movers to move household effects;

2. Cost of moving the family including all travelling expenses;

3. Cost to move personal items such as a car or trailer;

4. Costs of up to 15 days temporary living accommodations in the new work location if the new residence is not ready;

5. Charges for alterations to furniture and fixtures that were part of the old home;

6. Costs of cancelling a lease;

7. Costs of discharging a mortgage;

8. Legal fees and transfer taxes to buy a new home;

9. Mortgage interest, property taxes, utilities and insurance to maintain the old residence after the employee has moved and the house has not yet sold;

10. Interest costs on bridge financing; and

11. Long-distance charges incurred to sell the former residence.

Taxable Benefits

> *. . . taxable benefits are goods or services provided to the employee at little or no charge . . .*

Taxable benefits are goods or services provided to the employee at little or no charge, or "in kind". For example, the employer may pay a portion of group health premiums, pay the costs of a holiday trip or extend funds at little or no interest to the employee as a loan. Actual amounts expended by the company are fully deductible by the business.

Taxable benefits must be reported on the "T4 Slip," and in most cases, will be subject to source deductions of CPP/EI and Income Tax throughout the year. In some case, such as low-interest employee loans, the difference between the "fair market value" of the benefit and a prescribed rate of interest charged by Revenue Canada, must be manually calculated every quarter and then added to the employee's individual records. Automobile expenses and allowances are subject to special rules, discussed later.

Most taxable benefits, if they are taxable supplies for GST purposes, will also contain a GST component which must be added to the employee's benefit on the "T4 Slip". Examples of the most common taxable benefits are shown in Table 6-4.

TABLE 6-4
COMMON TAXABLE BENEFITS

TAXABLE BENEFIT	DESCRIPTION
1. Personal Use of employer's motor vehicle	This will be discussed in more detail in "Automobile Benefits" later in this chapter.
2. Gifts that exceed $100 in a year ($200 in the year an employee marries)	In cash or in kind, the amounts are taxable. Gifts given in kind must be valued at their "fair market value".

(continues)

TABLE 6-4
(continued)

TAXABLE BENEFIT	DESCRIPTION
3. Value of holidays, prizes and other awards	Vacations paid by the employer, and trips to an employer's vacation property, will be taxable on their "fair market value", unless it can be shown that the employee's presence was required for business purposes. The employee must be engaged in business activities at least for a part of every day. For prizes or rewards relating to sales work, the "fair market value" of the incentive is considered to be remuneration for tax purposes, unless the amount qualifies as a bursary, fellowship or scholarship. In such cases a T4A slip would be filed, and the employee could qualify for a special $500 exemption.
4. Frequent Flyer program points used for personal use	Credits accumulated by employees under their business activities and then used for personal enjoyment of employee and/or his or her family are taxable. Where the employer has no control over this, it is the responsibility of the employee to report the benefit on his or her tax return.
5. Travelling expenses of employee's spouse	Taxable to the employee, not the spouse, unless it can be shown the spouse was engaged in the business activities of the employee during the trip.
6. Premiums under a provincial hospital plan	Where the employer pays all premiums, the full amount is taxable to the employee, whether the amount is paid directly into the fund or to the employee.
7. Tuition fees paid by the employer	Any amounts paid by the employer, or reimbursed to the employee must be reported as income, unless the course was undertaken on the initiative of the employer and the course was taken during company time while the employee was being paid to take it. If the course is taken on the employee's own time, it is presumed it is for the benefit of the employee, not the employer and then the costs are taxable. If the educational institute provides a reduced rate to your employees, it is the "fair market value" that must be added to income, not the amount the company paid. The student may be eligible to claim an offsetting tuition fee tax credit on his or her tax return, or transfer the credits to a supporting individual in some cases.

(continues)

TABLE 6-4
(continued)

TAXABLE BENEFIT	DESCRIPTION
8. Reimbursement of cost of tools	Required for employment, must be included in income.
9. Interest free and low interest loans	The benefit is calculated as the difference between the prescribed rate of interest in effect at the time of the loan and the rate charged to the employee. In the case of a shareholder's loan, repayment within specific time frames will prevent income inclusion of the loan itself. In such cases, an "imputed interest" charge must be calculated as per the prescribed rate described above. If the shareholder's loan is not repaid in the required time period, (one year from the end of the lending corporation's tax year), it will be included in the employee's income in the year it was taken out. Future repayments of the loan will qualify for a tax deduction on Line 232 of the tax return. Loans to shareholders are not included in income if it can be shown that they are used to purchase a home, previously unissued fully paid-up shares of the capital stock of the corporation, or an automobile used for employment.
10. Financial counselling	This will be taxable unless it is for re-employment, or retirement.
11. Group insurance: group life, sickness, accident	The benefits of group life or sickness plans are now fully included in income if the premiums are paid by the employer. Once the employee draws benefits from a plan whose premiums were co-funded by the employer, and the amounts are properly included in the employee's income, the amount of any premiums paid by the employee all the way back to 1968 can be used as a tax deduction. In the case of employee pay-all plans, benefits received during illness or other interruption, will not be taxable to the employee.
12. Parking Provided	The "fair market value" is taxable
13. Income Tax preparation services	The "fair market value" of the service is taxable.

While often taxable benefits are assessed at year end by the employer, this practice is incorrect and could expose the employer to penalties for failure to withhold and remit the source deductions.

All taxable benefits are included in gross income on the "T4 Slips". They can then be allocated to special information boxes for the information of the employee and Revenue Canada.

Impact of the GST

As you may recall from earlier chapters, a supply of goods or services for GST purposes can be made by sale, rental, transfer, barter, exchange, licence, lease, gift, disposition, or as a taxable benefit to an employee. The general definition of a taxable property includes any property, real or personal, movable or immovable, tangible or intangible, corporeal or incorporeal, a right or interest of any kind, a share and a choice in action.

Not subject to the GST are:

(a) the sale of a person's personal effects;

(b) the sale of "exempt" supplies (see below);

(c) sales under $30,000 (unless the business has elected to be a registrant for GST purposes anyway);

(d) the sale of certain real estate outside of a commercial activity;

(e) supplies made outside of Canada by non-residents not carrying on business in Canada; and

(f) supplies of rights to explore or exploit a natural resource.

The following categories of supplies you may be providing to your employees are not subject to the GST because they are "exempt". No GST is collected on them, and no ITC is claimable on the cost of making or providing them:

(a) most health care services,

(b) child care services,

(c) legal aid services, and

(d) educational instruction services provided by public and private trainers (although an election may be made to collect and remit the GST).

... anytime you provide a taxable property ... for ... your employee, no ITC will be claimable ...

Anytime you provide a taxable property exclusively for the personal consumption or benefit of your employee, no ITC will be claimable. However, even in these cases, the GST component of the benefit must still be added to the employee's income, even if the employer cannot take an offsetting ITC. So, if a taxable benefit is provided to the employee, and that benefit is considered a taxable supply under the GST rules, you will have to assess a GST component on the employee's "T4 slip". You are considered to have collected the GST from the employee; you must then remit it on your GST form in the normal manner.

If you cannot claim an ITC for a taxable benefit (*i.e,* if you provide a supply exclusively for the personal consumption of the employee), then you will not be required to remit GST for that benefit. Certain financial institutions can elect not to make a GST remittance if they are allowed only partial ITC claims. However, the GST component on any taxable benefits supplied to the employee must be reported as income.

The good news is that the employee may turn around and claim a GST Rebate if he or she can show that required, unreimbursed employment expenses were tax deductible on "Line 212" — "Union Dues" or "Line 229" — "Other Employment Expenses" of the tax return.

(Note: Effective for 1996 and future years, any tax payable by the employer in purchasing or leasing an employer-provided automobile must be included in calculating the taxable benefit of the employee. More on that topic follows in this chapter.)

AUTOMOBILE BENEFITS

. . . a motor vehicle . . . may create taxable income, if the employee uses the automobile for personal driving . . .

A motor vehicle that is made available to an employee, and is accessible to the employee or under the employee's control, may create taxable income, if the employee uses the automobile for personal driving. It is possible, for example, to provide your spouse with a business-owned vehicle, if that spouse works as an employee in your business.

At the outset, it is most important to note that if the employee does not use the vehicle for personal driving, there will be no taxable benefit, even if the vehicle was available for personal use.

What Is Meant by Personal Driving?

This can include the use of the employer-provided vehicle for any travel other than for business purposes, such as a weekend trip to the cottage, a trip to the bank or grocery store for personal reasons, and most importantly, driving to and from work.

Driving from home to a client's place or other point of call is considered to be business travel. The same is true of the drive home: travel to a client's point of call before driving home will establish a business purpose for the entire trip home.

A motor vehicle is generally defined as an automobile, including a station wagon or van that is designed to carry not more than the driver and eight passengers on highways and streets.

How Does an Automobile Benefit Arise?

Taxable automobile benefits can occur in the following instances:

1. When the company or its owners provide a vehicle to their employees, partners or shareholders,

2. In certain circumstances when the company pays the operating costs of the vehicle, or

> *. . . the*
> *employee may*
> *make certain*
> *arrangements*
> *to reduce*
> *the taxable*
> *benefits . . .*

3. In certain circumstances when the company pays an allowance in addition to an employee's remuneration.

Any taxable amounts will be subject to source deductions for CPP, Employment Insurance and Income Taxes in the normal manner. However, the employee may make certain arrangements to reduce the taxable benefits.

Employer-Provided Vehicles

When an employer provides a vehicle to the employee, shareholder or partner, a "stand-by charge" is calculated in one of two ways, depending upon whether the car is owned or leased by the company.

COMPANY-OWNED VEHICLES

The taxable standby charge is calculated as

- 2% of the cost of the vehicle ×
- (the number of days in the calendar year that the car was available to the employee ÷ 30) ×
- a special reduction if personal kilometers driven were less than 1,000 in the month and the automobile is used at least 90% for business purposes.

Example

Taylor provided her son Jackson, a company-owned vehicle to help her in their real estate business. Jackson works as Taylor's assistant in listing and showing homes. Taylor works as an independent agent with an affiliation to a national real estate company, and receives a "T4A" slip for her commissions. She has only her office in the home to work from. She pays Jackson a salary to work as her assistant. The vehicle cost $23,456, all costs inclusive.

The standby charge is calculated as 2% of $23,456 or $469.12 × 365 ÷ 30 = $5707.63. Jackson would see a taxable benefit added to his employment income in this amount and Taylor would write the vehicle off in the normal manner against business income.

Note that in the case of automobile salespeople, the standby-charge is reduced to 1.5% of the cost of the automobile. Such a cost is calculated as follows:

The greater of:

(a) the average cost of all automobiles acquired to sell or lease in the year, or

(b) the average cost of all new automobiles acquired to sell or lease in the year.

To qualify, the salesperson, or leasing agent must meet the following criteria:

1. the person must be employed principally to sell or lease autos,

2. the auto must be available to the individual or his or her relative, and

3. the employer must have acquired at least one auto during the year.

COMPANY-LEASED VEHICLES

The taxable standby charge is calculated as

— 2/3 of the monthly lease costs ×
— the number of days in the calendar year the car was available to the employee divided by 30 ×
— a special reduction for personal use less than 1000 kilometres per month where the vehicle was used at least 90% for business purposes.

Example

Same as before, except Taylor decides to lease the car for Jackson. She pays $300 each month or $3,600 for the year.

The standby charge is
2/3 × $300 × 365 ÷ 30 = $2,433.33 taxable benefit.

Here is how the special reduction of the taxable benefit would work. Assume that Jackson used the car for personal purposes for an average of 200 kilometers per month, but he drove the car for business purposes 2,000 kilometers per month. His business use was therefore at least 90%. In this case he can calculate a reduction to his automobile standby charge:

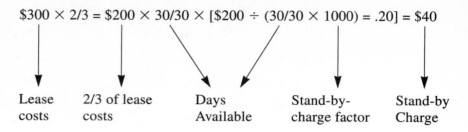

$$\$300 \times 2/3 = \$200 \times 30/30 \times [\$200 \div (30/30 \times 1000) = .20] = \$40$$

| Lease costs | 2/3 of lease costs | Days Available | Stand-by-charge factor | Stand-by Charge |

Instead of adding $200 a month to his taxable income, this taxpayer would add only $40.

An employee may also reduce the standby charge by making reimbursements for the personal component directly to the employer within 45 days of the end of the year.

Calculating Operating Benefits

There is one more taxable benefit that may need to be calculated. This is called an "operating cost benefit". This will apply where the company also pays the employee's, partner's or shareholder's operating expenses relating to personal use. The general benefit is calculated at a fixed rate of 13¢/km of personal use, effective the 1996 tax year; 14¢/km for 1997.

Operating Expenses are defined by Revenue Canada to be the costs of fuel, maintenance, car washes, oil, grease and servicing, repairs, licenses, insurance and certain leasing costs, but not depreciation or financing costs.

There will be no benefit calculated if the employee reimburses the company for all operating expenses within 45 days of the end of the year, including the GST component. Partial payments may also be made and deducted from the calculation of the benefit.

An optional method of calculating the operating cost benefit is also available. The operating costs can be reduced by one-half the standby charge, before reimbursements. This optional calculation can be used if the following conditions are met:

1. A standby charge is being added to the person's income,

2. The vehicle is being used more than 50% of the time for business, and

3. The employee notifies the employer in writing before the end of the tax year.

Your total benefit to be included in Box 14 and 28 of the employee's "T4 Slip" will be the standby charge, the GST component on the standby charge and the operating benefit.

TABLE 6-5
STEPS IN CALCULATING THE OPERATING BENEFIT

Step 1: Where there is no reimbursement or option calculation elected:

Personal Kilometers Driven _____ × .13 = $_____ A*

Step 2: If the vehicle is used at least 50% for business and the employee makes a written request before year end to use this method:

$\left(\begin{array}{c}\text{Standby Charge + Employee Reimbursements}\\ \text{Attributed to Standby Charge}\end{array}\right)$ × 50% = $_____ B

Use amounts from either Step 1 or 2 above (A or B) $_____ C

Less employee reimbursements attributed to operating $_____ *
cost benefit*

Operating Cost Benefit $_____ D

Note: Amount D is considered to include GST & PST, so no further calculation is required.

*No benefit is included in income if full reimbursement is made within 45 days of year end.

Calculating Payroll Deductions on Standby Charges and Operating Benefits

> *. . . the company is expected to estimate the yearly value of these benefits in advance . . .*

The company is expected to estimate the yearly value of these benefits in advance and then prorate the amount of taxable benefit to each pay period. The resulting amounts are added to the employee's salary to arrive at the correct deductions for Income Tax, Canada Pension Plan and EI premiums.

At the end of the year, when you know what the standby charge actually will be, you would recalculate the benefit based on the actual availability of the auto to the employee and the number of kilometres it was actually driven. The last pay cheque can be adjusted based on this new information.

While an employee's taxable benefit is reported on a "T4 Slip"; a shareholder's will be reported on a "T4A" in Box 28 "Other Income", unless that shareholder is also an employee, in which case, the amounts are reported on a "T4 Slip".

AUTOMOBILE ALLOWANCES

Moira works as a nurse who makes house-calls in her husband's business "Doctors on the Run". She supplies her own car for this work, and is paid a salary under an employment agreement she has with her husband, Mitchell, who runs his practice out of their home.

Under Moira's contract of employment, she is entitled to reimbursement of her auto costs. There are several different ways that the reimbursement of costs of an employee-provided vehicle can be treated, depending on circumstances:

1. An employer may reimburse the employee for specific amounts spent.

2. An employer may pay the employee an allowance, which may or may not be taxable.

3. An employer may not pay anything at all towards expenses

Reimbursements

A reimbursement occurs when an employer pays an employee for specific amounts expended in the course of conducting the employer's business. These amounts are generally not subject to tax or withholding. The employee would be required to submit an expense report and all receipts relating to the items purchased, and this will form part of the employer's regular company expenses. This would include the costs of operating the vehicle for business purposes.

. . . an "accountable advance" is an amount given . . . for expenses . . . to be incurred by the employee . . .

An "accountable advance" is an amount given to the employee for expenses that are to be incurred by the employee on the employer's business and for which receipts and vouchers must be produced for amounts spent. Such an accountable advance is not taxable.

A set periodic amount (such as an automobile allowance of $250 a month) may be deemed reasonable and therefore not taxable if the following conditions are met:

1. There is a "start of the year agreement" between the employer and employee that the employee will receive so much for each kilometre driven in the course of an office or employment.

2. There is "year-end accounting" where the total periodic advances received are compared to the amount per kilometre paid times the number of kilometres actually driven. If advances exceed the per kilometre reporting, the employee must reimburse the employer for the difference. It is not acceptable to simply report the excess amounts on the employee's "T4 Slip" as a taxable benefit.

Allowances

An allowance is any periodic or other payment that is received by the employee from an employer, in addition to salary or wages, where it is not necessary to account for the money's use. Such allowances may be calculated either by reference to distance travelled or number of days away or other time basis. Allowances may be considered either taxable or non-taxable, depending on circumstances.

TAX-FREE OR "REASONABLE ALLOWANCES"

A reasonable allowance is one that is based solely by reference to the number of kilometres the vehicle was used for business purposes in the year. As well, the employee cannot be reimbursed in whole or part for expenses paid for this vehicle. However, reimbursements for supplementary business insurance, parking, toll or ferry charges only can be made without jeopardizing the tax-free status of the allowance.

If these two conditions are not met, the whole amount of the allowance must be included in computing the employee's income, and source deductions are required.

The employer would generally pay a specific rate per kilometre. The maximum amounts that can be deducted as an expense of the employer are the following (current as of the time of writing) :

33¢ /km for the first 5,000 kilometers (for 1996),*

27¢ /km thereafter, and

4¢ /km extra in each case for travel in the Yukon and North West Territories.

TAXABLE ALLOWANCES

Taxable allowances are generally those which are not considered to be reasonable by virtue of the fact that they were not calculated on actual kilometres driven for business use and no reimbursement was given for the use of the vehicle (with the exception of supplementary business insurance, parking, ferry & tolls). See Table 6-6.

TABLE 6-6
TAXABLE ALLOWANCES

TYPE OF ALLOWANCE	HOW TO REMIT AND REPORT
1. Solely based on per-kilometre rate	Not taxable; no source deductions
2. Flat rate allowance	Taxable, and subject to source deductions. Employee may be able to claim deductions for expenses on "Line 229" of "T1 General" return. In such cases, employer must sign "Form T2200".
3. Unreasonable per-kilometre rate	as above in #2
4. Flat rate and reasonable allowance (Make source deductions)	Flat rate amount is included in income; while the reasonable per-kilometer amount is not. Employee may claim expenses on personal tax return if both allowances are included in income.

* For 1997, add 2¢/km.

When Payroll Deductions Can Be Waived

. . . payroll deductions can be reduced or eliminated . . . if a written request is made . . .

Payroll deductions can be reduced or eliminated on allowances if a written request is made to the tax department. In this request indicate:

1. An estimate of allowances you will receive in the year,

2. An estimate of business kilometers you expect to drive,

3. An estimate of your auto expenses for the year, and

4. The amount of money for which the waiver is being requested.

Bulk waivers for groups of employees may be obtained. Check with Revenue Canada for their preferred format and the contact person to whom these waivers should be sent.

Spouse's Travel

If a spouse travels with the employee on company business, any payment or reimbursement of the spouse's travelling expenses will be considered a taxable benefit to the employee unless the spouse was travelling on company business activities.

Part-Time Employees

. . . Revenue Canada considers driving to and from the place of employment to be a personal expense . . .

Revenue Canada considers driving to and from the place of employment to be a personal expense. However, subsection 81 (3.1) of the Income Tax Act provides that an allowance or reimbursement of travelling expenses paid to a part-time employee for travelling to and from the employee's part-time job shall not be included in income if the following conditions are met:

1. the employer and employee are not related,

2. throughout the period of part-time employment the employee has other employment or was carrying on a business,

3. the amounts paid were in respect of the part-time employment other than expenses incurred in the performance of the part-time job, and

4. the duties were performed at a location not less than 80 kilometres from the employee's place of residence and the principal place of employment.

Deducting Automobile Expenses on the Individual Tax Return

Sometimes, an employee may deduct auto expenses on the income tax return, following the rules under section 8(a)(h.1) of the Income Tax Act. This will be allowed if the employee is not in receipt of a "reasonable tax-free allowance" described earlier.

When an allowance received is considered not reasonable, and therefore taxable, the employee may include the allowance in income as a taxable benefit, and then deduct related auto expenses. It is Revenue Canada's view that an allowance is "unreasonably low" if the business portion of the expenses, based on kilometres driven, exceeds any allowance received. Such expenses would include operating costs, capital cost allowance and interest costs.

In such a case, the employee would be required to include "Form T2200" — "Declaration of Employment Conditions" in his or her tax return, signed by the employer. This form would verify the conditions of employment and any allowances received, for the purposes of making an expense claim on the tax return. (*See* Appendix 11.)

Reasonable Travelling Expenses of Salespersons and Clergy

A non-taxable allowance may be paid to employees who were employed to sell property or negotiate contracts for the employer, as well as to members of the clergy. The allowances received by salespeople must be:

(a) reasonable, that is, based on the number of kilometres for which the vehicle was used for business purposes (The employee must submit to the employer a record of employment kilometres driven. If this requirement is not met, the amounts are taxable and a deduction for auto expenses on the individual's tax return must be made instead.);

(b) for travelling expenses;

(c) received in a period in which the employee was selling property or negotiating contracts for the employer; and

(d) the sole reimbursement, other than reimbursements for supplementary business insurance, parking, toll or ferry, on a tax-free basis.

If these conditions are not met, the allowances must be included in income. Where they are included in income, the employee may make an offsetting deduction for all expenses incurred for the purposes of earning income.

In the case of clergy, the clergy member must be in charge of, or ministering to, a diocese, parish or congregation and the allowance must have been for transportation expenses occurring due to the discharge of duties of the office or employment.

From the employer's perspective, travelling allowances are treated differently from out-of-pocket expenses which are reimbursed and, if backed by vouchers, tax-free to the employee and fully deductible by the employer. Allowances paid to employees that are not in excess of 33¢/km for the first 5,000 kilometers and 27¢/km thereafter (with additional 4¢/km allowed in the Yukon and NWT), are fully deductible by the employer. Unreasonable allowances (those not supported by per-kilometre logs) are fully deductible by the employer and fully taxable to the employee.

HOW TO MAKE SOURCE DEDUCTIONS

Now that you know the rules determining which income sources are taxable and which are not, it's time to learn the specific rules about making source deductions. This is particularly interesting in light of the introduction of a new "Employment Insurance System," proposed to begin on January 1, 1997.

That is probably a good place to start this discussion. The new system has eliminated the concept of minimum and maximum insurable earnings. In the past we contributed to the Unemployment Insurance system as illustrated in Table 6-7.

TABLE 6-7
HISTORY OF UI PREMIUMS AND RATES

	1985	1986	1987	1988
Maximum Contributions	$562.12	$604.76	$647.92	$690.56
Maximum Insurable Earnings	$23,920	$25,740	$27,560	$29,380
UI Rate	2.35%	2.35%	2.35%	2.35%

	1989	1990	1991	1992	1993	1994	1995
Maximum Contributions	$613.47	$748.80	$892.84	$1,107.60	$1,162.20	$1,245.19	$1,271.40
Maximum Insurable Earnings	$31,460	$33,280	$35,360	$36,920	$38,740	$40,560	$42,380
UI Rate	1.95%	2.25%	2.525%	3%	3%	3.07%	3%
Employer's Portion	$858.86	$,1048.32	$1,249.98	$1,550.64	$1,627.08	$1,743.56	$1,779.96

For 1996, the maximum EIC (formerly UIC) contributions were $1150.76 based on Maximum Insurable Earnings of $39,000 for 52 weeks at a rate of 2.95%. A special reduction of EI benefits payable is allowed when the employer maintains an "approved wage loss replacement plan". A separate employer number must be obtain from Revenue Canada and separate remittances must be made for employees covered under the plan.

Starting in 1997, employers will be required to withhold EI premiums for each dollar of insurable earnings. At this time, EI will become an hours-based system. Employees will require 420 to 700 hours of work to collect EI benefits. This will make the employment of many part-time or casual workers insurable for the first time. Premium rates for EI are set annually at year end.

Effective June 30, 1996, unemployed persons will be able to earn up to 25% of their benefit rates each week. Claims for maternity, parental and sickness benefits will have no allowable earnings. Starting January 1, 1997, unemployed persons will be allowed to earn 25% of their benefit rates or $50 each week, whichever is higher, before their benefits are affected.

As well, employees who earn $2,000 or less during a tax year will be able to claim a refund on their tax returns of the EI premiums they have paid. The employer, however, will still have to remit his or her portion of EI premiums on these types of earnings. Yet even here there is transitional relief: small employers who remit less than $30,000 in employer premiums in 1996 will be able to claim a refund of EI premiums paid for casual employees as long as they pay at least $500 more in premiums for 1997 and 1998. A maximum refund of $5,000 will be available.

Under this new system, the premium payable by employers and employees will be based on an annual maximum for insurable earnings. For the years 1997 to 2000, this will be $39,000. This maximum will apply to each job the employee holds, even if this is with different employers. This means that each employer will withhold for EI purposes until the $39,000 income level is reached. An employee who earns $750 a week or less will have premiums withheld all year long.

Overpayments to EI that are made because an employee works for several employers during the year will be recoverable by filing an income tax return at year-end. However, once again the employer gets stung: there are no refunds for you, even if your employee has already maxed out by contributing on earnings of $39,000 or more made with another employer.

There will be another income tax related change due to the new system. Persons whose net income in 1996 exceeds $48,750 will be required to repay up to 30% of their benefits. However, starting January 1, 1997, if there are more than 20 weeks in a person's EI claim history, the claimant will be required to repay a portion of EI benefits received during the year when net income exceeds $39,000, up to a maximum of 100% of amounts received. A sample of this significant calculation appears in Table 6-8.

. . . employers will be required to withhold EI premiums for each dollar of insurable earnings . . .

TABLE 6-8
TAX-BACK OF EI BENEFITS FOR NET INCOME OVER $39,000
— JAN. 1, 1997

WEEKS OF REGULAR BENEFITS IN THE PAST 5 YEARS	MAXIMUM PORTION OF BENEFITS THAT CAN BE TAXED BACK ON YOUR INCOME TAX RETURN
20 or less	30%
21–40	50%
41–60	60%
61–80	70%
81–100	80%
101–120	90%
over 120	100%

In addition, for 1997 only, employers should prepare themselves to report earnings for their employees under both the 1996 and 1997 rules. Total earnings for the last 20 insurable weeks before January 1, 1997 will be reported, as well as the total number of insured weeks in 1996. Human Resource Development Canada will then automatically convert these weeks to hours to meet the new criteria of hours worked.

At the time of writing draft regulations were being prepared and the system was in a proposal stage only. What this means for home-based business owners, is that every hour an employee works will count for the purposes of making remittances into the Employment Insurance program. And for employees, drawing from EI now can have restrictions in the future.

The Canada Pension Plan

. . . the Canada Pension Plan . . . is funded by . . . both employees and employers . . . The Canada Pension Plan is a federal-government administered pension savings plan that is funded by equal contributions from both employees and employers. The plan came into existence in 1966 and distributes benefits, based on contributions made, to those who retire, those who are disabled and dependants who survive a contributor's death. For these reasons, the CPP is an important safety net, one whose viability is challenged as we move into the 21st Century. At the time of writing, an overhaul of the CPP was being discussed, so that its survival in the wake of an aging population, could be guaranteed.

The history of the maximum premiums that have been payable to the CPP is shown in Table 6-9.

TABLE 6-9
HISTORY OF CPP MAXIMUM PREMIUMS

	1985	1986	1987	1988
Maximum Contributions	$379.80	$419.40	$444.60	$478.00
Maximum Pensionable Earnings	$23,400	$25,800	$25,900	$26,500
Basic Exemption	$ 2,300	$ 2,400	$ 2,500	$ 2,600
Subject to Contribution	$21,100	$23,400	$23,400	$23,900
Rate of Contribution	1.8%	1.8%	1.9%	2%

	1989	1990	1991	1992	1993	1994	1995
Maximum Contributions	$ 525	$574.20	$632.50	$ 696	$752.50	$ 806	$850.50
Maximum Pensionable Earnings	$27,700	$28,900	$30,500	$32,200	$33,400	$34,400	$34,900
Basic Exemption	$ 2,700	$ 2,800	$ 3,000	$ 3,200	$ 3,300	$ 3,400	$ 3,400
Subject to Contribution	$25,000	$26,100	$27,500	$29,000	$30,100	$31,000	$31,500
Rate of Contribution	2.1%	2.2%	2.3%	2.4%	2.5%	2.6%	2.7%

For 1996, the maximum pensionable earnings are $35,400, with a basic exemption of $3,500, and a contribution rate of 2.8%.* Employers, are required to match the employee's contributions. CPP premiums do not have to deducted from those who make less than $4,250 in agriculture, forestry, trapping, fishing, hunting, horitculture or lumbering employment, employment of a child under 18, residence benefits of clergy, severance pay or death benefits.

The following circumstances indicate that CPP is not payable by the employee:

1. The employee is under the age of 18.

2. The employee is over the age of 70.

3. The employee has started to receive a retirement or disability benefit from the CPP.

4. The employee is deceased.

---

* For 1997 pensionable earnings increase to $35,800, the Basic Exemption remains at $3,500 and the contribution rate increases to 2.925%.

In the last three instances, CPP premiums are payable until the month of the event. CPP is remitted for teenagers in the month after they turn 18. A sample calculation is shown in Table 6-10.

TABLE 6-10
CALCULATION OF REQUIRED CPP CONTRIBUTIONS —
PARTIAL YEAR ELIGIBILITY

CPP Premiums are prorated if taxpayer turns 18, 70, died in the year or started to receive a pension from the Canada Pension Plan.

To calculate the eligible months:

1. Where taxpayer turned l8, number of months after birthday   _____

2. Where taxpayer turned 70, number of months prior to & including B-Day   _____

3. Where taxpayer died, number of months prior to & including mo. of death   _____

4. Where CPP pension received, no. of months pension not receivable   _____

To Calculate Required Amt.	Prorated by 1/12	# mos. above	Maximums	Taxpayer's amounts
1. Max. Pensionable Earnings	$2,950 × (mos.) _____		$35,400	_____ (1)
2. Actual Earnings fr. Box 26 or 14 (Do not prorate.)		"		_____ (2)
3. Lesser of 1 and 2				_____ (3)
Less Basic Exemption	$291.67 × (mos.) _____		$ 3,500	_____
Earnings Subject to Contribution			$31,900	_____
× CPP Rate for 1996				× .028
Required Contribution			$893.20	_____

TAX SAVINGS FOR FAMILY BUSINESSES

. . . overhead is low, time is maximized and support systems are great . . .

It is enlightening and often surprising to see how quickly a home-based small business can grow and prosper. Overhead is low, time is maximized and support systems are great . . . a recipe for success.

Once that success comes your way, you will soon see how far-reaching the tax system is as a whole, and that in general, there is continuity and equity across the lines between individuals and corporations. The self-employed individual does have a good degree of flexibility in influencing the timing of income and expenses with decision-making throughout the year, and in splitting income between family members, depending upon the circumstances within the individual business itself.

You should be discussing, on an ongoing basis, the changing nature of your business enterprise with your tax accountant, to see whether the current business organization — proprietorship, partnership or corporation or any combination thereof — can give you and your family the best tax position.

The opportunity to split income with other family members working in your home-based business, is by far the most attractive benefit of the home-based family business. (There are some who might argue it is one of the only advantages, given the long hours and the financial risk most proprietors are willing to work and take in building their enterprises.)

▶ *. . . the*
opportunity to
split income . . .
is by far the
most attractive
benefit . . .

In actual fact, in most family businesses, family members usually participate in the pursuit of income. The challenge is, to properly document these activities in order to meet Revenue Canada's requirements for tax deductibility and to stay clear of the Attribution Rules and the General Anti-Avoidance Rules discussed earlier.

We have previously outlined that in order to stay onside with Revenue Canada, one must follow the rules of reasonableness, documenting work actually done by family members with time cards and/or employment contracts, in a business that has a reasonable expectation of profit, and which would have hired a stranger to do the same work. Assuming all of these circumstances exist, the results of income splitting, can be astounding.

To give you some benchmarks, each family member may make up to $6,456 (the "Basic Personal Amount") before remittances for income tax are required. Therefore a family of four could earn $25,824 in taxable income before any income taxes would have to be paid to the federal government.

To stay in the lowest federal/provincial marginal tax bracket, each family member can earn a taxable income of $29,590. (For a refresher on marginal tax rates, see "How Income is Taxed in Canada," in Chapter Two). If there are two spouses and two teenaged children working in the family business, a combined total of $118,360 in taxable income can be made ($29,590 × 4) at the lowest possible tax rates. Each person would pay approximately $6,690 in federal/provincial taxes, for an effective tax rate of 23%. (Keep in mind the first $6,456 is not subject to tax and that actual rates would vary from province to province.) Under this scenario, the family tax liability would be approximately $26,760 ($6,690 × 4).

If only one family member, on the other hand, alone brought in $118,360, the family tax liability would be approximately $48,000 . . . an increase of $21,240 in the family net tax liability. The moral . . . it makes much more sense for four people in a family to make $29,590 each than for one person to make $118,360! In fact, by arranging your affairs in this manner, it's almost like having one more invisible person working for you, earning $21,240 more for your family unit, in tax savings.

So, with a better understanding of our progressive tax system and our effective and marginal tax rates, you can now decide how to remunerate yourself, your partners and your employees within the framework of the law so as to pay the least amount of taxes possible. Work with your tax advisor in setting up your remuneration structure, and the documentation requirements, and follow them meticulously. It's really worth it.

Below are some ways you can reduce the withholding taxes you make from your employee's cheques. These tax reducers can help you to maximize the cash-flow generated from your family business.

Letters of Authority

Any time that a taxpayer will have a significant number of other tax deductions on his or her personal tax return, an application can be made to Revenue Canada to have source deductions reduced. This can happen if the following provisions apply to the taxpayer:

1. There are loss carryovers available for claiming on this year's return;

2. The following deductions will be claimed on this year's return:
   (a) RRSP contributions will be made,
   (b) Child Care Expenses will be claimed,
   (c) Moving Expenses are deductible,
   (d) Allowable Business Investment Losses can be claimed,
   (e) Carrying Charges are significant,
   (f) Repayments of EI, or other social benefits erroneously paid to you can be deducted,
   (g) Alimony or Maintenance payments are being made,
   (h) Northern Residents Deductions will be claimed, or
   (i) Overseas Employment Tax Credits will be claimed.

3. Any other provisions that will reduce the taxpayer's taxable income.

. . . a letter is forwarded . . . requesting that tax deductions be waived . . .

A letter is forwarded to Revenue Canada, requesting that tax deductions be waived on the salary or wages, the name and address of the employer is outlined, and, in the case of alimony or RRSP contributions, the name of the recipient or plan holder is outlined.

The employer will then receive a letter of authority from Revenue Canada waiving the requirement for tax deductions on the income in question. The process of obtaining the waiver takes about three weeks.

When Tax Is Not Deducted

Tax is not deducted on:

1. casual employment for a purpose other than the normal trade or business,

2. the benefits received from wage loss replacement plans (these amounts are not subject to withholding tax, but are taxable. A special deduction for premiums paid by the employee since 1968, may be taken on the tax return. The company should be prepared to give the employee a

record of such premium payments made to wage loss replacement plans that are jointly paid for by employer and employee.),

3. the first $10,000 paid in the form of a death benefit, and

4. income earned by Status Indians employed on the reserve.

When Tax Can Be Reduced

There are six special forms that can be filed by employees in order to reduce the income tax that is deducted, or to reduce the tax they will eventually pay, all of which require interaction with a company official or payroll clerk.

TD1X STATEMENT OF REMUNERATION AND EXPENSES

This form is generally used by commissioned salespeople who are employees. Without this form, the payroll clerk is required to deduct income taxes on commissions paid in the period received; however, the salesperson often has out-of-pocket expenses which are deductible on the tax return. This form must be filed by January 31 of the new year, or within one month with a new employer, or within one month of changes either in remuneration and expenses, or personally (*i.e.,* marriage, divorce, *etc.*).

> *. . . the employer is responsible if a fraudulent form is accepted . . .*

(Note: The employer is instructed to contact the tax department if dubious claims are filed by the sales force; the *employer* is responsible if a fraudulent form is accepted.)

TD5 APPLICATION FOR REDUCTION IN AUTOMOBILE STANDBY CHARGE

The standby charge added to income as a taxable benefit of an employee who uses an employer-provided vehicle for personal use, may be reduced if the automobile is used at least 90% of the time for business purposes and the total kilometers it is used for personal use is less than 1,000 per month. This benefit was discussed in detail in "Automobile Benefits," earlier in this chapter.

T2200 DECLARATION OF EMPLOYMENT CONDITIONS

As a business owner, you may be called upon to sign this common form, for any employee who is required under the contract of employment to pay his or her own expenses for the use of an employee-owned vehicle, home-office, payment for a substitute or assistant, or for supplies directly used up in their work. The employer must verify whether the employee was required to work away from the place of business, for how long, how remuneration is paid, and whether an allowance was paid. With this signed form, the employee will be able to claim income tax deductions for the out-of-pocket expenditures.

TL2 CLAIM FOR BOARD AND LODGING

If you run a long-distance trucking company from your home, and hire drivers, you will encounter this form. It must be completed by the employer of a long-distance transport employee who is responsible for paying the cost of meals and lodging while en route and away from the employer's place of business for at least four hours.

Runs of less than 10 hours in a day (round trip) warrant only one meal claim; and a maximum of three meals in a 24-hour period are claimable using a flat rate/meal expense or "simplified method". A log book of trips is required for the eventuality that the employee is audited.

The employer must verify that the company's principal business is the transportation of goods, passengers or both, give the name of the collective agreement that governs the employee's employment, if any, state whether or not subsidized meals are available to this employee, indicate whether an allowance for meals and lodging is paid, and whether any of such allowance was reported on the "T4 Slip".

ANNUALIZATION OF INCOME TAX REMITTANCES ON BONUS PAYMENTS

An employer who paid bonuses, vacation pay, overtime pay or retroactive pay increases to the employees must deduct CPP, EI and Income Taxes. However, special rules will ease the tax burden. First, be aware that income tax is levied on the total remuneration for the year for each employee, less certain deductions (*See* "Letters of Authority," earlier in this chapter.)

When a bonus is paid in one period, it generally bumps the recipient into a high marginal tax rate, with the result that a higher percentage of tax is taken from the bonus due to the one-time receipt. It is possible to annualize the required tax remittance, with the overall result that the employee receives more of the bonus in his or her hands.

INSTALMENT PROFILES

. . . it is most important . . . that bonus payments are properly calculated . . .

If you are paying a bonus to one of your employees, it is most important for 1994 and future years, that bonus payments are properly calculated according to periodic payment requirements. If at the end of a tax year the employee owes tax of $2,000 or more on his or her tax return, because not enough tax was remitted at source during the year, the employee will become liable for making quarterly instalment payments to Revenue Canada. This would require the self-remittance of income tax on March 15, June 15, September 15 and December 15, even if the majority of the employee's taxes were deducted at source.

CHAPTER SEVEN

Special Tax Rules for Specific Business Ventures

Nobody can do it for you.
— *Ralph Cordiner*

...business you operate, there are some ...dual business types. It is always best ...business with your tax professional. ...special tax provisions for those in a

...ss is usually in the form of fees for services. This will generally include the professional practice of an accountant, dentist, doctor, lawyer, veterinarian or chiropractor. Such a professional may carry on business as an individual sole-proprietor, a partner or a corporation. Only certain professionals are allowed to incorporate. (You will have to check provincial legislation in your own province for more information.)

> ...*only certain professionals are allowed to incorporate* ...

Special Tax Forms for Professionals

For tax purposes, the income from professional services is reported on "Form T2032" — "Statement of Professional Activities," shown in Appendix 4.

Accounting Methods

Prior to 1972, professionals were able to use the cash method of reporting income; that is, income was taxable when actually received and expenses were deductible when they were actually paid. Now only farmers and fishermen are allowed to compute their net profits using the cash method.

Election to Exclude Work-in-Progress

After 1971 professionals were required to use the accrual method of accounting. Using this method, income is generally reported when it becomes receivable, whether or not payment has been received, and expenses are deductible when incurred, whether or not they have been paid. Until 1983, professionals could value "work-in-progress" at the end of the year at nil. Work-in-progress is work that has been started but is not yet completed.

For 1983 and future years, professional businesses were required to use the accrual method of accounting for income and expenses, but certain professionals may use a "modified accrual" method, in which the value of work-in-progress may be excluded in one year and added to income the next. Work-in-progress may be excluded by filing an election in the returns of accountants, dentists, lawyers, medical doctors, chiropractors or veterinarians. Once made, permission must be received from Revenue Canada to revoke the election.

Fiscal Year-Ends

An unincorporated professional practice is required to conform to a fiscal year-end of December 31 in reporting income and expenses, unless there is a valid non-tax reason to maintain a non-calendar year-end. These new rules came into effect as of the 1995 tax year. (For more information, *see* "Choosing a Fiscal Year-End," in Chapter Two.)

Fees Received in Advance of Services

▶ *. . . it is the date on the bill or invoice . . . that is used to determine when the income should be reported . . .*

Should you receive fees in advance, the amounts received must be reported as income, but a reasonable reserve may be set up for services that are reasonably anticipated to be rendered after the end of the year. It is important to point out that in reporting fee income, it is the date on the bill or invoice for services that is used to determine when the income should be reported.

Expenses of Professional Practices

Operating and capital expenses are treated much the same way for professionals as for regular businesses and follow similar rules for reasonable expectation of profit and onus of proof. There are special circumstances, however, that must be taken into account for professionals.

AUTOMOBILE EXPENSES

These are deductible under the rules discussed in Chapter Six. However, in the case of a dentist, or other professional, auto expenses for driving to and from the home to an off-site office will generally not be allowed.

BOOKS AND PROFESSIONAL LIBRARIES

Professional library fees are deductible, but generally the costs of purchasing a library is a depreciable asset in Class 8 at 20%. The cost of professional periodicals and library books purchased individually will generally be allowed as an operating expense.

CONVENTIONS

The costs of up to two conventions per year are deductible. (*See* "Maximizing Claims for Entertainment and Promotion," in Chapter Four.)

DEPRECIATION

The same rules apply to the write-offs for depreciable properties of a professional. Assets specific to the professional include:

1. Class 8: Furniture, fixtures, professional library, medical and dental instruments that cost more than $200;

2. Class 10: a vehicle that cost less than $24,000 (plus PST/GST)* after August 1989; over this Class 10.1 is used;

3. Class 12: medical and dental instruments costing less than $200; and

4. Class 13: leasehold interests.

HOME OFFICE

Costs are only deductible if a space is set aside exclusively for the purposes of earning income, and it is used on a regular and continuous basis for meeting clients. The deductions, which can include portions of property taxes, interest, insurance, utilities, repairs and maintenance, and so on, cannot be used to increase or create a loss.

---

* 25,000 after 1996.

INSURANCE

Malpractice insurance is tax-deductible, as is fire insurance on business property.

LICENCES

Annual fees paid to professional and scientific associations or societies are deductible; however entrance fees to a professional society are not. (*See* "Goodwill and Other Intangible Assets," in Chapter Five.)

POSTAGE AND OFFICE OR MEDICAL SUPPLIES

These are tax-deductible, and can include the costs of necessary laundry services.

RENT

These costs are tax-deductible.

RESERVES FOR DOUBTFUL ACCOUNTS AND BAD DEBTS

The amounts are deductible.

SALARIES OF PARTNERS, SPOUSES AND OTHERS

Salaries paid to clerical staff, para-professionals, salaried professionals and other assistance are deductible.

SUPPLIES

For the home office are tax-deductible.

TELEPHONE AND COMMUNICATIONS

These are tax-deductible, although the cost of equipment over $200 is generally depreciated.

Lawyers' Trust Accounts

If a lawyer receives an advance for services to be rendered in the future, the amount is not considered to be income, unless it is a retainer, which the lawyer can keep whether or not the services are rendered. In the former case, the amount held in trust becomes taxable when the lawyer has performed the

. . . if a lawyer receives an advance . . . the amounts are not considered to be income, unless they are a retainer . . .

services and has a legal right to the funds. Generally speaking interest earned on such accounts is considered to be the income of the client, unless there is a specific and different arrangement made between the lawyer and the client.

Where funds are deposited with a lawyer by a litigant for safekeeping and investment, pending court order or settlement, income earned on the account is considered to be income of the trust and will be recognized as such by the beneficial owner when the recipient is determined.

Disbursements on behalf of a client which are chargeable directly to funds advanced are not deductible by the lawyer as they are considered to be expenses of the client.

PARTNERSHIPS

A partnership is a relationship you have with one or more people in conducting a common business for profit. From a tax viewpoint, the partnership itself will not pay tax on its net income; rather the amounts are flowed through to each partner, each of whom must file a personal income tax return to report his or her share of the net income or loss.

A partnership with six or more members must file "Form T5013" to report income from the partnership to its members. A partnership with five or fewer members, where none of the members are involved in another partnership, need not file this special form. Should one of the partners of the group of five or fewer partners belong to another partnership, "Form T5013" must again be filed, on or before March 31 following the calendar year in which the fiscal period of the partnership ended, if all the members are individuals.

In the case of a professional partnership, an election may be made to exclude work-in-progress from income, under the same rules discussed in earlier chapters. However, the election must be made on behalf of all the partners by one partner who is authorized to act upon all of them.

Because the net profits of the partnership are flowed out to its members for tax reporting, the tax preparer must complete a "Business or Professional Income and Expense Statement" that is common for all, and then adjust the partner's share of the income for any expenses that were not included in the partnership statement and for which the individual partner was not reimbursed. This can include, for example, auto expenses, certain wages or entertainment expenses.

Example

Don and Kevin run Two Friends Moving Services out of their homes. Each partner has a computer, which the partnership owns and depreciates, and each partner uses his own vehicle for busi-

ness. Don is the partner who makes the sales calls, and he spends his own money when entertaining clients.

Don and Kevin would each file an identical income and expense statement for the partnership itself. The net income from the partnership, which is split on a 50-50 basis according to their partnership agreement, is now adjusted on each individual return. Don would calculate his individual auto expenses and reduce his share of the partnership according to that calculation and the entertainment expenses he is allowed to deduct. Kevin would reduce his share of the net income with the business portion of his own auto expenses.

As a result, each partner would have a different net income figure listed on the personal income tax return.

GST Rebate

Members of a partnership may be able to claim a GST Rebate on "Form GST-370" (*See* Appendix 8.) by filing a tax return. A refund of GST paid on any individual expenses paid outside the partnership — such as some of the auto and entertainment expenses discussed above may be possible. The rebate is allowed if the partner is a member of a GST-registered partnership, and the expenses are not GST-exempt.

Distribution of Income

Income or losses are reported by the individual partners; not the partnership; whether or not there were actual distributions. In general, income and losses of the partnership will affect the cost base of the partnership interest. (See the explanations below.)

It is usual for partnership agreements to divide profits and losses on the basis of the partners' individual interest in the partnership. As well, salaries may be paid to partners. If this is so, no deduction is claimable for partners' salaries or for interest on their capital contributions. As well, any drawings from the partnership are ignored in computing the income and expenses of the partnership. Check with your tax advisor about the technical details before laying out your personal remuneration package within the partnership.

It is also possible for partners to continue to allocate income or losses of a partnership to a retired partner or his or her spouse, estate or heirs.

The following are excluded from the computation of partnership income: proceeds of disposition of resource properties; deductions for Canadian oil and gas property expenses; depletion allowances or exploration and development expenses; and resource allowances for oil, gas and mineral resources.

These amounts are generally claimed by the individual partners, not the partnership itself.

When a Partnership Interest Is Acquired

The interest a partner has in the partnership is considered to be a capital asset. This interest can be acquired when a partner becomes a member, by contributing cash or property, or by acquiring another partner's interest.

A partner may dispose of the interest in a partnership by transferring it to another taxpayer or by receiving a full payment from the partnership itself for the partnership interest itself.

The original cost of the partnership interest forms the adjusted cost base and to this is added any undrawn profits.

Adjusted Cost-Base Computations

A record of the following transactions are required to properly compute the adjusted cost base of the partnership interest, as shown in Table 7-1.

TABLE 7-1
SOME COMMON ADDITIONS AND DEDUCTIONS TO ACB

AMOUNTS TO BE ADDED TO ACB	AMOUNTS TO BE DEDUCTED FROM ACB
1. Share of annual partnership income after 1971, excluding income allocated to a retired partner who is deemed to be a member of the partnership. To compute annual income: (a) include the whole gain on the disposition of eligible capital property. (b) include the whole gain of a capital property including a listed personal property. (c) do not use the grossed-up amount of taxable dividends from taxable Canadian corporations.	1. Losses allocated to partners. Limited partnership losses — defined as the excess loss over the at-risk amount — will only be deductible from the ACB of a partnership interest when they are deducted from the individual partner's taxable income.
2. Capital dividends of a partnership, which is any capital dividend in which the partnership holds stock and the share of any life insurance capital dividend received.	2. A partner's share of Canadian exploration and development expenses, and Canadian oil and gas property expenses.

(continues)

TABLE 7-1
(continued)

AMOUNTS TO BE ADDED TO ACB	AMOUNTS TO BE DEDUCTED FROM ACB
3. Life insurance policy proceeds received on the death of an insured.	3. The partner's share of charitable gifts or political contributions made by the partnership.
4. Contributions of capital.	4. The portion of partnership capital losses.
5. Rights or things.	5. Withdrawals of capital from the partnership.
6. Capital gains on a residual interest in the partnership.	
7. Certain property transferred into a partnership by an individual who becomes a member of the partnership.	

"Form T2065" — "Determination of Adjusted Cost Base of a Partnership Interest" may be obtained from Revenue Canada to compute the adjusted cost base of the partnership interest at the time of disposition. When a partnership interest is sold, the difference between the ACB and the proceeds of disposition will equal the taxpayer's capital gain or loss.

The comments above reflect legislation in effect at the time of writing only. You should speak to your tax advisor about any pertinent revisions to legislation that may affect your adjusted cost-base computations.

Negative Adjusted Cost Base

If ever the adjusted cost base of the partnership becomes negative, a capital gain is immediately generated, if the taxpayer has ceased to be a member of the partnership, or if the partner is a limited partner in a limited partnership for fiscal periods ending after February 22, 1994. Otherwise, the negative amount is only treated as a capital gain when the partnership interest is disposed of.

Transfers and Dispositions of Partnership Interests

> *. . . if a partnership is dissolved, there is a deemed disposition of . . . assets . . .*

A transfer or sale of an interest in a partnership will trigger a capital disposition. If a partnership is dissolved, there is a deemed disposition of the partnership assets. Special rules exist where a partner dies or retires. See Table 7-2.

TABLE 7-2
EFFECTS OF TERMINATION ON ACB

1. Upon Death of Partner	(a) If the deceased was a retired partner, it is possible that another person may receive the deceased's residual interest in the partnership at a cost equal to the proceeds deemed to have been received by the deceased. This transaction may generate a negative ACB in the deceased's partnership interest account, resulting in a capital gain.
	(b) On death of a partner, the residual interest is deemed to be disposed of for proceeds equal to "fair market value" unless the interest is transferred to a spouse.
2. Upon Retirement (*See* IT 242 for full commentary on retired partners.)	(a) Where all the rights to a partner's interests in a partnership have not been satisfied at the time of retirement, the partner is considered to have a "residual interest," where all the same additions and deductions to the ACB of the partnership interest will apply. Any amounts received in full or partial satisfaction of a residual interest will reduce the ACB and any negative amount will be reported as a capital gain, and the ACB is adjusted to zero. A residual interest is disposed of when the final payment is made.
	(b) Where an income allocation is made to a retired partner, such income must be reported by the retired partner in the tax year in which the fiscal year of the partnership ends.
3. Upon Termination of Partnership	Where all property of the partnership is distributed to the partners the partnership is deemed to have been dissolved, and the assets of the partnership distributed at "fair market value".
4. Upon Sale or Transfer	The transfer of assets from a partnership to a partner is generally treated as a sale at "fair market value". (Also see new "Stop Loss Rules" in Chapter 5.)

CHANGES FROM PROPRIETORSHIP TO PARTNERSHIP

The major issue to consider when a proprietorship becomes a partnership and vice versa is how the assets will be treated for tax purposes.

Proprietorship to Partnership

If all members of the partnership are Canadian, special tax-free rollovers of the assets of the partnership will be allowed. However, if there is even one non-resident partner, all asset transfers must be at "fair market value".

Where a partnership has acquired property from a taxpayer who was a member of the partnership immediately after such a transfer, the partnership is deemed to have acquired the property at its "fair market value" at the time of transfer. The taxpayer is deemed to have disposed of the property at the same amount, unless there is an election by all the members of the partnership, to acquire the property at an agreed upon amount that results in a tax-deferred rollover. In this case, "Form T2059" — " Election on Acquisition of Property by a Canadian Partnership" must be filed.

Transfers Between Partnerships

. . . a majority interest partner . . . is entitled to more than one-half of the partnership's income . . .

New rules introduced in the April 26, 1995 Technical Notes will prohibit a loss on the transfer of property to a partnership of which the transferor is a majority interest partner. A majority interest partner is someone who is entitled to more than one-half of the partnership's income from all sources for the immediately preceding fiscal period. Instead of adding the loss to the adjusted cost base, it will be deferred until the earliest of these three events:

1. a subsequent disposition of the property to a person who is not related or affiliated to the transferor,

2. there is a deemed disposition due to change of residence or change of taxable status, or

3. in the case of a corporation, the acquisition of the corporation's control.

Where the capital cost of property transferred to the partnership exceeds the taxpayer's proceeds of disposition, the capital cost is the figure used as the new capital cost to the partnership, which is deemed to have claimed capital cost allowance for the difference.

FARMERS AND FISHERMEN

. . . special tax provisions . . . make life a little more difficult for start-up farming ventures . . .

In the latest year that taxation statistics were available (1993-94), there were close to 240,000 farm returns filed in Canada, reporting net farming income of $1.9 billion. Of these, 80,750 returns were non-taxable. Another 65,220 returns reported off-farm employment earnings of $860,750.

With close to one-third of all farm returns showing losses, there are special tax provisions that make life a little more difficult for start-up farming ventures. It all revolves around whether the farm is a hobby farm or a viable business with a reasonable expectation of profit.

The net profits of farmers and fishermen are taxed in much the same manner as other unincorporated business. These enterprises will be subject to the same fiscal year-end rules that apply to all other businesses, although, most farming and fishing enterprises have a December 31 year-end. Some of the unique provisions for farmers and fishermen are discussed below.

Accounting Methods

One of the major differences between "Farming and Fishing" enterprises and other businesses is that the cash method of reporting income and expenses may be used. That is, income is reported when received and expenses are deducted when paid. This means that post-dated cheques are generally included in income on the earlier of the date the debt is payable or the date the cheque is cashed. A partnership can use the cash method only if all partners agree to it.

Farmers may wish to use the accrual method of reporting income, and this is acceptable. Under the accrual method it is necessary to value your inventory and keep track of it. Use one of the following three methods for valuation of livestock, crops, feed and fertilizer:

1. "Fair market value"

2. Lower of cost or "fair market value"

3. Unit base prices (Use "Form T2034" — "Election to Establish Inventory Unit Prices for Animals")

Inventory is not included in income if the cash method of reporting income and expenses is being used.

If the taxpayer wishes to change from the accrual to the cash method of accounting, this can be done simply by starting to use the cash method on the next return and attaching a statement showing the adjusting entries to income and expenses. However, if a change from cash to accrual is being made, permission must be granted from the Director of the local District Tax Office, after receipt of a letter from the taxpayer requesting the new treatment.

Instalment Tax Payments

▶ *. . . a self-employed farmer or fisherman needs to make only one instalment payment . . .*

Another difference in tax treatment of farmers and fishermen is the payment of instalments during the year. A self-employed farmer or fisherman needs to make only one instalment payment and that is due on December 31. Other unincorporated businesses are required to make quarterly instalments. Instalment payments will be required if the difference between federal and provincial taxes payable, and the amount of tax withheld at source plus provincial credits exceeds $2,000 in the current and the two immediately preceeding tax years.

Cash-Basis Losses

Finally, if a farmer is using the cash method of reporting income, it is necessary to perform a Mandatory Inventory Adjustment if there is a net loss from the business that is not a restricted farm loss, and if you have inventory on hand at the end of the year. This will be discussed in more detail later.

Definition of Income Sources

The income and expenses of a farmer are reported on "Form T2042" — "Statement of Farming Activities". Revenue Canada requests that you enter the percentage of the partnership you own. (*See* Appendix 4.)

Farm Income

Farming income is reported next, and can include: Farm Support Payments; Gifts; Sharecropping; Woodlots; and Specific Revenue Producers. Let's have a look at what each of these entails.

FARM SUPPORT PAYMENTS

For 1991 and subsequent years, payments or refunds of premiums for "gross revenue insurance programs" under the Farm Income Protection Act and other special programs must be included in income. Use "Line 8120" of the "Farming Income and Expense Statement". (GRIP is currently being phased out in all provinces except Ontario.) Form "AGR-1" is available to report any farm support payments received from most government agriculture programs. Income, grants or subsidies received and shown on this slip are generally reported as income on the "Farming Income and Expense Statement"("Form T2042"). Any investment income is reported on "Line 130" — "Other Income".

GIFTS

. . . when someone gives you a payment "in kind" . . . you must include the "fair market value" of such items in your income . . .

If you give away livestock or other inventory that would usually be sold, an amount equal to the "fair market value" of the item must be included in income, as you would have previously written off the costs as an expense. When someone gives you a payment "in kind" ; that is, some roasting chickens in exchange for custom work you may have performed, you must include the "fair market value" of such items in your income.

SHARECROPPING

If you rent out land to someone in return for a share of the products grown, you must include as income the amounts received. This is generally regarded as "rental income" as opposed to active business income.

WOODLOTS

Income received from the sale of trees, lumber, logs, poles or firewood must be reported. A depletion allowance can be claimed on the woodlot, and amounts received for removal of standing trees will be considered to be capital receipts. These special rules are described in more detail in Revenue Canada's IT 373.

SPECIFIC REVENUE PRODUCERS

The Industry Codes that identify sources of farming revenues are outlined in the *Farming Income Guide,* which is available free of charge from your local Tax Services Office. There are six main categories of farming revenues:

1. Livestock Farms (cattle, dairy, feedlot, hog, poultry and eggs, sheep & goats);

2. Other animals (fur and skin, honey and other apiary, horse and other equine);

3. Field Crops (dry field peas or beans, forage crops, grain corn, oilseeds, potatoes, small grains, tobacco, wheat and other field crops);

4. Fruit and Other Vegetable Farms (fruit, other vegetables);

5. Other specialty farms (greenhouse products, mushrooms, nursery products, other horticultural specialties); and

6. Combination Farms (Field crop combinations, fruit and vegetable combinations, livestock combinations, livestock, field crop and horticultural combinations).

Other Recent Tax Changes

The following is a summary of recent farming provisions that have been amended in the Income Tax Act.

MODIFICATION OF CASH METHOD DEDUCTIONS FOR CERTAIN PREPAYMENTS

Under the cash method of reporting income, amounts are generally deducted when paid. This can include certain prepaid amounts, for example, the prepayment of rents or insurance. In the April 26, 1995 Technical Amendments introduced by the Finance Department, the deduction for such prepaid expenses can be made in advance for only the current year and one more year. The portion of amounts paid for tax years that are two or more years after payment, must now be deferred and deducted in those future years. For example, if $5,000 was prepaid for five consecutive years of insurance coverage, $2,000 could be deducted in 1995 and then $1,000 in each year 1997, 1998 and 1999. To be deductible, the amount is required to have been paid in a preceding tax year and cannot be deductible in computing income of the business for any other year. These rules will not apply to prepayments of inventory items.

LAND IMPROVEMENT COSTS

. . . expenditures, such as clearing land and constructing unpaved roads, are deducted as a current expense by farmers . . .

Expenditures, such as clearing land and constructing unpaved roads, are deducted as a current expense by farmers. A farmer may claim less than the full cost of these expenses in the year they are incurred (effective for fiscal periods since 1988). He or she will be allowed to carry forward and use the remaining undeducted amounts in a subsequent year. This is significant to farmers who have little or no net income in the year the expenditure is made, as it allows the deferral of the write off to a year when there is taxable income. As well, the cost of laying or installing a land drainage system will be deductible, whether it is composed of tile or other materials.

LIVESTOCK INCOME TAX DEFERRAL PROGRAM

On June 30, 1988, then-Finance Minister Wilson announced a tax-deferral program for farmers who had to deplete their breeding herds of grazing livestock because of drought conditions.

Farmers will be required to include the proceeds received for the forced destruction of breeding animals in income. However, an offsetting deduction may be taken to defer tax on such sales to the next tax year. Qualifying areas will be determined every year upon recommendation by the Minister of Agriculture. Specifically, the deferral will apply to proceeds from the sale of breeding herds (cattle, bison, goats, sheep) over 12 months old and held for breeding purposes. After 1990, deer, elk and other grazing ungulates are included. Horses may qualify under certain circumstances. The proceeds must be reduced by the cost of the animals, which all must be over 12 months old.

If sales resulted in a reduction in the breeding herd of more than 15% and less than 30%, 30% of the proceeds are eligible for deferral. Ninety percent of the proceeds are eligible for the deferral for sales that exceeded 30% of the animals in the herd.

PRIOR-YEAR DEFERRALS

If you no longer live in a prescribed drought area, previously deferred amounts must be included in the current fiscal year. If you live in such an area in the current fiscal year and are carrying prior-year deferrals, all such amounts, may be deferred to next year.

(Note: The deferral of income will not apply in a year in which the taxpayer dies or where at year-end the taxpayer is a non-resident, unless he or she carried on business throughout the year in Canada.)

A further deferral is allowed in cases where there is forced destruction of livestock under statutory authority. Any amounts deducted from income in one year must be added to income in the following year.

RESTRICTED FARM LOSSES

Farmers whose chief source of income is not from farming are currently restricted to a maximum farm loss write off of $2,500 plus one-half of the next $12,500 (total $8,750). This means that a loss of $15,000 will qualify for a loss write off of $8,750. Before 1989, this loss limitation stood at $2,500 plus one-half of the next $5,000 of losses (total $5,000).

Also be aware that if you have a capital gain, perhaps from farmland sold during the year, interest or property taxes that were included in any restricted farm losses of prior years that have not yet been deducted, may be used to reduce the capital gain, but not to create or increase a capital loss on the sale of the farmland.

FARMERS AND THE GST

Most farmers should become GST registrants. This is because most supplies produced by farmers are zero-rated; that is, no GST is charged by the farmer on the sale of supplies, but a GST input tax credit can be claimed. This amounts to a recovery of GST paid on purchases incurred in producing supplies.

Examples of zero-rated supplies are livestock used to produce wool or food, grains, seeds (not garden seeds) and fodder crops, share cropping and unprocessed fish. The sale or transfer of farmland is taxable if the purchaser is a developer or unrelated individual. A special election may be made for the purchaser to claim taxes charged, offset by GST input tax credits claimed if the operation is "a going concern". If a farmer transfers land to a relative or former spouse for that person's personal use, no GST is charged. GST paid is deducted as part of an expense, but input tax credits recovered must be added to income.

WESTERN GRAIN TRANSITION PAYMENTS

In the 1995 tax year, owners of farmland on which grain is grown qualified for a one-time transition payment in a collective amount of $1.6 million, to partially offset the anticipated drop in land values due to the previously subsidized freight rates in Canada. The payments were made to those who owned farmland in Manitoba, Saskatchewan, Alberta, the Peace River District or Creston-Wynndel Areas of B.C. On the tax return, such payments were handled as follows:

(a) Farmland that is capital property — the adjusted cost base of the farmland has to be reduced by the amount of the transition payment.

(b) Farmland that is held as inventory for resale — the transition payment is considered to be "assistance" in respect of the cost and to be received in the course of earning income from a business, which means full income inclusion.

(c) Payments to those who lease farmland from the owner — the amount must be included in the income of the recipient and not in the income of the owner of the farmland.

It is interesting to note that this one-time transition payment brought prairie cash income up to unusually high levels, and therefore also increased the taxes collected for the 1995 tax year.

Farm Expenses

Farm expenses are reported on "Lines 8206" to "8246" of "Form T2042," and can include the following:

1. Building and fence repairs;

2. Cleaning, levelling and draining land;

3. Crop insurance, GRIP and stabilization premiums;

4. Machinery expenses including gas, diesel fuel and oil, repairs, licenses and insurance;

5. Interest on farm loans, mortgages, vehicles;

6. Professional fees;

7. Property taxes;

8. Rent for land buildings or pastures;

9. Salaries, wages and benefits, including employer's contributions;

10. Memberships and subscription fees;

11. Livestock purchased;

12. Utility bills for farm buildings;

13. Seeds, plans, feed, supplements, straw and bedding, pesticides, veterinary fees and breeding fees;

14. Capital cost allowance on assets owned;

15. 50% of meals and entertainment costs; and

16. Office supply costs.

HOME EXPENSES

Certain household expenses can be claimed as a business expense on the tax return under the general provisions for home workspace expenses. This includes heat, electricity, insurance, maintenance, mortgage interest, property taxes and other expenses, prorated for the business/personal-use portions and subject to the restrictions that no loss can be increased or created using the home-offices expenses.

TELEPHONE BILLS

Long-distance calls that are personal in nature may not be deducted. Circle all personal calls on every monthly phone bill and use the rest of the bill as a deduction, if you have a separate business phone. If there is no separate phone, the monthly rental charge is usually considered a personal expense.

. . . if there is no separate phone, the monthly rental charge is usually considered a personal expense . . .

DEDUCTIBLE WAGES FOR SPOUSE

After January 1, 1980, salaries paid to a spouse in a family business became fully deductible, provided the wage was reasonable and for work actually done in the operation. (As of January 1, 1993; includes common-law spouse.) The spouse may contribute to and receive benefits from the Canada Pension Plan.

Effective September 1, 1989, all persons employed by spouses must have Employment Insurance (formerly Unemployment Insurance) premiums withheld and remitted. In order to be eligible to collect benefits, however, it must be shown that a valid contract of employment existed and would have existed had the parties not been related. It is important to note that Revenue Canada has the responsibility to determine "insurability" of family members once an EI benefits claim is made. This means a several week delay in benefits as the department reviews pay, conditions, length, type and importance of the work done by the relative on behalf of the Department of Human Resources Development.

. . . employment by a person who controls more than 40% of the issued voting shares is not insurable . . .

Employment by a person who controls more than 40% of the issued voting shares is not insurable; neither is employment of a spouse unless the remuneration is tax-deductible under the Income Tax Act (see comments below), nor is a salary level that is unreasonably high. Contact Revenue Canada for more information.

A "T4 Slip" must be issued for the spouse, as for all other employees, showing gross income, total source deductions, and a completed "T4 Summary" (a form that balances your total source remittances with the amounts actually due to Revenue Canada). The "T4 Slips" must be sent out to Revenue Canada and employees by the last day of February of the new year.

WAGES PAID TO CHILDREN

The same general rules apply to children's wages (that is, reasonable wages must be actually paid for services that were necessary in producing income and that would have required the services of outside help). The farmer must also contribute a portion of the premiums paid by the child to the Employment Insurance Commission (or Canada Pension Plan if child is 18 or over) on the monthly remittance form. The employer's portion is a deductible expense. There are some important points to remember when paying your children:

(a) If the children are under 18, no Canada Pension Plan deductions are made.

(b) If you pay your children by cheque, the tax department will accept your cancelled cheque as a legitimate receipt.

(c) Receipts signed by the child are required if you pay cash.

(d) If you give your child livestock or grain in lieu of money for the payment of wages, the child must report the value of this livestock or grain on his or her tax return as income. In order to claim the wage expenses, you will be required to include in your gross sales income the value of this property given to your child.

(e) The value of board may not be claimed as an expense if this is supplied to any child who is dependent upon you for support.

VEHICLE COSTS

The most important part of claiming any vehicle expenses is to keep a distance log, which can record your total business driving for the year. To make a claim on your return, you will need to know the "Total Business Kilometres" driven and divide that by the "Total Kilometres" driven in the year. The size of deductible expenditures for your vehicles depends on how many you have and what they are used for. Restrictions on certain expenses apply to passenger vehicles. If purchased after June 17, 1987, such cars will be restricted to a capital cost allowance ceiling of $20,000 and a maximum monthly interest expense of $300. Leasing restrictions may also apply (as discussed in earlier chapters). For passenger vehicles purchased after August 31, 1989, the capital cost allowance ceiling has been raised to $24,000 (plus GST and PST), and after 1996 to $25,000 (plus GST and PST).

Farm trucks or vans, on the other hand, are "motor vehicles" that will be exempt from these restrictions if they are designed to carry the driver and two passengers and are used primarily (which means more than 50% of the time to transport equipment or goods or 90% or more to transfer equipment, goods, or passengers) for the purpose of earning income.

NON-ALLOWABLE EXPENSES

Non-allowable expenses include:

(a) Replacement or improvement of assets (these must be capitalized);

(b) Principal payments on borrowed money, including repayments of a loan for tile drainage;

(c) The value of animals that have died during the year (When they are purchased, the cost is written off as an expense.);

(d) Expenses for a personal garden or upkeep of livestock gifted to children; and

(e) Costs of paving a road (three-quarters of these are capitalized — Class 17-8%).

NEW RULES ON CAPITAL GAINS DEDUCTION

The February 22, 1994 federal budget may have eliminated the $100,000 Capital Gains Exemption for gains realized on capital property after budget day. However, the Super Exemption of $500,000 on the disposition of small business shares and qualified farm property will remain untouched, and available for now.

The Super Exemption may be used on the gains generated by the disposal of shares of the capital stock of a small business corporation owned by the individual or partnership related to him or her. A small business corporation is a Canadian-controlled private corporation in which all or substantially all of the assets are used in an active business carried on primarily in Canada. The shares must be owned by such an individual through the 24 months immediately prior to the disposition. During the holding period, more than 50% of the "fair market value" of the corporation's assets must have been used in an active business.

Qualifying farm property, on the other hand, refers to farm property acquired after June 17, 1987, including real property owned by the taxpayer, spouse or child for at least 24 months immediately before sale. A gross revenue test must by met; that is, in at least two years prior to disposition, gross income earned by the individual by active farming operations, must exceed net income from all other sources. In addition, all or substantially all of the fair value of the farm assets must by used in active business operations for at least 24 months prior to disposition.

On farms acquired before June 17, 1987, the Super Exemption will be allowed if the farmland and buildings were used in an active farming business in Canada in the year of sale, and at least five years prior to the disposition.

Tax Treatment of Farm Inventory

Farmers who have suffered a cash loss are subject to the Mandatory Inventory Adjustment if they own "purchased inventory" at year-end. This is inventory such as livestock, fertilizer, chemicals, fuel, seed; anything bought and paid for and used to sell to customers or in the business operation itself. The reason for its implementation is primarily that farm losses can no longer be increased or created by purchasing farm inventory.

> *. . . at their option, farmers who have livestock, may claim an "optional inventory provision" . . .*

At their option, farmers who have livestock, may claim an "optional inventory provision," in order to plan to reduce future income. The basic idea behind the inventory adjustments is that "valued inventory" is added to the net loss calculated after expenses are deducted, and adjustments are made to include the value of saleable goods consumed, personal use of expenses deducted, as well as expenses paid to a partner. This has the effect of decreasing the current-year cash loss to zero, if that much inventory is held. (It is not a requirement to use the value of inventory to create positive income.) In the following year, any amounts added to income are allowed as a tax deduction. These inventory adjustments are not applicable in the year a farmer has died.

Deducting Farm Losses

Farm expenses are deductible only if there is a profit motive involved. They must also be reasonable in relation to the size and scope of the farming operation. Both the purchase of the farm and the expenses incurred in its operation must have been made with the intent to earn income.

Under current rules, Revenue Canada groups farm losses into three categories:

1. Losses from a full-scale farming operation (the taxpayer spends all of his or her time and effort in the operation of the farm and farming is the chief source of income): These losses are deductible in full against other income the taxpayer may have.

2. Farm losses claimed against other income when it is clear that the taxpayer's chief source of income is not farming: The losses are subject to special limitations.

3. Farm losses claimed against other income when it is questionable whether a business actually exists: These losses are not deductible at all, as the activities are considered to be a hobby.

The first thing a tax auditor must determine in allowing or disallowing your losses is whether you are making a legitimate attempt at earning income from your operation. Sometimes this can be a difficult decision, for example, in the case of first-year farmers who must invest large sums of money in the purchase of assets, and perhaps work off the farm to support the operation. The tax department will look at a number of conditions as proof that a viable operation exists.

Proof of a Viable Operation

There are a number of factors that will be considered in determining the viability of of a farm operation.

1. Gross and net income from the farming operation and amount of capital invested;

2. The Size of the Property Used for Farming. Your losses may be disallowed if:
   (a) Your property is too small to project any hope of profit,
   (b) You have made no attempt at farming or developing your land, and/or
   (c) You have no intention of using more than a fraction of the land over a period of years. (There must be potential for profit that you can document and justify with cash-flow statements and budgets for the future.);

3. The Time Spent on the Farming Operation. Losses will generally be allowed if:
   (a) You have farming background experience and spend most of your time on the operation during the busy months,
   (b) You make commitments for the future expansion of the farm, and/or
   (c) You qualify for some type of provincial assistance.

4. Other Sources of Income: Generally speaking, if your chief source of income is from other sources, losses may be restricted or disallowed. If forced to earn income elsewhere in a bad year, full losses may be allowed if it can be proven that farming is still your chief source of income and that it is your intention to continue spending most of your time and money on the future of the farm.

5. Cash-flow generated, including gross and net income; and

6. Your personal involvement and experience.

Ensuring Full Farm Losses Are Allowed

The most important steps to take to ensure your full farm losses are allowed by Revenue Canada are:

1. Determine whether you are a "full-time" farmer or a farmer subject to the restricted loss rules.

2. Keep all receipts in meticulous (preferably in chronological or numerical) order.

3. For full-time farmers, any losses not claimable in one taxation year may be carried back three years or carried forward 10 years and applied against other income. Restricted farm losses may also be carried over for the same periods but are deductible against farm income only in those years.

Capital Dispositions

Special rules exist for farmers in the following instances.

LAND THAT INCLUDES A PRINCIPAL RESIDENCE

Your principal residence can be defined as a house, cottage, condo, duplex, apartment, trailer, mobile home or houseboat owned solely or jointly with another person and that is inhabited by you, your spouse, former spouse and children at some time during the year.

For those homeowners whose property includes land surrounding the principal residence, approximately one acre (one-half hectare) of land surrounding the home and used for personal use and enjoyment is considered to be a part of your tax-exempt principal residence. In some cases, more than this amount of land can be claimed; for example, if a minimum lot size larger than one acre was imposed by your municipality at the time you acquired the home. Special rules are in place for calculating the exempt portion of farm properties. That is, one of two methods can be chosen to determine the exempt portion of the gain due to the principal residence:

Method 1: Calculate the capital gain on principal residence separately from each farm property.

Method 2: Determine the capital gain on your land and your principal residence. To the gain, apply a tax reduction of $1,000 plus $1,000 for each year after 1971 in which the property was your principal residence and you were a resident of Canada. If this method is chosen, attach a note to the tax return indicating you are electing this method under Subsection 40(2)(c)(ii) of the Income Tax Act. (Have a look at IT 120.)

TRANSFERS TO SPOUSE AND CHILD

When a farmer dies, a tax-free rollover of farm assets will be allowed on transfers to the spouse, children or grandchildren. This means that no capital gain or loss or terminal loss or recapture will generally arise on the tax return of the deceased. However, to qualify, the property must have been used principally in an active farming business.

. . . the meaning of "child" has been extended . . . The meaning of "child" has been extended to include persons who, before reaching age 19, were under the control and custody of the taxpayer and dependent upon him or her. This will include nephews, nieces and in-laws. The cost of acquisition of the property is equal to the deceased's deemed proceeds of disposition.

As well, farm rollovers from a child to a parent would be allowed in cases in which the child dies leaving a surviving parent.

Property eligible for such transfers includes property leased by a taxpayer to the family farm corporation. A special election is available to transfer depreciable property on death (including buildings, equipment, or other depreciable property used in business). This may be done in any amount between the "fair market value" of the property and its undepreciated capital cost at the time of transfer. Eligible capital property (ECP) can be transferred at any amount between "fair market value" and

$$5/4 \times \frac{Cumulative}{Eligible\ Capital} \times \frac{\text{``Fair Market Value''} \text{ of Property}}{\text{``Fair Market Value''} \text{ of all Eligible Capital Property}}$$

Other capital property, such as land, may be transferred at any amount between the "fair market value" and the adjusted cost base immediately prior to death.

FISHING ACTIVITIES

Fishing income sources reported by taxpayers who make their living from the sea, are broken down on the "Statement of Fishing Activities" — "Form T2121", into the following groupings:

1. Fish products (fish, lobster, scallops, *etc.*). You must report income earned on the high seas in Canadian dollars, at the exchange rate in effect at the time of sale.

2. Other marine products. This includes the sale of Irish moss, herring scales, herring roe, seal meat and flippers, seaweed, kelp, roe on kelp, and so on.

3. Grants, credits and rebates. Including input tax credits, investment tax credits, bonuses from boat owners, and so on.

4. Subsidies from all federal, provincial, municipal or joint programs.

5. Compensation for loss of fishing income or property.

6. Other income. This can include debts that are paid with a part of a catch. Add the "fair market value" of the catch into income in these cases.

Fishing Expenses include all expenses incurred on each boating trip, including the expenses of calculating the crew shares. Also included:

1. home-office expenses and office supplies;

2. cost of travel between the home and the fishing boat;

3. costs of bait, ice and salt;

4. costs of salary, wages and benefits;

5. fuel for the boat and equipment;

6. fishing gear such as gloves, small knives, rubber or oilskin clothing, *etc.*;

7. insurance premiums paid for fishing boat and equipment;

8. interest on money borrowed to earn fishing income;

9. food stocked on the boat to feed crews;

10. costs of renewing your annual license;

11. costs of nets and traps, buoys, anchors and radar reflectors (These costs can be capitalized or put into inventory.);

12. legal, accounting and other professional fees;

13. fishing boat repairs;

14. costs of small tools less than $200;

15. telephone expenses for long-distance and costs of separate business phone;

16. CCA on fishing assets:

Asset	Class	Rate
Fishing Boats	7	15%
Accelerated Rates:		$16\frac{2}{3}$% Thereafter $13\frac{1}{3}$%
Leasehold Interests	13	straight-line method

HOME-BASED BABYSITTERS

One of the most common home-based businesses is often started by a parent who takes in several of the neighbor's children to supplement family income, while looking after his or her own pre-schoolers.

Like other proprietors, a self-employed babysitter may deduct various business expenses against income earned from the babysitting enterprise, provided there is a reasonable expectation of profit from the enterprise. It is very important that the enterprise is formalized for tax purposes. That is, a separate bank account should be set up for the business, and all income and expenses should be carefully tracked.

Your Deductions

Remember that the proprietor is taxed on net business income; what is left after the expenses of the business are deducted. In the case of the home-based babysitter, there are many deductions to take: portions of rent, mortgage interest, property taxes, utilities and repairs would be deductible, according to the amount of floor space used in the babysitting business and the number of hours the daycare centre is open. Additional deductions for food, toys and supplies related to the business would also be deductible.

One of the most important criteria in legitimizing your business expenses in an enterprise that uses the principal residence and personal effects to the degree that babysitters do, is to keep a meticulous record of the personal-use component of your expenses.

Food costs, for example, may prove to be a problem to track. If all food consumed by the children could be purchased separately, the full food bills could be deducted. However, in most cases, food is purchased at the same time for both family and business consumption. Therefore, in a separate book of account, the babysitter should keep a record of food items to feed the children and then prorate the total food bill accordingly.

Toys could be handled in the same way. If the babysitter's children play with the toys after the others have gone home, a "time allocation" of the expenses may be made. That is, the total cost of the toys times the number of hours the daycare centre is open in the year divided by the total number of hours in the year, would give you the tax-deductible portion of the toy costs. If the toys are not used personally by the family, a 100% claim is possible.

To make a deduction for expenses of the home (if there is no area exclusively set aside for the business), use the following formula:

... deductible home expenses can circumvent the restrictions imposed under "home workspace" rules ...

$$\text{Total Operating Expenses} \times \frac{\text{Square footage of home used in business}}{\text{Total square footage of the home}} \times \frac{\text{No. of hours daycare is open in the year}}{\text{Total hours in the year}}$$

$$= \text{Deductible Amounts}$$

It would appear that deductible home expenses can circumvent the restrictions imposed under home workspace rules. That is, because the home is an integral part of the babysitting enterprise, expenses for the business portion of operating expenses such as mortgage interest, property taxes, maintenance, repairs and utilities should all be listed separately on the "Income and Expense Statement". In that way, such expenses can be used to reduce income or increase or create a business loss, the latter of which is not allowable under the home workspace claim. However, if the taxpayer also has an office in the home in which bookkeeping and billings or other preparatory work is done, the normal rules would apply. (*See* "General Anti-Avoidance Rules," in Chapter Three.)

Like other self-employed persons, the babysitter can begin making contributions on his or her own behalf to the Canada Pension Plan based on net income of the business. As well, RRSP contribution room can be built up based on 18% of net income of the business. Using this latter tax deduction, the self-employed babysitter can often reduce income below the Basic Personal Amount.

Once all the applicable deductions are taken from babysitting income, it is possible that the babysitter's net income, which is used in computing the Spousal Amount, is low enough for a full or partial claim by the spouse. If net income is just over the threshold limits, a Registered Retirement Savings Plan could be purchased for the self-employed spouse, if this spouse reported earned income last year. The results would be a greatly reduced net income, resulting in a possible Spousal Claim for the higher-income earner, and possibly increased refundable tax credits such as the Child Tax Benefit.

Finally, when issuing receipts, remember to break down how much money the parents paid for children under seven, and those over six so that parents can take advantage of higher allowable deduction limits for preschoolers.

Summary: Deductible Child Care Expenses

Accounting Costs	Cost of Field Trips
Advertising	Food
Art Supplies	Household Costs
Auto Expenses	Insurance
Bank Charges	Postage
Blankets	Repairs
Books	Soap and Shampoo
Capital Cost Allowances	Telephone
Diapers	Towels and Toothbrushes
Employee Expenses	Toys
Medical Supplies	Training Courses

Be sure to keep track of all of these items carefully, and if travelling is involved, such as trips to the grocery store to pick up food and other supplies for the children, the expenses of taking the children on field trips, or to make deposits of the babysitting income, make sure an auto log is kept up, in order to write off a portion of gas and oil, maintenance, insurance, license fees, car washes, leasing or interest costs, capital cost allowance and parking of the vehicle.

TAXATION OF INVESTORS AND TRADERS

We have previously discussed that different types of income receive different tax treatment in Canada. (*See* "How Income Is Taxed in Canada," in Chapter Two.) Sometimes those income types are "blurred" in the eyes of the opposing parties: the taxpayer and Revenue Canada.

This is particularly so when there is a question about whether a profit is an "income" profit, or simply a "gain on an investment". In the former case, 100% of net income is added to income; in the latter, 75% of the capital gain is added to income.

Investor or Trader?

. . . at what point in time does an "investor" become a "trader"? . . .

At what point in time does an "investor" become a "trader"? There are specific guidelines that Revenue Canada must follow before they can arbitrarily classify your transactions as income-producing. Major factors in determining whether a gain is classed as capital or income in nature include:

- the taxpayer's intention at the time of purchase of the asset,
- the relationship of the sales transaction to the taxpayer's ordinary line of work or business,
- the frequency of similar transactions,
- the period of ownership,
- improvements or developments to make the property more saleable, and
- income generated by the asset during the period it is owned.

Gains or losses from the disposition of a share or debt obligation such as a bond or note might also be taxed either as "income" or "capital" gains (or losses). A taxpayer may elect that every security of this and future years be treated as "capital" in nature, qualifying for capital gains treatment on disposition. The election cannot be rescinded once made on "Form T123". This election is not available to those who are traders or dealers in securities, banks, credit unions and others, including non-residents.

Factors that will help determine whether the taxpayer is a "trader" in the business of buying and selling securities include the frequency of the transactions, period of ownership, knowledge of the securities market, the time spent on the market, and advertising to purchase shares. If the taxpayer has used special information not available to the public in order to make a "quick profit," Revenue Canada will likely assess the transaction "an adventure or concern in the nature of trade". In the past, the courts have dealt with many cases concerning the income-versus-capital-gains question.

Other rules are in place for "capital" dispositions of the proprietor. Capital gains and losses will never form part of the individual's business income, unless the transactions are reclassified as "income" in nature, as explained above. This is so even if the capital gains results from the sale of business property. An individual or proprietor must report capital gains and losses on a calendar-year basis, no matter what he or she has chosen as the business' fiscal year-end.

For tax purposes, capital assets are classified into a group of assets, some of which are subject to specific tax rules.

Personal-Use Property

This includes all properties owned by the taxpayer for personal use or the use of individuals related to him or her. It includes cars, boats, furniture, and all personal effects. A special rule allows you to ignore capital gains or losses on certain dispositions.

. . . Do not use personal-use property losses to reduce capital gains realized on other property during the year . . .

Proceeds of disposition and adjusted cost base of personal-use property are deemed to be at least $1,000 for purposes of computing any capital gain upon disposition. This $1,000 Rule eliminates the reporting of small transactions.

Losses on the disposition of such properties including your personal home or cottage, are not deductible as they are considered a personal expense. Do not use personal-use property losses to reduce capital gains realized on other property during the year.

Residences

In Canada, capital gains on the disposal of your principal residence are tax exempt. However, since 1982 a family unit is allowed only one tax-exempt principal residence each year. This means that gains accruing on the second and subsequent residences are subject to capital gains tax on disposition. As long as you "ordinarily inhabited" your residences at some time in the year, you may choose or "designate" one of them as your principal residence each year.

Vacant Land

The disposal of vacant land follows the same general rules as for any other non-depreciable property. However, there has been some confusion about the deductibility of interest and property taxes paid on vacant land held by the taxpayer. Should these expenses be deducted on an ongoing basis during the period of ownership, or upon sale of the property?

If no income source is being collected from the land, the interest and property taxes paid can neither be deducted nor added to the adjusted cost base. However, taxpayers who earn rental income from vacant land can claim property taxes and interest as tax-deductible expenses, but only to the extent of rental income reported. A rental loss can neither be created nor increased by these expenses. Should the expenses be restricted, the excess interest and property taxes may be added to the land's adjusted cost base for use in calculating any subsequent capital gain or loss on disposition.

When it comes to "sets" of personal-use property that are disposed of in more than one transaction, they will be treated to be a single personal-use property to which the $1,000 Rule applies. A set is a number of properties that belong together or are related to each other, such as a number of silver glasses.

Depreciable Properties

Disposition of depreciable properties, those on which the taxpayer has claimed or was entitled to claim capital cost allowance, can trigger income tax consequences, in the calendar year in which a disposition occurs.

A capital gain occurs on the disposition of depreciable property only if it is disposed of for more than its original capital cost and is limited to any gain since "valuation day" if it was owned on December 31, 1971. There can be no capital losses on the disposition of depreciable property.

. . . there can be no capital losses on the disposition of depreciable property . . .

Recapture of depreciation previously claimed may result if one or more assets in the class is disposed of for proceeds exceeding the undepreciated capital cost of that class. The overstated depreciation is therefore added to income of the year. Assets sold for less than their undepreciated capital cost will usually be written off on the capital cost allowance schedule. (*See* Chapter Five)

On Class 10.1, luxury vehicles (those costing over $20,000, or $24,000 if acquired after September 1, 1989) neither recapture nor terminal loss is allowed on disposition.

Other Capital Properties

These include mutual funds, stocks and bonds, debentures, promissory notes, and commodities and can include gains on the sale of foreign currencies in excess of $200. (This might affect business travellers and tourists. The $200 exemption does not apply to sales of foreign securities, which are treated in the normal manner.)

Identical Properties

Taxpayers sometimes will also purchase shares of the same or identical class of the capital stock of a corporation, but at varying times. They may also sell such identical shares at different times and at varying prices. Such transactions within the same group of shares require the computing of an "average cost" of the shares each time there is a purchase, in order to properly compute any gain or loss at disposition. To calculate the average cost, add the adjusted cost base of all the shares in the group and divide by the total number of shares held.

... for identical properties, any capital gains or losses are based on a "first-in, first-out rule," ...

New rules on debt forgiveness, introduced in the February 22, 1994 budget, will complicate this calculation somewhat. Where a debt owing on the identical property is forgiven, the adjusted cost base of the whole group must be reduced. For identical properties, any capital gains or losses are based on a "first-in, first-out rule," that is, the assets held the longest are considered to have been disposed of first.

Qualified Small Business Corporations

The sale of shares of a Canadian-controlled small business orporation, where mostly all (90% or more) of the assets are used in an active business carried on primarily in Canada, will be reported on "Schedule 3". Shares must be held throughout a 24-month period before disposition, and in that period more than 50% of the "fair market value" of the corporation's assets must have been used in an active business in order to qualify for the $500,000 Capital Gains Exemption.

Qualified Farm Property

The disposition of real property owned (for a full 24 months prior to disposition) by an individual or spouse, children, grandchildren or parents, certain trusts and partnerships, and interests in a family farm partnership corporation is reported on "Schedule 3" under "Qualified Farm Property" and will qualify for the $500,000 Capital Gains Deduction if the property was actively used in the course of carrying on a farm business.

Farm property acquired after June 17, 1987 will be considered qualified farm property if all or substantially all (90%) of the "fair market value" of the property was used throughout the 24 months immediately before its disposition by the qualifying individuals named above in the business of farming. (The property need not be so used at the time of disposition.) As well, for at least two years during ownership, the gross revenue of the individual who used the property in the active business of farming must have exceeded income from all other sources in the year in order to qualify for the deduction.

Farm property acquired before June 18, 1987 will qualify for this classification if it was used by individuals, partnerships or corporations defined above in the year of disposition or in at least five years in which the property was owned by the taxpayer, the spouse, children, grandchildren, great-grand-children, parents or a family farm partnership in which the people named owned an interest. All other "non-qualified" property that does not meet these definitions is reported under "Real Estate" and/or depreciable property.

Eligible Capital Property

This is generally intangible property that can accumulate value within a business. Examples include goodwill, customer lists, trademarks or patents, licenses or quotas. These are acquisitions that are capital in nature in that they are not deductible as current expenses, but at the same time do not belong to a prescribed class for capital cost allowance purposes. (*See* "Goodwill and Other Intangible Assets" and "Patents and Other Properties with a Specific Lifespan," in Chapter Five.)

For expenses after 1987, three-quarters of the costs of these expenses are put into a separate class on the Capital Cost Allowance schedule, subject to a 7% declining-balance rate. When a disposition occurs, three-quarters of the Proceeds of Disposition are recorded in the class, generally creating a negative balance. For most eligible capital property dispositions that occur in 1995 and later years, this negative balance will be included in business income.

However, the capital portion of eligible capital property used in qualified farm businesses will continue to be eligible for the $500,000 Super Capital Gains Exemption. While recaptured deductions previously taken must still be included in business income, any excess negative balance remaining on disposition will be treated as a capital gain, which will qualify for the $500,000 deduction. This excess will be reported on "Schedule 3" as a capital gain. This is a very complicated transaction that should be discussed with your tax advisor before you make your final decision to sell your eligible capital property.

Application of Losses

Capital losses are first used to reduce any capital gains of the year. If an excess loss remains after application to capital gains, or, if there are no capital gains in the year, we have what is known as an "Allowable Capital Loss".

APPLICATIONS OF LOSSES DURING THE TAXPAYER'S LIFETIME

Losses incurred after May 23, 1985 cannot be used to reduce other income of the year. However, they may be carried back or forward and applied to capital gains in what is known as the "carry-over years": three years back, and then forward indefinitely until used up.

Prior to the May 23, 1985 budget, up to $2,000 of net allowable capital losses were deductible against all other income reported in the year. Excess losses of up to $2,000 incurred prior to this date may still be carried forward and applied to net income in the carry-over year, until used up. However, such amounts must be reduced by net capital losses claimed in previous years and must exceed total capital gains deductions claimed in prior years. These old losses will be adjusted for the new inclusion rates, as will other capital losses, as described below.

Net Capital Losses

TABLE 7-3
NET CAPITAL LOSSES

Prior to 1972	No tax consequences
1972 to 1987	Total Capital Losses of the year × 50%
1988 and 1989	Total Capital Losses of the year × $66\frac{2}{3}$%
1990 and subsequent years	Total Capital Losses of the year × 75%

Net allowable capital losses may be carried back and applied against taxable capital gains in the previous three years, or carried forward and applied against taxable capital gains in the future, indefinitely, until used up.

Report the capital disposition on which a loss occurred on "Schedule 3". To carry back or carry forward an unabsorbed loss, Revenue Canada "Form T1A" is used, and must generally be filed by April 30.

(Note: As previously mentioned, the application of a net capital loss carry-back will result in the reduction of any capital gains deduction claimed in the year. It is generally not a good idea to apply the loss carry-back provision to such a year. This is because Revenue Canada will remove the capital gains deduction in the year in question, but will not apply the loss carry-back to the taxable income until the date of filing the "T1A Form". This could cause you to incur expensive interest penalties. As well, it is important to note that late filing penalties applicable to the tax return for the year in which the loss is being applied will not be reduced by the loss carry-back. Neither will the tax threshold for your quarterly instalment payment be affected by loss carry-backs.)

Because of the varying inclusion rates that have been in place over the years for capital gains, net capital losses that are carried backwards or forwards and applied to taxable capital gains in the carry-over year must be adjusted to take into account the rules of the day. If, for example, a loss is carried forward from a year in which the capital gains inclusion rate was lower (*i.e.,* 50% or 662/3%), the net capital loss must be increased.

To bring forward a loss that was incurred in a prior year, (1972 to 1995) and use it to offset capital gains of the current year, claim such a loss on "Line 253" of the tax return.

LOSS APPLICATIONS IN THE YEAR OF DEATH

There are special rules in the year of death. Unused capital losses can be applied against other taxable income of the year, usually to the great advantage of the beneficiaries overall. Therefore, meticulous lifetime tracking of losses is desirable for maximum estate planning opportunities.

> ▷ *. . . therefore, meticulous lifetime tracking of losses is desirable for maximum estate planning opportunities . . .*

In the year of death, a net capital loss can be used to reduce all taxable capital gains in the three years immediately before death. Use "Form T1A". If there is an excess, the remaining amounts can be used to reduce all other income of the year on the final return, or all other income of the year immediately prior to the year of death. From these losses, however, any capital gains deductions previously used must first be subtracted.

Alternatively, the taxpayer may choose not to carry back the losses to reduce taxable capital gains of prior years. All the losses can be applied against all income of the year of death or immediately preceding year or both. Again, all capital gains deductions previously claimed must first be subtracted from the loss balance.

Many taxpayers are unaware of these very lucrative provisions that can result in little or zero taxes payable for the year of death and the year before death. Always ask the client whether any net capital loss balances were dropped from the carry-forward procedure in the past, or missed entirely to recover these for future use.

Special Situations

You and your tax advisor should plan for the special situations that are discussed below.

CHANGE IN USE

A conversion of a business property to personal use may result in a capital gain or loss, based on the "fair market value" of the asset at the time of conversion.

FORGIVEN DEBT

When a debt is extinguished, settled or forgiven, the excess of the debt remaining over what you actually paid down was previously used only to reduce the following "tax attributes" to which you are entitled:

1. Your non-capital losses of prior years,

2. Your net capital losses of prior years,

3. Your farm losses of prior years,

4. Your restricted farm losses of prior years,

5. The capital cost of your depreciable property, or

6. The adjusted cost base of non-depreciable capital property you own.

New rules introduced in the February 22, 1994 budget changed these existing rules in a number of ways (*See* "Amounts to Be Included in Income for Tax Purposes," in Chapter Two).

EXPROPRIATION

When a property is expropriated, generally the following occurs:

1. The owner is notified of the intent to expropriate.

2. The plan is filed with the land titles office. At this time the title to the property will vest in the expropriating authority although the right to possession may occur later.

3. There is agreement on the amount of compensation to be paid to the owner.

4. The compensation is paid to the owner.

Upon notice of intent to expropriate, the owner may start negotiating for the best price. The time that Revenue Canada considers the proceeds of disposition to be received is the earliest of:

1. the day the taxpayer has agreed to an amount as full compensation,

2. the day the compensation is determined by a court or tribunal,

3. the day that is two years following the day the property is taken away if there was no appeal to a competent tribunal or court, or

4. the time the taxpayer is deemed to have disposed of the property at death.

The taxpayer is deemed to have owned the property continuously until the earliest of these dates. The compensation received will be allocated to the specific assets that were expropriated (*i.e.,* buildings, fixtures, goodwill, *etc.*) The compensation may also take into account inconvenience, disturbance, disruption or loss of business, cost of relocation including legal or moving fees, and legal, appraisal and other costs incurred to determine fair compensation. Any such amounts may form a part of the proceeds of disposition of the property.

Any interest expense being paid on the property that is expropriated will continue to be claimable if the property was used to earn income from a business or property. In the case of expropriated depreciable property, the proceeds of disposition may be reduced by legal fees and interest costs if not previously used to reduce adjusted cost base.

Any interest paid on the compensation for expropriated property, must generally be included in income, although may sometimes be considered part of the proceeds of disposition. If the expropriating authority later changes its mind and gives the property back to the owner, the owner may have a valid claim for damages. Such damages will be taxable as business or property income if they replace such losses. (For more information, *see* IT 271R.)

BUSINESS INVESTMENT LOSSES

Business Investment Losses arise when shares or debt of a small business corporation are disposed of at a loss, or when the corporation becomes bankrupt or insolvent, as long as the corporation was a small business corporation when it became bankrupt. The loss must first qualify as a capital loss.

A portion of such losses can be deducted on "Line 217" from "Other Income" of the year to the following maximums:

1987 and prior years	1/2 of losses incurred
1988 and 1989	2/3 of losses incurred
after 1989	3/4 of losses incurred

Losses are reduced by the adjusted (grossed up) capital gains deductions previously claimed by the taxpayer to the extend that such gains have not been used to reduce other Business Investment Losses. If there is an excess loss after application to other income of the year, such an excess will be treated as a non-capital loss, which may be carried back and applied against income in the previous three years and then carried forward seven years.

Excess losses still remaining after the seven-year carry forward become capital losses that can be carried forward indefinitely. However, as a capital loss, these amounts are only deductible against taxable capital gains, and the appropriate rules will apply.

A new rule introduced in legislation on July 13, 1990 will allow payments made by taxpayers under an arm's length guarantee of debts of a small business corporation to be claimed as a business investment loss even if the corporation has ceased to operate. This will be effective on payments made after 1985 provided the corporation was a small business corporation both at the time the debt was incurred and at any time in the 12 months before an amount first became payable under the guarantee.

Any taxpayer who has incurred a business investment loss would be wise to seek the help of a qualified tax practitioner. Any capital gains deduction that may be claimable by the taxpayer will be affected by business investment losses deducted. As well, Business Investment Losses available will be converted to capital losses to the extent of capital gains deductions previously claimed.

(Note: The forgiven amount of a commercial debt must be used to reduce a debtor's non-capital loss carry-forwards, farm loss carry-forwards, and restricted farm loss carry-forwards. Any unapplied forgiven amounts still remaining can then be applied to non-capital losses arising from Allowable Business Investment Losses, and then any net capital losses of each prior year. In these cases, losses from the earliest tax year must be reduced first.)

The portion of any forgiven amount applied to these types of losses must be multiplied by the income inclusion fraction used in the year the loss occurred (3/4 for losses incurred in 1990 and future years).

Because of the complexity behind the disposition of assets, it is always best to discuss your intentions for the future of your home-based business with your tax advisor, who can inform you of the possible tax consequences, which can influence the timing of your dispositions, and often the asking price.

NETWORK MARKETING AND DIRECT SELLERS

Network marketing and direct selling as a distributor of products and services has become a hugely popular way for people to go into business for themselves. Run primarily out of their own homes, Canadians are signing up to sell "positions" and products in everything from health care and cleaning products to jewelry and auto parts. There are those who sell long-distance telephone services at a discount, and others who sell make-up and skin care.

The biggest tax problem in these ventures is whether the profit margin on the sale of goods and services is high enough for a reasonable expectation of profits to occur. It is often expected that there will be losses in the start-up year, when sales revenues may not yet be matched with purchases of products by your potential customers. But beyond this, watch your gross income, after purchases, carefully.

. . . it is often expected that there will be losses in the start-up year, . . .

If, after reporting your annual income and deducting the cost of goods sold, you are always in a negative position, there are some serious problems in your business venture. You are either buying too much stock that is left unsold year after year, which will put you in a cash-flow bind, or if you are successful in clearing out most of your inventory each year, the profit margins coming back to you may simple be too slim for a reasonable expectation of profit.

Cost of Inventory Items and Sales Aids

A second problem revolves around the acquisition of "sales kits" or demonstration aids that are acquired from the direct seller. Sometimes their costs may not be fully deductible, and this can make for an unpleasant surprise at tax audit time. These costs could be considered a "capital or asset acquisition" with a useful or enduring life of more than one year if they are not held for resale. In other words, the costs would not be fully deductible if used as "capital property".

This is where a Business Journal can really pay off, should you run into an auditor who wishes to invoke capital treatment. For example, the cost of the catalogues given to the potential customers would be considered a tax-deductible promotional expense . . . but only if your clients get to keep them. If you collect them and reuse them generally over a period of years, an auditor could dispute your claim. The cost of customized business forms or other promotional or instructional items would be fully deductible though.

Persons entering these types of ventures are notoriously naïve of the "personal-use component rules". The cost of your inventory held for resale will be tax-deductible, but only to the extent that it is resold to a customer for revenues that you are reporting as income. Any items you use personally must be added back into income, if they are expensed.

GST Implications

These rules were discussed in detail in "Special GST Rules for Unique Businesses," in Chapter Three. Briefly, as an independent sales contractor, affiliated with a direct seller, you will not be required to remit GST if the direct seller has been approved by Revenue Canada to use the Alternate Collection Method. That is, the direct seller will charge you the GST and remit it on your behalf. You, on the other hand, will charge your customer the GST, but be allowed to keep it, as you have already previously remitted it on the original transaction.

The direct seller is not required to charge GST on sales aids supplied to independent salespersons, unless any of the exclusive products are used as capital property.

If your direct seller is not approved, you must register once your sales exceed $30,000. You can check with your local Tax Services Office to see if the direct seller has been approved.

In any event, keep meticulous tract of all invoices that verify your inventory purchases, so that you can back up your GST remittances through the direct seller to Revenue Canada.

You can, however, register with Revenue Canada to claim back the costs of GST paid on other inputs you may be required to buy in carrying out your business activities.

Provincial Sales Taxes

Check with your local provincial Department of Finance for remittance requirements on the products that you are reselling to the public, if the direct seller is not making these remittances on your behalf. Any amounts collected and remitted would be deducted from your gross income for tax purposes.

To close, it is worth repeating that certain key conditions must be met to satisfy the tax auditor who may be looking at your books sometime in the future. Here are some pointers on common concerns that independent sales contractors often have.

NEVER MIX PERSONAL AND BUSINESS FUNDS

Open a separate bank account no matter how infrequent your start-up activities are. Sometimes taxpayers who have a part-time home-based business will have a line of credit on their personal accounts, for use in their business enterprises. This might make sense from a cash-flow point of view, as interest costs on the line of credit are reduced whenever a paycheque from employment is deposited.

This set-up will spell trouble for you, though, in a tax audit. First, it opens all your personal transactions up to scrutiny by the auditor. This is not necessary. Second, it may cause your auditor to question whether this is truly a business, or simply a hobby with no reasonable expectation of profit.

Keep your business and personal affairs completely separate. Set up a separate line of credit for the business; and, if you must make personal contributions to the account, set these up as equity contributions to the business on a formal basis. You will then be able to draw out any repayments of personal equity on a tax-free basis, when the business can afford to pay you back.

KEEP AN AUTO LOG AND KNOW WHICH TRIPS ARE TAX DEDUCTIBLE

Driving to meetings with potential participants in your venture, company sales meetings, sales demonstration meeting, picking up your products, delivering your products, making bank deposit or mail runs, entertaining potential customers . . . all distance driven to and from these events is considered to be "business driving" for tax purposes. Keep track of it in your Auto Log (*See* Appendix 10), as the onus of proof is on you, to claim the correct proportion of total expenses for your car.

PROPER USE OF HOME FOR STORAGE AND OFFICE WORK

Portions of your mortgage interest, property taxes, rent, insurance, utilities and other home operating expenses may be tax-deductible provided that the home-office space is used exclusively to earn business income. It must be used on a regular and continuous basis for the meeting of clients, or customers or it must be the principal place of business.

The tax-deductible portion of these expenses is based on the square footage of the home used exclusively in the business enterprise. Often resellers of products and services will state that half their home is used in the storage and distribution of their products, and will then proceed to write off 50% of all their home costs. This is acceptable only if the area is not used for personal purposes at all and is sectioned off from the rest of the house. So, if you store your boxes of products in the basement next to the laundry area, Revenue Canada could disallow the claim for the entire space as it is not "exclusively" set aside for business purposes. Legitimize your tax-deductible expenditures by separating the business portion of your home from the rest.

. . . Revenue Canada could disallow the claim for the entire space as it is not "exclusively" set aside for business purposes . . .

Remember too, that if you are reporting operating losses from your business ventures, your home-office expenses will not be claimable, as you cannot create or increase a business loss with your home-office expenses. In such cases, the home-office expenses are carried forward for use as a business deduction against net income in the future.

PROPER USE OF MOTOR HOME FOR BUSINESS TRAVEL

Associations with large direct selling organizations often involves attendance at national or international conferences. People often wonder about the tax deductibility of such trips and, whether an investment in a motor home would be a little easier if there were a way to write it off on the tax return.

There are a couple of important things for you to know here. First, a self-employed person may only write off the costs of two conventions per year. This includes travel to and from the convention, expenditures for the costs of staying in a hotel and 50% of meals and entertainment. Receipts and documentation are required, and must be converted to Canadian dollars for reporting on the Canadian return. The costs of taking accompanying family members to the convention will not be deductible under the "business portion" of the trip, unless the family members are actively involved in the business.

If a family vacation is "added on" to the trip, any costs for travel beyond the convention site and resulting hotel, meals and other costs associated with that portion of the trip will not be tax-deductible.

If you buy a motor home and use it in making the trip, the costs of purchasing that motor home may be tax-deductible, but only in a very limited scope. First, the home must be scheduled for Capital Cost Allowance purposes. Is this a Class 10 "motor vehicle" (no limitation on the capital cost) or a Class 10.1 "passenger" or luxury vehicle (capital cost is limited to $24,000 ($25,000 after 1996) plus PST and GST)? To be classified as a Class 10 asset, the motor home, with the capacity to seat four to nine people, would have to be used more than 90% of the time to transport goods or equipment or passengers to avoid the restrictions. If the motor home seats one to three people, it would have to be used 50% of the time to transport goods or equipment. This time usage must be supported by an accurate distance log.

So, while you may be able to claim a tax deduction for your motor home costs, what you are looking at claiming, is only the proportionate operating and fixed costs, based on distance travelled for business purposes over total distance travelled in the year.

PROPER USE OF HOME COMPUTER

These costs are tax-deductible if you are using the computer in your business. Because the computer is a capital asset, it must be scheduled into Class 10 and is subject to a maximum CCA rate of 30% and subject to the half year rule. If this computer is in your son's bedroom and is used for video games and family Internet fun, the costs will not be deductible. If the computer is in your exclusively set-aside home workspace, and it is occasionally used by the kids for fun, claim a personal-use component, based on the time the computer is used for personal purposes, to stay onside with Revenue Canada.

PROPER USE OF HOME TELEPHONE

This is always a problem come tax time, if you don't know the rules. The monthly rental for the home telephone is not deductible at all if it is used for personal use by the family members. Only the long-distance portion of the calls and any specific business costs, such as yellow page ads charged to that line, will be tax-deductible.

If, however, you have a separate business line installed in your home, or a separate fax line or modem line for business purposes, both the monthly rental and the long-distance and other costs will be fully deductible. Cellular phone air-time costs are generally tax-deductible in full if used for business purposes. The costs of the phone itself must usually be capitalized, as it has a useful life of more than one year.

PROPER USE OF HOME CLEANING SERVICES

Provided that only the proportion of the costs of maid services that relate to the exclusively set-aside office space are claimed, you should have no problems with Revenue Canada. After all, you would normally be allowed to deduct the full amount of cleaning costs if you were renting an office space downtown. Again . . . don't try to write off the personal portion of such expenses.

PROPER USE OF TELEVISIONS, VCRS AND OTHER AUDIO OR VIDEO EQUIPMENT

If your business presentations involve the projection, viewing or listening to video or audio tapes, the costs of a television, VCR or other such equipment may be tax-deductible, based on the same business-personal rules. That is, the costs would be capital in nature, usually classified in Class 10 with a CCA rate of 20%, and you would have to show, based on each time the equipment is used, the business-use component of the asset. If the asset is used exclusively for business purposes in your exclusively-set aside business area, and there is no personal-use component at all, and you can show this, the asset will be considered a business asset wherein the deductions for depreciable assets will be deductible under normal rules. (*See* Chapter Five for details).

Musicians, entertainers, producers, writers, journalists, and others whose income depends upon this equipment will of course be able to write off the acquisitions as capital expenditures in the business enterprise. Stay onside with Revenue Canada by allocating personal-use to services such as cable TV, that is enjoyed by the whole family or general newspaper subscriptions. Specific industry publications will usually be tax-deductible.

ENTERTAINING AT HOME

. . . taxpayers often wonder whether the costs of entertaining clients at home at a dinner party are tax-deductible . . .

Taxpayers often wonder whether the costs of entertaining clients at home at a dinner party are tax-deductible. The answer is yes, provided that receipts are kept and food and liquor items used specifically for the event are circled. Family staple items or other groceries to be used after the event must be excluded from the costs. Just like entertaining in a commercial establishment, all identified business-related costs are subject to the normal 50% restriction on all meals and entertainment.

When entertaining or meeting for business purposes, always keep receipts — even if you have met only for coffee and donuts — and write the name of your business associate and the reason for the meeting on the back of the receipt.

In closing, you should be aware that in the province of Quebec, costs of a home office will be further restricted to 50% of the normal tax-deductible expenditures, if proposals announced in 1996 are passed into law. Our federal government is looking at current rules for claiming home expenses with a critical eye. It would not be surprising to see similar restrictions on the federal return in the future.

CHAPTER

EIGHT

A Tax-Wise Plan for Wealth Creation

Dreams are free
— Unknown

GUIDELINES FOR THE TAX-WISE

In examining the tax strategies for a home-based business, we have learned that different situations often require different approaches. There are, however, some basic guidelines that every taxpayer — regardless of his or her situation — would be wise to follow. And if you do follow them, they will help you create a sound audit-proof organization; split income among family members; defer income; and offset profits — all within the framework of the law.

Know Your Tax-Free Zone

Remember, every Canadian resident must file a tax return and report world income in Canadian funds if income exceeds allowable deductions and tax credits. And every Canadian resident may take advantage of a Basic Personal Amount of $6,456. This is true for every one of your family members as well. Therefore, a family of four has a minimum Tax-Free Zone of $25,824 (4 × $6,456). To maximize wealth creation, this is the minimum productivity level each family member should strive for in accumulating tax-free earnings.

In the case of seniors, depending on income level, an additional age amount of $3,482 may be available to bring the Tax-Free Zone of a person over the age of 64 to a maximum of $9,938, or $19,876 per couple. Certain other non-refundable tax credits found on page 3 of the return can also reduce taxes payable. (See Appendix 5)

Split Business Income to Family Members

In most family businesses, family members work for the enterprise, either doing occasional overflow work or in a more direct role. Because of the Tax-Free Zone each individual has, be aware that any work that a family member does for you in your business can and should be paid for under the same terms and conditions a stranger would be paid for equal work. This is a legitimate way to split income. The payor takes a tax deduction for the payments made to the family member, thereby reducing business income; and the family member may even receive this money tax-free, if taxable income — that is, income after all deductions — is under the Basic Personal Amounts and other Non-Refundable Tax Credits.

Pay Your Own Source Deductions

. . . this will have to be a self-directed form of discipline to develop an emergency fund . . .

As a proprietor, you now know that you will be required to remit both the employer's and the employee's portion of Canada Pension Plan premiums based on the net income of the business (gross income less allowable tax deductions). This is payable when you file your tax return. Because you will not be allowed to contribute to Employment Insurance, you may wish to start a special savings plan to cover yourself in case of business failure. This will have to be a self-directed form of discipline to develop an emergency fund because you have no safety net to fall into, if your business fails.

Finally, you may also have to remit tax instalment payments to Revenue Canada periodically during the year.

Create Your Own Retirement Plan

No one will help you provide for your retirement, either. Fortunately 18% of your net income from the business last year, may be contributed to an RRSP. Keep this fact in mind when you are deciding the level of your net income with your discretionary deductions, such as Capital Cost Allowances. Make a commitment to saving at least 18% of your net income for retirement purposes each and every month.

Protect Yourself in Case of Disability

Don't forget the disability insurance. You may one day need it in order to have an income source should you become disabled. There are many private plans to choose from. Your contributions will not be tax deductible now, but, should you have to draw on the plan, your benefits will be tax-free. It may also be wise to buy a medical plan if you can afford this. Should you belong to an industry association, you may find low group rates for such plans.

Protect Your Family in Case of Your Death

Life insurance coverage is important when you're on your own. Be sure to maximize this opportunity when you are still healthy and insurable. Certain life insurance policies also provide for an investment component . . . they allow you to accumulate savings on a tax-deferred basis and increase the value of the insurance benefit at the same time. This is something to look into once you are maximizing your RRSP contributions and you are looking for ways to shelter extra disposable income.

Nurture Your Business Interests

Properly nurtured, a home-based business is a true asset . . . with the owner-manager steering and driving it to two specific results:

(a) to make profits that will meet ongoing survival needs for both the family and the business; and

(b) to build equity, that will provide capital gains upon disposition in the future.

When you see your business as having a life of its own, it is easy to make growth-oriented decisions that are right for the business, rather than for the individuals who run it. By keeping this tip in mind, your decisions will be focused on expectation of future profits, and this will also keep you onside with Revenue Canada's audit probes.

Always Make Decisions With a Tax Viewpoint

By knowing your marginal tax rate, and how much you will give up to Revenue Canada at the height of your success, you will be able to plan your financial legacy. Every individual tax receipt you keep is potentially worth somewhere between 27¢ and 50¢ on the dollar in tax savings. Income splitting and tax-assisted retirement savings techniques can work in your favor as well. Especially when you are surviving extended periods of losses, be meticulous about claiming every possible deduction and credit. Such losses could save you thousands of dollars in taxes owing on future profits.

Pay Tax in the Province in Which Your Business Is Located

. . . your business profits may be taxed in the business's province of residence . . .

Despite the fact that you are required to file a tax return based on the province you lived in as at December 31, your business profits may be taxed in the business's province of residence. This can make a substantial difference if you live in Manitoba, for example, but ranch in Alberta. The net income from the ranch can be taxed at the lower Alberta rates by filing "Form T2203" — "Tax In Respect of Multiple Jurisdictions". (*See* Appendix 3.)

Everything Has a Value . . . Including Your Tax-Exempt Principal Residence

It is important that you value your income-producing assets for tax purposes. Income producing assets are usually scheduled for Capital Cost Allowance purposes. (*See* Chapter Five.) You may, for example convert an asset from personal to business use, and vice versa. In such cases, you will need to know the "fair market value" of the asset. That is, what someone would be willing to pay for the asset on the open market at the time of conversion. Your tax professional will ask you for this documentation come tax time.

As a general rule, however, the home out of which you run your business should not be depreciated on the tax return. That is because the profits on the disposition of a principal residence are exempt from tax. The only exception to this tax exemption applies when the residence owner has claimed Capital Cost Allowance on the building to reduce taxes. In such cases, the profits on the portion of the home that was depreciated in the past will be subject to capital gains treatment. You should try to avoid this.

Try to employ these guidelines in your tax planning strategies — they will serve you well.

MAXIMIZING YOUR TIME, ENERGY AND MONEY

Probably the most difficult thing about starting and running your own business is the need to be so multi-faceted in your daily activities. In the days before you can afford to hire the right number of employees to help you, you may need to be the creator, the public relations firm, the sales agent, the quality control manager, the complaint department, the deal-maker, the bookkeeper, the analyst, the conciliator, the office manager, the secretary, the communicator . . . as well as the mom or dad, the husband or wife, the son or daughter and the best friend of those around you who give your life meaning. Quite often, all of these demands exist while you are investing your savings, with little or no immediate return for your efforts. Managing all of that is a very tall order.

It really causes one to think carefully about the precious resources of time, energy and money. The home-based business owner should be questioning each and every activity embarked upon, as one that will either produce revenues or equity in the firm. If neither of those goals is achieved now or in the future with the efforts you are expending, there is really not much reason to waste your precious resources and rob yourself of time with your favorite people and things.

A small business owner, above all else, needs to take special care of him or herself. You should be constantly recreating your personal energies to move your company forward to its next achievement. If you want your revenues to grow, you must also be building a management team that can help you take your enterprise to the next level. Creation and recreation; a constant evolution; an investment in the future, this is what you strive for.

Perhaps the second most difficult task of the hands-on business owner, is to let someone else take over the day-to-day tasks, so that you can concentrate on building the equity in the business. Manage your human resources to build revenues; then concentrate on increasing market share in your particular niche area to increase the value in your business for the future. That's when the many unpaid hours invested in the start-up, may eventually pay off.

. . . to make this happen, you need to schedule "thinking time" . . .

To make this happen, you need to schedule "thinking time". This is the time you make to take a look at "The Big Picture". It's the time you stop "doing" for a moment; it's the time that you stop the car, review the distance travelled, and plan for the road ahead.

Ask yourself, for example, just how much money you'll need to adequately protect yourself in case of disability, or death. What will happen to your family if you are disabled? How will the medical bills be paid if you don't have a medical insurance plan? Are you protected by a long-term disability insurance plan?

Once you have yourself adequately protected from the unexpected, ask yourself this question: How much money do I need to live the lifestyle I'd like to have in my retirement? Is this $60,000 a year, $75,000 a year? Less? More? What is that magic number that will give me the security I need to live a long and happy retirement? That's what you are working for today.

Many people make the mistake of mixing up their retirement goals with their estate planning goals. It is very important that you separate the two. Your retirement planning goals are for you. Your estate planning goals are for the dependants you leave behind.

Think about that for a moment. In Canada today, tax deferred retirement savings, such as RRSP contributions, are taxable when withdrawn. If you should die before you can use up your retirement savings, one of two things will happen: if you have a spouse, your accumulations will usually roll over on a tax-free basis to that person, who is then taxed on the withdrawals he or she takes. But once the second surviving spouse dies, the government steps in and invokes the "deemed disposition rules" on the death of that person. The accumulated RRSP amounts become fully taxable, and depending on the size of the registered plan up to 50% of the savings or more may be lost to taxes before your children or other beneficiaries get anything.*

It is most important for you, the small-business owner, to adequately plan for retirement by making tax-deductible RRSP contributions based on the net profits of the business throughout your active period of life. No one else will do it for you; you have no other unemployment insurance or company pension plans to fall back on; so you have to create your own.

But as far as your estate planning goes, be aware that life insurance policy proceeds can be received by your beneficiaries on a tax-free basis. When

---

*Note there are special rules for dependent children and those who are mentally or physically infirm.

your days are over, it may make sense to provide a completely tax-free life insurance benefit for those left behind.

... these policies can also be used to accrue tax-free investment earnings ...

Life insurance can also be used to pay for the tax on deemed disposition of your assets upon your death. These policies can also be used to accrue tax-free investment earnings. That is, interest-bearing investments held outside of an RRSP are subject to taxes as interest income is accrued, whether or not it is paid to the taxpayer. In the case of many life insurance policies, cash values may accumulate on a tax-free basis until withdrawal or death.

You may wish to revisit your general insurance needs now that you are in business for yourself.

You may be asking yourself, how do I come up with the money for all of this? That's the tough part, of course. But it all boils down to making choices ... to maximize your precious resources of time, energy and money. Consider drawing up a basic blueprint for wealth creation (Table 8-1), in which you project out your income and expenditure patterns for your family over your lifetime. This can really put your efforts into perspective. For example:

TABLE 8-1
WEALTH CREATION BLUEPRINT

Monthly Earnings	$4,200
Annual Before-Tax Earnings	$50,400
Productivity Period	40 Years
Projected Lifetime Earnings	$2,016,000 (Before Taxes)

That's a lot of money to divide up between current expenditures, savings and estate planning. How does one start to break it down to meet the goals and objectives that have been set? A sample plan is shown in Table 8-2. Adjust the ratios to make the numbers real for you:

TABLE 8-2
SPENDING ASSESSMENT PROJECTION

COSTS	RATIO	MONTHLY	ANNUAL	LIFETIME
Taxes	30%	$1300	$15,600	$624,000
Shelter	12%	500	6,000	240,000
Food	12%	500	6,000	240,000
Clothing	5%	200	2,400	96,000
RRSP	18%	750	9,000	360,000*
Non-RRSP	12%	500	6,000	240,000*
Other Consumer Goods	11%	450	5,400	216,000
Total	100%	$4200	$50,400	$2,016,000

*Pre-tax principle only; 30% savings factor: 18% tax assisted (RRSP); 12% savings from tax paid dollars

And so, with a little bit of time to sit down and chart out your tax and financial plans, you and your family will reap many rewards from the sacrifices you make in building your business. Be sure to speak to your professional advisors about the best long-term and short-term financial plans for your own unique situation.

A competent professional can examine your personal and business situation using the most up-to-date information about the law. You can't be an expert at everything. It may ultimately be to your advantage to recruit a professional team that can help you grow and prosper. The first step in building this team, is to find someone who can answer the simplest questions without making you feel intimidated.

> *. . . find someone who can answer the simplest questions without making you feel intimidated . . .*

Benjamin Disraeli once said, "As a general rule, the most successful person in life is the one who has the best information". Make sure that you have the best tax information for the growth and development of your home based business; and know how to minimize the taxes you and your family must pay. If you do so, you will likely find your wealth multiply and your dreams become reality.

I sincerely hope that this book has provided you with some insights into arranging your affairs within the framework of the law, and enables you to maximize the return on your investment of time and money.

Good luck in all of your endeavors.

Appendix 1

T137 REQUEST FOR DESTRUCTION OF BOOKS AND RECORDS

| Revenue Canada / Revenu Canada | **REQUEST FOR DESTRUCTION OF BOOKS AND RECORDS** | T137 Rev. 95 |

- For use by an individual, his or her authorized representative, or the authorized representative of a corporation, trust, or partnership.

- Generally, you have to keep your books and records for at least six years after the end of the taxation year to which they relate. For more information, as well as the sections of the *Income Tax Act, Income Tax Regulations, Unemployment Insurance Act,* and *Canada Pension Plan* that apply, see Information Circular 78-10, **Books and Records Retention/Destruction**.

- Send your request for permission to destroy books and records to the Director of your tax services office.

Name of individual, corporation, trust, or partnership

Address of individual, corporation, trust, or partnership

Social Insurance Number, Corporation Account Number, Partnership Identification Number, or Business Number

REASON FOR REQUEST

Books, records, or other documents to be destroyed:

OTHER INFORMATION

1. Fiscal periods for which destruction of records is being requested   from: Day Month Year   to: Day Month Year

2. Have all returns for the taxation years involved been filed?   ☐ YES   ☐ NO

3. Is there a *Notice of Appeal* or *Objection* outstanding?   ☐ YES   ☐ NO

4. Type of documents

   ☐ Non-microfilmed or non-imaged records

   ☐ Microfilm or image records (roll film, microfiche, microtypes, micro card, aperture cards, acetate jackets, etc.)

5. Other pertinent information:

CERTIFICATION

I hereby certify that the information given in this request is true, correct and complete in every respect.

_____
(signature of individual or authorized representative)

_____
(position or office)

Date   Day   Month   Year

Telephone number   Area code

Printed in Canada.   Français au verso.

Appendix 2

T1ADJ ADJUSTMENT REQUEST

✦✦ Revenue   Revenu
Canada   Canada

T1 ADJUSTMENT REQUEST

T1-ADJ(E)
Rev. 96

● Use this form to request an adjustment (a reassessment) to an individual income tax return.
● See the back of this form for information on how to complete it.
● Send the completed form to the Enquiries & Adjustments Division of your tax centre. You can find the address listed under "Revenue Canada" in the Government of Canada section of your telephone book.

A | Identification

| DEPARTMENTAL USE |

Social insurance number

Adjustment request for the
19_____ tax year
(complete a separate form for each year)

PS
N   [ ] – [ ] – [ ] – [ ] [ ]

Full name: (please print your given name first, surname last)

Address: (please print)
☐ same as on the return
☐ or:

CORLOC # [ ] – [ ] [ ] [ ] [ ]   Ack. [ ]   St.Code

Assessor   Date   Rev.   Date

B | Authorization - complete this area if a person or firm is preparing this request for you; otherwise, go to Area C.

Name and address of person or firm preparing this request: (please print)

Letter of authorization (or Form T1013, *Consent Form*) for the year under review:

was submitted previously   ☐

is attached   ☐

C | Adjustment details

Using your copy of your tax return and your *Notice of Assessment* or *Reassessment*, list below the details of your requested change.
If you have received an assessment or reassessment notice with an amount that is different from the amount on the return, use the amount stated on the notice.
See the back of this form for information about required documentation and for examples of how to complete this area.

Line number from return or schedule	Name of line from return or schedule	Previous amount	±	Amount of change	Revised amount

Other details or explanations (attach an extra sheet if required)

D | Certification

I certify that the information given on this form and on any documents attached is, to the best of my knowledge, correct and complete.

_____   _____
Date   Client's/Representative's signature

(Home) (_____) _____
(Business) (_____) _____
Telephone

You can get more copies of this form from any Revenue Canada office.   Ce formulaire existe aussi en français.

HOW TO COMPLETE THE FORM

Area A: Identification
- Complete this area in full so that we know exactly who you are and what return you want us to reassess.

Area B: Authorization
- Complete this area if you are authorizing a person or firm to make this request on your behalf.
- You have to authorize us to discuss your tax matters with this person or firm by providing a signed letter or Form T1013, *Consent Form*. You do not have to provide a letter or Form T1013 if there is already one on file.
  Note: You can get Form T1013 from any Revenue Canada office.

Area C: Adjustment details
- Please provide all details for each change you request (you do not have to show a recalculation of your taxes).
- Show any losses in brackets (e.g., self-employed business loss).
- If you are changing a line on which you already claimed an amount (see Example 1, below) and you did not previously provide the supporting documentation, you now have to provide supporting documentation for the entire revised amount.
- Supporting documentation may include receipts, schedules, or other relevant documents. Your request may be delayed if you do not provide all required information with this form.
- You can get more information about Revenue Canada's rules and policies for reassessments in Information Circular 75-7R3, *Reassessment of a Return of Income*. You can get IC 75-7R3 from any Revenue Canada office.
- Following are two examples of how to complete this area.

Example 1
Mary filed her 1995 return reporting the following information:
Employment income $28,600
Union dues $500
After receiving her *Notice of Assessment*, Mary received an additional T4 slip. It showed $200 in income and $20 for union dues. To request a change to her return, Mary will complete Area C as follows:

Line number from return or schedule	Name of line from return or schedule	Previous amount	+ -	Amount of change	Revised amount
101	Employment income	28,600	+	200	28,800
212	Union dues	500	+	20	520

Note: Even though Mary did not submit receipts with her tax return for the original union dues claim of $500, she must now submit those receipts along with her additional T4 slip.

Example 2
In certain situations there may not be a line number to use when requesting a change. Complete the form as shown in the following example.
John filed his 1995 return, claiming the goods and services tax (GST) credit. When he received his *Notice of Assessment*, John realized that he had not claimed the credit for his infant son, born on December 15, 1995. Since there is no line number for this claim, John will complete Area C as follows:

Line number from return or schedule	Name of line from return or schedule	Previous amount	+ -	Amount of change	Revised amount
–	GST credit - number of children	0	+	1	1

Area D: Certification
- Make sure either you or your authorized representative signs and dates the request for a change to your return.

Appendix 3

T2203 TAX IN RESPECT OF MULTIPLE JURISDICTIONS

Revenue   Revenu
Canada   Canada

T2203(E)
Rev. 95

CALCULATION OF TAX FOR 1995 – MULTIPLE JURISDICTIONS

- Use this form to calculate your tax if:
  - you resided in a province on December 31, 1995, and all or part of your business income for the year was earned and is allocable to a permanent establishment outside that province or outside Canada; or
  - you were a non-resident carrying on business in one or more provinces.
- If you ceased to reside in Canada during 1995, your province of residence on December 31, 1995, is the province you lived in on the last day you resided in Canada.
- Attach one completed copy of this form to your 1995 income tax return.
- If an allocation of the federal forward averaging tax credit is being made, also complete and attach one copy of Form T2203A.
- If minimum tax applies, complete and attach Forms T691A and T691.

Part I – Income Allocated to Various Jurisdictions

Net income (from line 236 of your return) . . . . 1.

Net income from self-employment including partnership income from line 122, and lines 135 to 143 of your return (excluding losses) . . . . 2.

Excess income (line 1 minus line 2; if negative, enter "0") . . . . 3.

Note: In column 2 below, allocate to your province of residence any net income from self-employment from line 2 above that is not allocable to a permanent establishment.

Note: In column 3 below, allocate to your province of residence the amount from line 3, if any. If line 3 is zero, calculate the allocations in column 4 by applying the percentages of the incomes allocated to the jurisdictions (including your province of residence) in column 2, to the net income on line 1. In column 5 below, determine the percentage for each jurisdiction on the basis of the income allocated in column 4.

(1) Jurisdiction	(2) Allocation of net income from self-employment (line 2 above)	(3) Excess income (line 3 above)	(4) Income allocated to jurisdiction (column 2 plus column 3)	(5) % of income allocated to jurisdiction
Newfoundland				
Prince Edward Island				
Nova Scotia				
New Brunswick				
Quebec				
Ontario				
Manitoba				
Saskatchewan				
Alberta				
British Columbia				
Northwest Territories				
Yukon Territory				
Other (outside Canada)				
Totals				**100%**

Part II – Net Federal Tax

Taxable income 4. _____ (from line 260 of your return)   See Part 2 of Schedule 1 of your return for the income tax percentages.

On the first _____ tax is . . . . 5.

On remaining _____ tax at _____ % is . . . . 6.

Total federal income tax on taxable income . . . . 7. ▶ 7.

Add: Tax adjustments (from line 500 of Schedule 1) . . . . 8.

Total . . . . 9. ▶ 9.

Subtract: Total non-refundable tax credits (from line 350 of your return) . . . . 10.

Overseas employment tax credit (from Form T626) . . . . 11.

Dividend tax credit: 13 1/3% of the amount on line 120 of your return . . . . 12.

Minimum tax carry-over (from Form T691) . . . . 13.

Total of lines 10 to 13 . . . . 14. ▶ 14.

Basic federal tax (line 9 minus line 14) . . . . 15.

16. **Allocation of basic federal tax to jurisdictions**

_____ % to Newfoundland $ _____	_____ % to Ontario $ _____	_____ % to N.W.T. $ _____
_____ % to P.E.I. $ _____	_____ % to Manitoba $ _____	_____ % to Yukon $ _____
_____ % to Nova Scotia $ _____	_____ % to Saskatchewan $ _____	_____ % to Other $ _____
_____ % to New Brunswick $ _____	_____ % to Alberta $ _____	The total allocated **must** equal
_____ % to Quebec $ _____	_____ % to British Columbia $ _____	line 15, "Basic federal tax".

Add: Federal surtax: 52% of the basic federal tax allocated to "Other" (from area 16) . . . . 17.

Federal tax before the federal foreign tax credit (line 15 plus line 17) . . . . 18.

Ce formulaire existe aussi en français.

T2203, page 2

Part II – Net Federal Tax (Continued)

Federal tax before the federal foreign tax credit (enter the amount from line 18 on page 1 of this form) . . . . **18.**

Subtract: Federal foreign tax credit (make a separate calculation for each country; refer to page 4 of this form for explanatory notes)

Non-business foreign income

1. Non-business income tax paid to a foreign country * . . . . $ _____ **(A)**

2. (a) Net foreign non-business income ** $ _____ / Net income *** $ _____ X Federal tax **** $ _____ = $ _____ **(B)**

Federal non-business foreign tax credit is the lesser of (A) and (B) . . . . $ _____ **(C)**

Business foreign income

1. Business income tax paid to a foreign country † plus any unused foreign tax credit for that country . . . . . . $ _____ **(D)**

2. (a) Net foreign business income †† $ _____ / Net income *** $ _____ X Basic federal tax ††† $ _____ = $ _____ **1)**

   (b) Federal surtax (line 17) (If you paid business income tax to more than one country, enter the proportion of line 17 that applies to each country.) . . . . $ _____ **2)**

   Total: Line 1) plus line 2) . . . . $ _____ **(E)**

3. Basic federal tax ††† plus federal surtax (line 17) . . . . $ _____

   Subtract: The amount from line (C), if any . . . . $ _____ = $ _____ **(F)**

Federal business foreign tax credit is the least of (D), (E), and (F) . . . . $ _____ **(G)**

Federal foreign tax credit: Line (C) plus line (G) . . . . **19.**

Federal tax: Line 18 minus line 19 . . . . **20.**

Subtract: Federal political contribution tax credit (from line 410 of your return) . . . . **21.** _____

Investment tax credit (from line 412 of your return) . . . . **22.** _____

Labour-sponsored funds tax credit (from line 414 of your return) . . . . **23.** _____

Total of lines 21 to 23 . . . . **24.** ▶ **24.**

Federal tax before the federal individual surtax (line 20 minus line 24) (enter this amount on line 417 of your return) . . . . **25.**

Refundable Quebec abatement: 16.5% of the basic federal tax allocated to Quebec (from area 16) (If you are using a return for residents of Quebec, enter this amount on line 440. For all other returns, enter this amount in the space above line 437) . . . . **26.**

If you have to complete Form T2203A, enter the amount on line 26, on line 3 of the T2203A, and do not enter it on line 440 of your return.

Federal individual surtax: Total of the basic federal tax (line 15), overseas employment tax credit (line 11) and net federal tax from line 20 of Form T541 (deceased person only) minus any adjusted federal forward averaging tax credit (line 12 of Form T2203A) . . . . **27.** _____

3% of the amount on line 27 . . . . **28.** _____

5% of (the amount on line 27 in excess of $12,500) . . . . **29.** _____

Individual surtax: Line 28 plus line 29 . . . . **30.** ▶ **30.**

Subtract: Additional foreign tax credit (make a separate calculation for each foreign country; refer to page 4 of this form for explanatory notes)

Non-business foreign income

1. Line (A) minus line (C) . . . . $ _____ **(H)**

2. Net foreign non-business income ** $ _____ / Net income *** $ _____ X Individual surtax (line 30) $ _____ = $ _____ **(I)**

Additional federal non-business foreign tax credit is the lesser of (H) and (I) . . . . $ _____ **(J)**

Business foreign income

1. Line (D) minus line (G) . . . . $ _____ **(K)**

2. Net foreign business income †† $ _____ / Net income *** $ _____ X Basic federal tax ††† plus Individual surtax (line 30) $ _____ = $ _____ **3)**

   Federal surtax (line 17) (If you paid business income tax to more than one country, enter the proportion that applies to this particular country) . . . . $ _____ **4)**

   Line 3) plus line 4) $ _____ **5)**

   Line 5 minus line (G) . . . . $ _____ **(L)**

3. Individual surtax (line 30) . . . . $ _____

   Subtract: The amount from line (J), if any . . . . $ _____ = $ _____ **(M)**

Additional federal business foreign tax credit is the least of (K), (L), and (M) . . . . $ _____ **(N)**

Additional federal foreign tax credit: Line (J) plus line (N) . . . . **31.**

Subtotal: Line 30 minus line 31 . . . . **32.**

Subtract: Additional investment tax credit (from Section II of Form T2038 (IND)) . . . . **33.**

Federal individual surtax (enter this amount on line 419 of your return) . . . . **34.**

T2203, page 3

Part III – Provincial Tax

Newfoundland: 69% of the basic federal tax allocated to Newfoundland (from Part II, area 16) . . . . **35.**

Prince Edward Island: 59.5% of the basic federal tax allocated to P.E.I. (from Part II, area 16) . . . . **(a)**

Add: 10% of (amount (a) in excess of $12,500) . . . .

Adjusted Prince Edward Island income tax . . . . ▶ **36.**

If you made a forward averaging election, calculate the adjusted Prince Edward Island tax on Form T2203A.

Nova Scotia: 59.5 % of the basic federal tax allocated to Nova Scotia (from Part II, area 16) . . . . **(a)**

Add: 10 % of (amount (a) in excess of $10,000) . . . .

Adjusted Nova Scotia tax . . . .

Subtract: Provincial foreign tax credit (from line 47) . . . .

Nova Scotia income tax . . . . **(b)**

Nova Scotia tax (use Form T1C(N.S.)TC to complete the calculation of Nova Scotia tax and enter the result here). . . . ▶ **37.**

Use amount (b) as amount (D) on Form T1C(N.S.)TC.
If you made a forward averaging election, calculate the adjusted Nova Scotia tax on Form T2203A.

New Brunswick: 64% of the basic federal tax allocated to New Brunswick (from Part II, area 16) . . . . **(a)**

Add: 8% of (amount (a) in excess of $13,500) . . . .

Adjusted New Brunswick income tax . . . . ▶ **38.**

If you made a forward averaging election, calculate the adjusted New Brunswick tax on Form T2203A.

Ontario: 58% of the basic federal tax allocated to Ontario (from Part II, area 16) . . . . **(a)**

Add: 20% of (amount (a) in excess of $5,500), plus . . . .

10% of (amount (a) in excess of $8,000) . . . . **=**

Adjusted Ontario tax . . . .

Subtract: Provincial foreign tax credit (from line 47) . . . .

Ontario income tax . . . . **(b)**

Ontario tax (use Form T1C(ONT.)TC to complete the calculation of Ontario tax and
enter the result here) . . . . **39.**

Use amount (b) as amount (E) on Form T1C(ONT.)TC.
If you made a forward averaging election, calculate the Ontario tax on Form T2203A.

Manitoba: 52% of the basic federal tax allocated to Manitoba (from Part II, area 16) . . . .

Add: Manitoba net income tax: 2% of "Net income allocated to Manitoba"
(from column 4 in Part I) . . . .

Manitoba income tax . . . . **(a)**

Manitoba tax (use Form T1C(MAN.)TC to complete the calculation of Manitoba tax and
enter the result here) . . . . **40.**

Use amount (a) as amount (C) on Form T1C(MAN.)TC. The reference to "Net income"
in the opening line of Section II of Form T1C(MAN.)TC should be read as "Net income allocated to Manitoba."

For residents of Manitoba, reduce "Net income allocated to Manitoba" by the amount deducted as an other payments
deduction (line 250 of your return) and by any foreign income exempt under a tax treaty (included on line 256 of your return).

Saskatchewan: 50% of the basic federal tax allocated to Saskatchewan (from Part II, area 16) . . . .

Add: Saskatchewan flat tax: 2% of "Net income allocated to Saskatchewan"
(from column 4 in Part I) . . . .

Basic Saskatchewan tax . . . . **(a)**

Net Saskatchewan tax (For residents of Saskatchewan, use Form T1C(SASK.) to complete the
calculation of Net Saskatchewan tax and enter the result here. Use amount (a) as "Basic Saskatchewan tax."
For all others, enter amount (a) here) . . . . **41.**

For residents of Saskatchewan, reduce "Net income allocated to Saskatchewan" by the amount deducted as an other payments
deduction (line 250 of your return) and by any foreign income exempt under a tax treaty (included on line 256 of your return).

Alberta: 45.5% of the basic federal tax allocated to Alberta (from Part II, area 16) . . . . **(a)**

Add: Alberta surtax: 8% of (amount (a) in excess of $3,500) . . . .

Add: Alberta flat rate tax: 0.5% of "Taxable income allocated to Alberta" . . . .

Adjusted Alberta income tax . . . . **(b)**

Alberta tax (use Form T1C(ALTA.) to complete the calculation of Alberta tax and enter
the result here) . . . . **42.**

Use amount (b) as "Adjusted Alberta income tax" on T1C(ALTA.).

"Taxable income allocated to Alberta" is the percentage allocated to Alberta in column 5 of Part I
applied to the taxable income (line 260 of your return).

British Columbia: 52.5% of the basic federal tax allocated to B.C. (from Part II, area 16) . . . .

Subtract: Provincial foreign tax credit (from line 47) . . . .

Adjusted British Columbia income tax . . . . **(a)**

British Columbia tax (use Form T1C(B.C.)TC to complete the calculation
of B.C. tax and enter the result here) . . . . **43.**

Use amount (a) as "Adjusted British Columbia income tax" on Form T1C(B.C.)TC.
If you made a forward averaging election, calculate the British Columbia tax on Form T2203A.

Northwest Territories: 45% of the basic federal tax allocated to Northwest Territories (from Part II, area 16) . . . . **44.**

T2203, page 4

Part III – Provincial Tax (Continued)

Yukon Territory: 50% of the basic federal tax allocated to Yukon Territory (from area 16) . . . . (a) _____

Add: 5% of (amount (a) in excess of $6,000) . . . . _____

Adjusted Yukon Territory income tax . . . . ▶ 45. _____
If you made a forward averaging election, calculate the adjusted Yukon Territory tax on Form T2203A.

Total of lines 35 to 45 . . . . 46. _____

Provincial foreign tax credit: From Form T2036 (apply this amount to your province or territory of
residence as of December 31) . . . . 47. _____

Provincial tax (For residents of Ontario, Manitoba, Saskatchewan, Alberta and British Columbia, enter the amount from line 46
on line 428 of your return. For other residents, enter the amount of line 46 **minus** line 47 on line 428 of your return) . . . . 48. _____

Explanatory Notes for Foreign Tax Credit

* **Non-business income tax paid to a foreign country** is the total income or profits taxes paid to that country (or to a political subdivision of the country) for the year (excluding business income tax), minus any part of such taxes that is deductible under subsection 20(11), or deducted under subsection 20(12) of the *Income Tax Act*. It does not include any part of such taxes that can reasonably be attributed to amounts that:
- any other person or partnership received or is entitled to receive from the foreign country;
- relate to employment income from that country for which you claimed an overseas employment tax credit;
- relate to taxable capital gains from that country for which you claimed a capital gains deduction;
- were deductible as exempt income under a tax treaty between Canada and that country; or
- were taxable in the foreign country because you were a citizen of that country, and relate to income from a source within Canada.

** **Net foreign non-business income**[1] is the total non-business income from the foreign country before deducting the foreign tax, minus allowable expenses and deductions relating to the foreign income (other than any deduction you claimed in respect of a dividend you received from a controlled foreign affiliate). Reduce this amount by any income from that foreign country for which you claimed a capital gains deduction, and by any income from that country that was deductible as exempt income under a tax treaty between Canada and that country. Also, reduce this amount by any part of employment income from that country for which you claimed an overseas employment tax credit. If the net foreign non-business income is greater than the net income, use the amount of net income in the calculation.

*** **Net income**[2] is the amount on line 236 of your return (or if you filed a Form T581 election, it is the amount on line 7 of that form) minus any:
- amounts deductible as an employee home relocation loan deduction (line 248 of your return);
- amounts deductible as a stock option and shares deductions (line 249 of your return);
- amounts deductible as an other payments deduction (line 250 of your return);
- net capital losses of other years claimed (line 253 of your return);
- capital gains deduction claimed (line 254 of your return); and
- foreign income deductible as exempt income under a tax treaty, or deductible as net employment income from a prescribed international organization (included on line 256 of your return).

**** **Federal tax** is the federal tax before the federal foreign tax credit (from line 18 of this form) plus any:
- overseas employment tax credit (line 11 of this form); and
- dividend tax credit (line 12 of this form);

and minus any:
- refundable Quebec abatement (for residents of Quebec only) (line 26 of this form); and
- tax adjustments for CPP/QPP disability benefits for previous years (included on line 8 of this form).

† **Business income tax paid to a foreign country** is the total of business income or profits taxes paid to that country (or to a political subdivision of the country) for the year and the unused foreign tax credits for that country for the seven taxation years before and the three taxation years immediately after this taxation year. It does not include any part of the business income tax that can be reasonably attributed to an amount that any other person or partnership has received or is entitled to receive from that country, or was deductible as exempt income under a tax treaty between Canada and that country.

†† **Net foreign business income**[1] is the total business income from the foreign country minus allowable expenses and deductions relating to the foreign income, and minus any part that was deductible as exempt income under a tax treaty between Canada and that country. If the net foreign business income is greater than the net income, use the amount of net income in the calculation.

††† **Basic federal tax** is the federal tax before the federal foreign tax credit (from line 18 of this form) plus any:
- overseas employment tax credit (line 11 of this form); and
- dividend tax credit (line 12 of this form);

and minus any:
- tax adjustments for CPP/QPP disability benefits for previous years (included on line 8 of this form), and
- federal surtax (line 17 of this form).

[1] Note: If you were a resident of Canada for part of the year, only include the income for the part of the year when you were a resident of Canada.

[2] Note: If you were a resident of Canada for part of the year, include the income for the part of the year when you were a resident of Canada, and your taxable income earned in Canada (before deductions in paragraphs 115(1)(d) to (f) of the *Income Tax Act*) as reported on your Canadian income tax return, for the part of the year when you were not a resident of Canada.

Printed in Canada

Appendix 4

BUSINESS STATEMENTS: T2124, T2032, T2042, T2121

T2124, page 1

Revenue Canada / Revenu Canada

STATEMENT OF BUSINESS ACTIVITIES

2

- For more information on how to complete this statement, see the income tax guide called *Business and Professional Income.*

Identification

Your name	Your social insurance number

For the period from:	Year	Month	Day	to:	Year	Month	Day	Was 1996 your final year of business? Yes ☐ No ☐

Name of business	Main product or service
Business address	Industry code (see the appendix in the *Business and Professional Income* guide)
City, town, or municipality, and province / Postal code	Partnership identification number
Name and address of person or firm preparing this form	Tax shelter identification number
Business number	Your percentage of the partnership %

Income

Sales, commissions, or fees		(a)
Minus – GST and/or provincial sales tax (if included in sales above)		
– Returns, allowances, and discounts (if included in sales above)		
Total of the above two lines		(b)
Net sales, commissions or fees (line a minus line b)	8123	▶
Reserves deducted last year		
Other income		
Gross income (total of the above three lines) enter on the appropriate line of your income tax return	8124	(c)

Calculation of cost of goods sold (enter business portion only)

Opening inventory (include raw materials, goods in process, and finished goods)	8200	
Purchases during the year (net of returns, allowances, and discounts)	8201	
Sub-contracts	8202	
Direct wage costs	8245	
Other costs		
Total of the above five lines		
Minus – Closing inventory (include raw materials, goods in process, and finished goods)	8203	
Cost of goods sold	▶	(d)
Gross profit (line c minus line d)	8125	(e)

Expenses (enter business portion only)

Advertising	8204
Bad debts	8205
Business tax, fees, licences, dues, memberships, and subscriptions	
Delivery, freight, and express	8211
Fuel costs (except for motor vehicles)	8212
Insurance	8213
Interest	8214
Maintenance and repairs	8215
Management and administration fees	8216
Meals and entertainment (allowable portion only)	8217
Motor vehicle expenses (not including capital cost allowance)	8218
Office expenses	8219
Supplies	8252
Legal, accounting, and other professional fees	8220
Property taxes	8221
Rent	8222
Salaries, wages, and benefits (including employer's contributions)	8223
Travel	8224
Telephone and utilities	8225
Other expenses	
Subtotal	
Capital cost allowance (from Area A on page 3 of this form)	8207
Allowance on eligible capital property	8246
Total business expenses (total of the above three lines)	▶ (f)
Net income (loss) before adjustments (line e minus line f)	8237

T2124 E (96) (Ce formulaire existe aussi en français.) 2035 **Canada**

T2124, page 2

Net income (loss) before adjustments (from line 8237 on the front)	(g)
Your share of line g above	(h)
Minus – Other amounts deductible from your share of net partnership income (loss) from the chart below	(i)
Net income (loss) after adjustments (line h minus line i)	(j)
Minus – Business-use-of-home expenses (from the chart below)	8235
Your net income (loss) line j minus line 8235 (enter on the appropriate line of your income tax return)	8243

Other amounts deductible from your share of net partnership income (loss)

Claim expenses you incurred that were not included in the partnership statement of income and expenses, and for which the partnership did not reimburse you.

Total (enter this amount on line i above)

Calculation of business-use-of-home expenses

Heat	
Electricity	
Insurance	
Maintenance	
Mortgage interest	
Property taxes	
Other expenses	
	Subtotal
Minus – Personal use portion	
	Subtotal
Plus – Amount carried forward from previous year	
	Subtotal 1
Minus – Net income (loss) after adjustments from line j above (if negative, enter "0")	2
Business-use-of-home expenses available for carry forward (line 1 minus line 2) if negative, enter "0"	
Allowable claim (the lower of amounts 1 or 2 above) enter this amount on line 8235 above	

Details of other partners

	Share of net income or (loss) $	Percentage of partnership %
Partner's name and address		
Partner's name and address		
Partner's name and address		
Partner's name and address		

Details of equity

Total business liabilities	8313
Drawings in 1996	8400
Capital contributions in 1996	8401

T2124, page 3, CCA SCHEDULE

Area A - Calculation of capital cost allowance claim

1 Class number	2 Undepreciated capital cost (UCC) at the start of the year	3 Cost of additions in the year (see Areas B and C below)	4 Proceeds of dispositions in the year (see Areas D and E below)	5 * UCC after additions and dispositions (col. 2 **plus** 3 **minus** 4)	6 Adjustment for current year additions (1/2 x (col. 3 **minus** 4)) If negative, enter "0"	7 Base amount for capital cost allowance (col. 5 **minus** 6)	8 Rate %	9 CCA for the year (col. 7 x 8 or a lower amount)	10 UCC at the end of the year (col. 5 **minus** 9)

Total CCA claim for the year (enter this amount, minus any personal portion, on line 8207 on page 1 of this form)

* If you have a negative amount in this column, add it to income as a recapture under "Other income" on page 1 of this form. If there is no property left in the class and there is a positive amount in the column, deduct the amount from income as a terminal loss under "Other expenses" on page 1 of this form. Recapture and terminal loss do not apply to a Class 10.1 property. For more information, read Chapter 4 of the *Business and Professional Income* guide.

Area B - Details of equipment additions in the year

1 Class number	2 Property details	3 Total cost	4 Personal portion (if applicable)	5 Business portion (Column 3 **minus** Column 4)

Total equipment additions in the year | 8304 |

Area C - Details of building additions in the year

1 Class number	2 Property details	3 Total cost	4 Personal portion (if applicable)	5 Business portion (Column 3 **minus** Column 4)

Total building additions in the year | 8306 |

Area D - Details of equipment dispositions in the year

1 Class number	2 Property details	3 Proceeds of disposition (should not be more than the capital cost)	4 Personal portion (if applicable)	5 Business portion (Column 3 **minus** Column 4)

Note: If you disposed of property from your business in the year, see Chapter 4 in the *Business and Professional Income* guide for information about your proceeds of disposition.

Total equipment dispositions in the year | 8305 |

Area E - Details of building dispositions in the year

1 Class number	2 Property details	3 Proceeds of disposition (should not be more than the capital cost)	4 Personal portion (if applicable)	5 Business portion (Column 3 **minus** Column 4)

Note: If you disposed of property from your business in the year, see Chapter 4 in the *Business and Professional Income* guide for information about your proceeds of disposition.

Total building dispositions in the year | 8307 |

Area F - Details of land additions and dispositions in the year

Total cost of all land additions in the year	8302	
Total proceeds from all land dispositions in the year	8303	

Note: You cannot claim capital cost allowance on land.

Printed in Canada

T2032, page 1

Revenue Canada / Revenu Canada

STATEMENT OF PROFESSIONAL ACTIVITIES

• For more information on how to complete this statement, see the income tax guide called *Business and Professional Income*.

3

Identification

Your name _____ Your social insurance number ___ – ___ – ___

For the period from: Year ___ Month ___ Day ___ to: Year ___ Month ___ Day ___   Was 1996 the final year of your professional business? Yes ☐ No ☐

Name of business _____ Main product or service _____

Business address _____ Industry code (see the appendix in the *Business and Professional Income* guide) _____

City, town or municipality and province _____ Postal code _____

Name and address of person or firm preparing this form _____ Partnership identification number _____

Tax shelter identification number _____

Business Number _____ Your percentage of the partnership ___ %

Income

Professional fees (includes work-in-progress) _____ (a)

Minus – GST and/or provincial sales tax (if included in fees above) _____ (b)
     – Work-in-progress, end of the year (See Chapter 2) _____

Total of the above two lines ▶ _____

Subtotal (line a minus line b) _____

Add – Work-in-progress, beginning of the year (See Chapter 2) _____

Adjusted professional fees (Total of the above two lines) **8123** _____

Reserves deducted last year _____

Other income _____

Gross income (total of the above three lines) enter on line 164 of your income tax return **8124** _____ (c)

Expenses (enter business portion only)

Expense	Code	
Advertising	8204	
Bad debts	8205	
Business tax, fees, licences, dues, memberships, and subscriptions		
Delivery, freight, and express	8211	
Fuel costs (except for motor vehicles)	8212	
Insurance	8213	
Interest	8214	
Maintenance and repairs	8215	
Management and administration fees	8216	
Meals and entertainment (allowable portion only)	8217	
Motor vehicle expenses (not including capital cost allowance)	8218	
Office expenses	8219	
Supplies	8252	
Legal, accounting, and other professional fees	8220	
Property taxes	8221	
Rent	8222	
Salaries, wages, and benefits (including employer's contributions)	8223	
Travel	8224	
Telephone and utilities	8225	
Other expenses		

Subtotal _____

Capital cost allowance (from Area A on page 3 of this form) **8207** _____

Allowance on eligible capital property **8246** _____

Total expenses (total of the above three lines) ▶ _____ (d)

Net income (loss) before adjustments (line c minus line d) **8237** _____ (e)

Your share of line 8237 above _____ (f)

Minus – Other amounts deductible from your share of net partnership income (loss) from the chart on page 2 of this form _____ (g)

Net income (loss) after adjustments (line e minus line f) _____

Minus – Business-use-of-home expenses (from the chart on page 2 of this form) **8235** _____

Subtotal _____ (h)

Plus – Net amount to be reported in respect of your reserve for 1971 accounts receivable (from the chart on page 2 of this form) _____ (i)

Your net income (loss) line h plus line i (enter on line 137 of your income tax return) **8243** _____

T2032, page 2

Other amounts deductible from your share of net partnership income (loss)

Claim expenses you incurred that were not included in the partnership statement of income and expenses, and for which the partnership did not reimburse you

Total (enter this amount on line f on page 1 of this form)

Calculation of business-use-of-home expenses

Heat

Electricity

Insurance

Maintenance

Mortgage interest

Property taxes

Other expenses

Subtotal

Minus – Personal use portion

Subtotal

Plus – Amount carried forward from previous year

Subtotal

Minus – Net income (loss) after adjustments from line g on page 1 of this form (if negative, enter "0")   1

Business-use-of-home expenses available for carry forward (line 1 minus line 2) if negative, enter "0"   2

Allowable claim (the lower of amounts 1 or 2 above) enter this amount on line 8235 on page 1 of this form

---

Reserve for 1971 accounts receivable (for professionals in practice before 1972 only)

Enter your 1995 reserve in respect of 1971 receivables

Minus – your 1996 reserve in respect of 1971 receivables

Your net amount to be reported in respect of 1971 receivables (enter this amount on line i on page 1 of this form)

Details of other partners

Partner's name and address	Share of net income or (loss) $	Percentage of partnership %
	Share of net income or (loss) $	Percentage of partnership %
	Share of net income or (loss) $	Percentage of partnership %
	Share of net income or (loss) $	Percentage of partnership %

Details of equity

Total business liabilities	8313	
Drawings in 1996	8400	
Capital contributions in 1996	8401	

T2032, page 3, CCA SCHEDULE

Area A - Calculation of capital cost allowance claim

1 Class number	2 Undepreciated capital cost (UCC) at the start of the year	3 Cost of additions in the year (see Areas B and C below)	4 Proceeds of dispositions in the year (see Areas D and E below)	5 * UCC after additions and dispositions (col. 2 **plus** 3 **minus** 4)	6 Adjustment for current year additions (1/2 x (col. 3 **minus** 4)) If negative, enter "0"	7 Base amount for capital cost allowance (col. 5 **minus** 6)	8 Rate %	9 CCA for the year (col. 7 x 8 or a lower amount)	10 UCC at the end of the year (col. 5 **minus** 9)

Total CCA claim for the year (enter this amount, minus any personal portion, on line 8207 on page 1 of this form) [ ]

* If you have a negative amount in this column, add it to income as a recapture under "Other income" on page 1 of this form. If there is no property left in the class and there is a positive amount in the column, deduct the amount from income as a terminal loss under "Other expenses" on page 1 of this form. Recapture and terminal loss do not apply to a Class 10.1 property. For more information, read Chapter 4 of the *Business and Professional Income* guide.

Area B - Details of equipment additions in the year

1 Class number	2 Property details	3 Total cost	4 Personal portion (if applicable)	5 Business portion (Column 3 **minus** Column 4)

Total equipment additions in the year 8304 [ ]

Area C - Details of building additions in the year

1 Class number	2 Property details	3 Total cost	4 Personal portion (if applicable)	5 Business portion (Column 3 **minus** Column 4)

Total building additions in the year 8306 [ ]

Area D - Details of equipment dispositions in the year

1 Class number	2 Property details	3 Proceeds of disposition (should not be more than the capital cost)	4 Personal portion (if applicable)	5 Business portion (Column 3 **minus** Column 4)

Note: If you disposed of property from your professional business in the year, see Chapter 4 in the *Business and Professional Income* guide for information about your proceeds of disposition.

Total equipment dispositions in the year 8305 [ ]

Area E - Details of building dispositions in the year

1 Class number	2 Property details	3 Proceeds of disposition (should not be more than the capital cost)	4 Personal portion (if applicable)	5 Business portion (Column 3 **minus** Column 4)

Note: If you disposed of property from your professional business in the year, see Chapter 4 in the *Business and Professional Income* guide for information about your proceeds of disposition.

Total building dispositions in the year 8307 [ ]

Area F - Details of land additions and dispositions in the year

Total cost of all land additions in the year	8302	
Total proceeds from all land dispositions in the year	8303	

Note: You cannot claim capital cost allowance on land.

Printed in Canada

T2042, page 1

T2042, page 1

Revenue Canada / Revenu Canada

STATEMENT OF FARMING ACTIVITIES

• For information on how to complete this statement, refer to the income tax guide called *Farming Income*.

Identification [5]

Name		Social insurance number				

For the period from:	Day	Month	Year	to:	Day	Month	Year	Was 1996 your final year of farming?	Yes [ ]	No [ ]

Farm name		Acres owned

Farm address		Acres farmed

Township or municipality and province		Postal code

Accounting method	Cash [ ]	Accrual [ ]	Main product or service	Industry code (see Chapter 2 of the *Farming Income* guide)

Name and address of person or firm preparing this form		Partnership identification number
		Tax shelter identification number

Business Number		–		–		Your percentage of the partnership	%

Income

Wheat			
Oats			
Barley			
Mixed grains			
Corn			
Canola			
Flaxseed			
Soya beans			
Other grains and oilseeds			
Total grains and oilseeds	**8100**	▶	
Fruit		8101	
Potatoes		8102	
Vegetables (excluding potatoes)		8103	
Tobacco		8104	
Other crops		8105	
Greenhouse and nursery products		8106	
Forage crops		8107	
Livestock sold			
- Cattle		8108	
- Swine		8109	
- Poultry		8110	
- Sheep and lambs		8111	
- Other animal specialties		8112	
Eggs		8113	
Milk and cream (excluding dairy subsidies)		8114	
Other commodities		8115	
Custom or contract work, and machine rentals		8116	
Insurance proceeds		8117	
Patronage dividends		8121	
Program payments			
- Dairy subsidies		8119	
- Crop insurance		8120	
- Other payments		8122	
Rebates		8134	
Other income			
Gross income (enter on line 168 of your income tax return)		8118 / 8124	

T2042 E (96)   (Ce formulaire existe aussi en français.)   0753   **Canada**

T2042, page 2

Gross income (from line 8124 on page 1) _____ a

Expenses (enter business portion only)

Building and fence repairs	8206	
Clearing, levelling, and draining land	8208	
Containers, twine, and baling wire	8209	
Crop insurance, GRIP, and stabilization premiums	8210	
Machinery expenses		
- Gasoline, diesel fuel, and oil	8212	
- Repairs, licences, and insurance	8232	
Other insurance	8213	
Interest	8214	
Motor vehicle expenses (not including CCA)	8218	
Office expenses	8219	
Legal and accounting fees	8220	
Property taxes	8221	
Rent (land, buildings, pasture)	8222	
Salaries, wages, and benefits (including employer's contributions)	8223	
Small tools	8257	
Custom or contract work, and machinery rental	8226	
Electricity	8227	
Feed, supplements, straw, and bedding	8228	
Fertilizers and lime	8229	
Heating fuel	8230	
Livestock purchased	8231	
Pesticides (herbicides, insecticides, fungicides)	8233	
Seeds and plants	8234	
Insurance program overpayment recapture	8255	
Veterinary fees, medicine, and breeding fees	8236	
Optional inventory adjustment included in 1995	8238	
Mandatory inventory adjustment included in 1995	8241	

Other expenses _____

_____

_____

Subtotal of all expenses

Capital cost allowance (from Area E on page 3)	8207	
Allowance on eligible capital property	8246	

Total farm expenses (total of the above three lines) ▶ b

Net income (loss) before adjustments (line a minus line b)	8237	
Optional inventory adjustment included in 1996	8239	
Mandatory inventory adjustment included in 1996	8240	

Total of the above three lines c

Your share of line c _____ d

Minus - Other amounts deductible from your share of net partnership income (loss) from the chart on page 4 _____ e

Net income (loss) after adjustments (line d minus line e) f

Minus - Business-use-of-home expenses (from the chart on page 4) 8235

Your net income (loss) (line f minus line 8235) 8243

Area A - Details of equipment additions in the year

1 Class number	2 Property details	3 Total cost	4 Personal portion (if applicable)	5 Business portion (column 3 minus column 4)

0753E2

Total equipment additions in the year 8304

T2042, page 3, CCA SCHEDULE

Area B - Details of building additions in the year   3

1 Class number	2 Property details	3 Total cost	4 Personal portion (if applicable)	5 Business portion (col.3 minus col.4)

Total building additions in the year `8306` |

Area C - Details of equipment dispositions in the year

1 Class number	2 Property details	3 Proceeds of disposition (should not be more than the capital cost)	4 Personal portion (if applicable)	5 Business portion (column 3 minus column 4)

Note: If you disposed of property from your farming business in the year, see Chapter 3 in the *Farming Income* guide for information about your proceeds of disposition.

Total equipment dispositions in the year `8305` |

Area D - Details of building dispositions in the year

1 Class number	2 Property details	3 Proceeds of disposition (should not be more than the capital cost)	4 Personal portion (if applicable)	5 Business portion (column 3 minus column 4)

Note: If you disposed of property from your farming business in the year, see Chapter 3 in the *Farming Income* guide for information about your proceeds of disposition.

Total building dispositions in the year `8307` |

Area E - Calculation of capital cost allowance (CCA)

Part XI properties (acquired after 1971)

1 Class number	2 Undepreciated capital cost (UCC) at the start of the year	3 Cost of additions in the year (see Area A on page 2 and Area B above)	4 Proceeds of dispositions in the year (see Areas C and D above)	5 UCC * after additions and dispositions (col. 2 plus 3 minus 4)	6 Adjustment for current year additions (1/2 x (col. 3 minus col. 4)) -if negative, enter "0"-	7 Base amount for CCA (col. 5 minus 6)	8 Rate (%)	9 CCA for the year (col. 7 x 8 or a lower amount)	10 UCC at the end of the year (col. 5 minus 9)

* If you have a negative amount in this column, add it to income as a recapture under "Other income" on the appropriate line on page 1 of this form. If there is no property left in the class and there is a positive amount in the column, deduct the amount from income as a terminal loss under "Other expenses" on page 2 of this form. Recapture and terminal loss do not apply to a Class 10.1 property. For more information, read Chapter 3 of the *Farming Income* guide.

Total CCA on Part XI properties ▶ _____ i

Part XVII properties (acquired before 1972)

1 Year acquired	2 Kind of property	3 Month of disposition	4 Cost (business portion)	5 Rate (%)	6 Allowance for this year	7 Total allowance for this and prior years

Enter the total of lines i and ii on line 8207 on page 2 of this form.

Total CCA on Part XVII properties ▶ _____ ii

0753E3

T2042, page 4

4

Area F - Details of land additions and dispositions in the year

Total cost of all land additions in the year	8302	
Total proceeds from all land dispositions in the year	8303	

Note: You cannot claim capital cost allowance on land. See Chapter 3 in the *Farming Income* guide.

Area G - Details of quota additions and dispositions in the year

Total cost of all quota additions in the year	8308	
Total proceeds from all quota dispositions in the year	8309	

Note: Quotas are eligible capital property. For more information about this kind of property, see Chapter 4 in the *Farming Income* guide.

Other amounts deductible from your share of net partnership income (loss)

Claim expenses you incurred that you did not include in the partnership statement of income and expenses, and for which the partnership did not reimburse you.

Total (enter this amount on line e on page 2 of this form)

Calculation of business-use-of-home expenses

Heat

Electricity

Insurance

Maintenance

Mortgage interest

Property taxes

Other expenses

Subtotal

Minus - Personal use portion

Subtotal

Plus - Amount carried forward from previous year

Subtotal

Minus - Net income (loss) after adjustments from line f on page 2 of this form (if negative, enter "0")   1

Business-use-of-home expenses available for carry forward (line 1 minus line 2) - if negative, enter "0"   2

Allowable claim (the lower of amounts 1 or 2 above) - enter this amount on line 8235 on page 2 of this form

---

Details of equity

Total business liabilities	8313	
Drawings in 1996	8400	
Capital contributions in 1996	8401	

Details of other partners

Partner's name and address	Share of net income or (loss) $	Percentage of partnership %

Printed in Canada

T2121, page 1

Revenue Canada / Revenu Canada

STATEMENT OF FISHING ACTIVITIES

T2121 (E)
Rev. 95

- For more information on how to complete this statement, see the income tax guide called *Fishing Income*.

4

Identification

Your name _____

Your social insurance number ___ - ___ - ___

For the period from: Day ___ Month ___ Year ___ to: Day ___ Month ___ Year ___

Was 1995 your final year of fishing? Yes ☐ No ☐

Boat name _____

Main specie _____

CFV licence # _____

Industry code (see Chapter 2 of the *Fishing Income* guide) _____

Name and address of person or firm preparing this form _____

Partnership identification number _____

Tax shelter identification number _____

Business number ___ - ___

GST account number _____

Your percentage of the partnership ___ %

INCOME

Fish products		
Other marine products		
Grants, credits, and rebates		
Subsidies		
Compensation for loss of fishing income or property		
Other income		
Sharesman income - List name of fishing boat and captain:		

Gross income (enter this amount on line 170 of your income tax return) | 8124 | (a)

EXPENSES (enter business portion only)

Bait, ice, salt		
Crew shares		
Fuel costs (except for motor vehicles)	8212	
Gear		
Insurance	8213	
Interest	8214	
Food	8217	
Licences		
Motor vehicle expenses (not including capital cost allowance)	8218	
Office expenses	8219	
Nets and traps		
Legal, accounting, and other professional fees	8220	
Salaries, wages, and benefits (including employer's contributions)	8223	
Repairs - Fishing boat		
- Engine		
- Electrical equipment		
Total of the above three lines		
Minus - Insurance recovery		
Your cost	8232	▶
Other expenses		
Subtotal		
Capital cost allowance (from Area A on page 2 of this form)	8207	
Allowance on eligible capital property	8246	

Total expenses (total of the above three lines) | ▶ | (b)

Net income (loss) before adjustments (line a minus line b) | 8237 |

Your share of line 8237 above | (c)

Minus - Other amounts deductible from your share of net partnership income (loss) from the chart on page 2 of this form | (d)

Net income (loss) after adjustments (line c minus line d) | (e)

Minus - Business-use-of-home expenses (from the chart on page 2 of this form) | 8235 |

Your net income (loss) line e minus line 8235 (enter on line 143 of your income tax return) | 8243 |

(Ce formulaire existe aussi en français.)

Printed in Canada

(see reverse)

T2121, page 2

Other amounts deductible from your share of net partnership income (loss)

Claim expenses you incurred that were not included in the partnership statement of income and expenses, and for which the partnership did not reimburse you

Total (enter this amount on line d on page 1 of this form)	

Calculation of business-use-of-home expenses

Heat		
Electricity		
Insurance		
Maintenance		
Mortgage interest		
Property taxes		
Other expenses	Subtotal	
Minus - Personal use portion	Subtotal	
Plus - Amount carried forward from previous year	Subtotal	1
Minus - Net income (loss) after adjustments from line e on page 1 of this form (if negative, enter "0")		2
Business-use-of-home expenses available for carry forward (line 1 minus line 2) if negative, enter "0"		
Allowable claim (the lower of amounts 1 or 2 above) enter this amount on line 8235 on page 1 of this form		

Details of equity

Total business liabilities	8313	
Drawings in 1995	8400	
Capital contributions in 1995	8401	

Area A - Calculation of capital cost allowance claim
Part XI properties (acquired after 1971)

1 Class number	2 Undepreciated capital cost (UCC) at the start of the year	3 Cost of additions in the year (see Areas B and C on page 3)	4 Proceeds of dispositions in the year (see Areas D and E on page 3)	5 UCC * after additions and dispositions (col. 2 plus 3 minus 4)	6 Adjustment for current year additions (1/2 x (col. 3 minus 4)) If negative, enter "0"	7 Base amount for capital cost allowance (col. 5 minus 6)	8 Rate %	9 CCA for the year (col. 7 x 8 or a lower amount)	10 UCC at the end of the year (col. 5 minus 9)

Total CCA on Part XI properties ▶ _____ (i)

* If you have a negative amount in this column, add it to income as a recapture under "Other income" on the appropriate line on page 1 of this form. If there is no property left in the class and there is a positive amount in the column, deduct the amount from income as a terminal loss under "Other expenses" on page 1 of this form. Recapture and terminal loss do not apply to a Class 10.1 property. For more information, read Chapter 3 of the *Fishing Income* guide.

Part XVII properties (acquired before 1972)

1 Year acquired	2 Kind of property	3 Month of disposition	4 Cost (business portion)	5 Rate %	6 Allowance for this year	7 Total allowance for this and prior years

Total CCA on Part XVII properties ▶ _____ (ii)

Enter the total of lines i and ii on line 8207 on page 1 of this form.

T2121, page 3

Area B - Details of equipment additions in the year

1 Class number	2 Property details	3 Total cost	4 Personal portion (if applicable)	5 Business portion (Column 3 **minus** Column 4)

Total equipment additions in the year **8304** |

Area C - Details of building additions in the year

1 Class number	2 Property details	3 Total cost	4 Personal portion (if applicable)	5 Business portion (Column 3 **minus** Column 4)

Total building additions in the year **8306** |

Area D - Details of equipment dispositions in the year

1 Class number	2 Property details	3 Proceeds of disposition (should not be more than the capital cost)	4 Personal portion (if applicable)	5 Business portion (Column 3 **minus** Column 4)

Note: If you disposed of property from your fishing business in the year, see Chapter 3 in the *Fishing Income* guide for information about your proceeds of disposition.

Total equipment dispositions in the year **8305** |

Area E - Details of building dispositions in the year

1 Class number	2 Property details	3 Proceeds of disposition (should not be more than the capital cost)	4 Personal portion (if applicable)	5 Business portion (Column 3 **minus** Column 4)

Note: If you disposed of property from your fishing business in the year, see Chapter 3 in the *Fishing Income* guide for information about your proceeds of disposition.

Total building dispositions in the year **8307** |

Area F - Details of land additions and dispositions in the year

Total cost of all land additions in the year	**8302**
Total proceeds from all land dispositions in the year	**8303**

Note: You cannot claim capital cost allowance on land.

Details of other partners

Partner's name and address	Share of net income or (loss) $	Percentage of partnership %
Partner's name and address	Share of net income or (loss) $	Percentage of partnership %
Partner's name and address	Share of net income or (loss) $	Percentage of partnership %
Partner's name and address	Share of net income or (loss) $	Percentage of partnership %

Appendix 5

T1 GENERAL 1996 TAX RETURN

Revenue Canada / Revenu Canada

T1 GENERAL 1996

Individual Income Tax Return

7

Step 1 – Identification

Attach your identification label here. Correct any wrong information. If you are not attaching a label, print your name and address below.

First name and initial

Last name

Address   Apt. or Unit No.

City

Province or territory   Postal code

Enter your province or territory of residence on December 31, 1996:

If you were self-employed in 1996, enter the province or territory of self-employment:

If you became or ceased to be a resident of Canada **in 1996**, give the date of:

entry   Day   Month   or departure   Day   Month

Enter your social insurance number if it is not on the label, or if you are not attaching a label:

Enter your date of birth: Day   Month   Year

Your language of correspondence:
Votre langue de correspondance :   English ☐   Fran•ais ☐

If this return is for a deceased person, enter the date of death: Day   Month   Year **1 9**

Check the box that applies to your marital status on December 31, 1996: We use it to determine the amount of certain credits and benefits.

1 ☐ Married   2 ☐ Living common-law   3 ☐ Widowed

4 ☐ Divorced   5 ☐ Separated   6 ☐ Single

If box 1 or 2 applies, enter your spouse's social insurance number if it is not on the label, or if you are not attaching a label:

Enter the first name of your spouse:

Check this box if your spouse was self-employed in 1996:   1 ☐

Do not use this area

Step 2 – Goods and services tax (GST) credit application

(You have to apply each year. See Step 2 in the guide to find out if you should apply this year.)

Are you applying for the goods and services tax credit? . . . . Yes ☐ 1   No ☐ 2

If *yes*, enter the number of children under age 19 on December 31, 1996 (if applicable) . . . .

If *yes*, enter your spouse's net income from line 236 of your spouse's return (if applicable) . . . .

Step 3 – Total income

Employment income (box 14 on all T4 slips)	**101**	
Commissions included on line 101 (box 42 on all T4 slips)	**102**	
Other employment income (see line 104 in the guide)	**104** +	
Old Age Security pension (box 18 on the T4A(OAS) slip and box 24 on the T4A(P) slip)	**113** +	
Canada or Quebec Pension Plan benefits (box 20 on the T4A(P) slip)	**114** +	
Disability benefits included on line 114 (box 16 on the T4A(P) slip)	**152**	
Other pensions or superannuation (see line 115 in the guide)	**115** +	
Employment Insurance benefits (box 14 on the T4U slip)	**119** +	
Taxable amount of dividends from taxable Canadian corporations (attach a completed Schedule 4)	**120** +	
Interest and other investment income (attach a completed Schedule 4)	**121** +	
Net partnership income: limited or non-active partners only (attach a completed Schedule 4)	**122** +	
Rental income Gross **160**	Net **126** +	
Taxable capital gains (attach a completed Schedule 3)	**127** +	
Alimony or maintenance income	**128** +	
Registered retirement savings plan income (from all T4RSP slips)	**129** +	
Other income (see line 130 in the guide) Specify:	**130** +	
Business income Gross **162**	Net **135** +	
Professional income Gross **164**	Net **137** +	
Commission income Gross **166**	Net **139** +	
Farming income Gross **168**	Net **141** +	
Fishing income Gross **170**	Net **143** +	
Workers' Compensation benefits (box 10 on the T5007 slip)	**144**	
Social assistance payments (see line 145 in the guide)	**145** +	
Net federal supplements (box 21 on the T4A(OAS) slip)	**146** +	
Add lines 144, 145, and 146 =	▶ **147** +	
Add lines 101, 104 to 143, and 147. This is your **total income. 150** =		

Do not use this area	605			600		

5006-R

T1 GENERAL, page 2

2

Step 4 – Taxable income

Enter your **total income** from line 150   200

Pension adjustment
(box 52 on all T4 slips and box 34 on all T4A slips)   **206**

Registered pension plan contributions (box 20 on all T4 slips and box 32 on all T4A slips)	**207**	
Registered retirement savings plan contributions (attach receipts)	**208**+	
Saskatchewan Pension Plan contributions (see line 209 in the guide)	**209**+	
Annual union, professional, or like dues (box 44 on all T4 slips, or from receipts)	**212**+	
Child care expenses (attach a completed Form T778)	**214**+	
Attendant care expenses (see line 215 in the guide)	**215**+	

Business investment loss (see line 217 in the guide)
Gross **228**   Allowable deduction **217**+

Moving expenses (see line 219 in the guide)	**219**+	
Alimony or maintenance paid	**220**+	
Carrying charges and interest expenses (attach a completed Schedule 4)	**221**+	
Exploration and development expenses (attach a completed Schedule 4)	**224**+	
Other employment expenses (see line 229 in the guide)	**229**+	
Other deductions (see line 232 in the guide) Specify:	**232**+	

Add lines 207 to 224, 229, and 232. **233**= ▶ –

Line 200 minus line 233 (if negative, enter "0"). This is your **net income before adjustments. 234**=

Social benefits repayment (if you reported income on line 113, 119, or 146, see line 235 in the guide)   **235**–   ●

Line 234 minus line 235 (if negative, enter "0"). This is your **net income. 236**=

Accumulated forward-averaging amount withdrawal (attach a completed Form T581)   **237**+

Add lines 236 and 237. **239**=

Employee home relocation loan deduction (from all T4 slips)	**248**	
Stock option and shares deductions (from all T4 slips)	**249**+	
Other payments deduction (if you reported income on line 147, see line 250 in the guide)	**250**+	
Limited partnership losses of other years	**251**+	
Non-capital losses of other years	**252**+	
Net capital losses of other years (1972 to 1995)	**253**+	
Capital gains deduction (see line 254 in the guide)	**254**+	
Northern residents deductions (attach a completed Form T2222)	**255**+	
Additional deductions (see line 256 in the guide)	**256**+	

Add lines 248 to 256. **257**= ▶ –

Line 239 minus line 257 (if negative, enter "0"). This is your **taxable income. 260**=

Foreign property reporting (see page 9 in the guide)

At any time in 1996, did you own any foreign property? .... **266**Yes ☐ 1   No ☐ 2

If **yes**, and if the cost amounts of all such property at any time in 1996 totalled more than CAN$100,000, file Form T1135.

Did you earn any income or realize any gains from foreign property in 1996? .... **267**Yes ☐ 1   No ☐ 2

If **yes**, include in calculating your income for 1996, the amount of the income earned, or gains realized.

At any time in 1996, did you receive funds or property from, or were you indebted to, a non-resident trust in which you were beneficially interested? .... **268**Yes ☐ 1   No ☐ 2

If **yes**, file Form T1142.

T1 GENERAL, page 3

3

> Before you mail your return, make sure you have attached here all required information slips, completed schedules, receipts, and corresponding statements.

Step 5 – Non-refundable tax credits

Basic personal amount	**claim $6,456.00**	**300**	
Age amount (if you were born in 1931 or earlier, see line 301 in the guide)		**301** +	
Spousal amount (see line 303 in the guide)			
Base amount	$ 5,918 | 00		
Minus: Your spouse's net income	−		
Spousal amount (if negative, enter "0") **(maximum claim $5,380)** =		▶ **303** +	
Equivalent-to-spouse amount (attach a completed Schedule 5) **(maximum claim $5,380)**		**305** +	
Amounts for infirm dependants age 18 or older (attach a completed Schedule 6)		**306** +	
Canada or Quebec Pension Plan contributions			
Contributions through employment from box 16 and box 17 on all T4 slips (maximum $893.20)		**308** +	●
Contributions payable on self-employment and other earnings (attach a completed Schedule 8)		**310** +	●
Employment Insurance premiums from box 18 on all T4 slips (see line 312 in the guide)		**312** +	●
Pension income amount (maximum $1,000; see line 314 in the guide)		**314** +	
Disability amount (claim $4,233; see line 316 in the guide)		**316** +	
Disability amount transferred from a dependant other than your spouse		**318** +	
Tuition fees (see line 320 in the guide)		**320** +	
Education amount (see line 322 in the guide)		**322** +	
Tuition fees and education amount transferred from a child (see line 324 in the guide)		**324** +	
Amounts transferred from your spouse (attach a completed Schedule 2)		**326** +	

Medical expenses (see line 330 in the guide; attach receipts)	**330**		
Minus: $1,614, or 3% of line 236, whichever is less	−		
Subtotal	=		
Minus: Medical expenses adjustment (see line 331 in the guide)	**331** −		
Allowable portion of medical expenses (if negative, enter "0")	=	▶ **332** +	

Add lines 300, 301, 303 to 326, and 332
(if this total is more than line 260, see line 335 in the guide) **335** =

Multiply the amount on line 335 by 17% = **338**

Donations and gifts (from the calculation below)   **349** +

Add lines 338 and 349. These are your **total non-refundable tax credits**. **350** =

Donations and gifts (see lines 340 and 342 in the guide)

Charitable donations (attach receipts and information slips)		**A**	
Calculate 50% of the amount on line 236			**B**
Taxable capital gains from 1996 gifts of capital property (included on line 127)		**C**	
Capital gains deduction claimed on 1996 gifts of capital property (included on line 254)	−	**D**	
Line C minus line D **339** =		**E**	
Calculate 50% of the amount on line E		+	**F**
Total charitable donations limit (add lines B and F)	=		**G**

Enter the amount from line A or line G, whichever is **less**	**340**		
Cultural, ecological, and government gifts (see line 342 in the guide; attach receipts)	**342** +		
Add lines 340 and 342. **344** =			
Enter $200 or the amount on line 344, whichever is **less**	**345** −	▶ multiply this amount by 17% = **346**	
Line 344 minus line 345 (if negative, enter "0") =		▶ multiply this amount by 29% = **348** +	

Allowable portion of donations and gifts (add lines 346 and 348)
Enter this amount on line 349 above. =

T1 GENERAL, page 4

Step 6 – Refund or Balance owing 4

Use Schedule 1, *Federal Tax Calculation*, to calculate your federal tax and your federal individual surtax.

Federal tax: If you are using **Method A** of Schedule 1, enter the amount from line 15, **or**
if you are using **Method B** of Schedule 1, enter the amount from line 30   406

Total federal political contributions (attach receipts) **409**		
Federal political contribution tax credit (from the calculation at line 410 in the guide)	**410**	•
Investment tax credit (attach a completed Form T2038 (IND.))	**412** +	•
Labour-sponsored funds tax credit Net cost **413**	Allowable credit **414** +	•
Add lines 410, 412, and 414. **416** =	▶ −	
Federal tax before federal individual surtax (line 406 minus line 416; if negative, enter "0") **417** =		

Federal individual surtax: If you are using **Method A** of Schedule 1, enter the amount from line 18, **or**
if you are using **Method B** of Schedule 1, enter the amount from line 40   **419** +

Add lines 417 and 419. This is your **net federal tax. 420** =	
Canada Pension Plan contributions payable on self-employment and other earnings from Schedule 8	**421** +
Social benefits repayment (enter the amount from line 235)	**422** +
Provincial or territorial tax (see line 428 in the guide)	**428** +
Add lines 420 to 428. This is your **total payable. 435** =	•

Total income tax deducted (from all information slips) **437**		•
Tax transfer for residents of Quebec (see line 438 in the guide) **438** −		•
Line 437 minus line 438 =	▶ **439**	
Refundable Quebec abatement (see line 440 in the guide)	**440** +	•
Canada Pension Plan overpayment (see line 448 in the guide)	**448** +	•
Employment Insurance overpayment (see line 450 in the guide)	**450** +	•
Refund of investment tax credit (attach a completed Form T2038 (IND.))	**454** +	•
Part XII.2 trust tax credit (box 38 on all T3 slips)	**456** +	•
Employee and partner GST rebate (attach a completed Form GST-370)	**457** +	•
Tax paid by instalments (see line 476 in the guide)	**476** +	•
Forward-averaging tax credit (from Form T581)	**478** +	•
Provincial or territorial tax credits (see line 479 in the guide)	**479** +	•
Add lines 439 to 479. These are your **total credits. 482** =	▶ −	

Line 435 minus line 482   =

If the result is negative, you have a **refund**.
If the result is positive, you have a **balance owing**.
Enter the amount below on whichever line applies.
We do not charge or refund a difference of less than $2.

Refund **484**   •

Balance owing 485   •

Amount enclosed 486

Attach a cheque or money order payable to
the Receiver General. **Do not mail cash.** Your
payment is due no later than April 30, 1997.

◤ Direct Deposit Request (see the guide for more information)

If you already use direct deposit, the service will continue.

Refund and GST credit – To start direct deposit, or to change banking information you
already gave us, attach a "void" personalized cheque, **OR**, complete the area below.

Branch number	Institution number	Account number
702	**703**	**704**

701 ☐ **Child Tax Benefit (CTB)** – Check this box to start direct deposit of your CTB
payments into the **same account** as your refund and GST credit. If you want your
CTB payments directly deposited into a different account, see line 484 in the guide.

I certify that the information given on this return and in any documents attached is correct, complete, and fully discloses all my income.	**490**	Person or firm paid to prepare this return.
Sign here _____	Name	
It is a serious offence to make a false return.	Address	
Area code		Area code
Telephone _____ Date	Telephone	

Do not use this area	**639**			•
	684			

Privacy Act Personal Information Bank number RCT/P-PU-005

Appendix 6

SCHEDULE 8   CANADA PENSION PLAN CONTRIBUIONS ON SELF-EMPLOYED EARNINGS

T1-1996	Calculating Canada Pension Plan Contributions on Self-Employment and Other Earnings	Schedule 8

Complete this schedule to determine the amount of your Canada Pension Plan (CPP) contributions if you reported:
- self-employment income on lines 135 to 143 of your return; or
- business or professional income from a partnership on line 122 of your return.

Also use this schedule to calculate your additional CPP contributions.
See lines 308 and 310 in the guide for more information.

Pensionable net self-employment earnings (amounts from line 122 and lines 135 to 143 of your return)		1
Earnings on which additional contributions are being made (attach a completed Form CPT20)	674 +	2
Subtotal (add lines 1 and 2; if the result is negative, enter "0")	=	3
Pensionable earnings from employment from box 14 or box 26 on all T4 slips	+	4
Total pensionable earnings (add lines 3 and 4)	=	5
Basic CPP exemption	claim $3,500 −	6
Earnings subject to contribution (line 5 minus line 6; if negative, enter "0") (maximum $31,900)	=	7
Multiply the amount on line 7 by 5.6%	=	8
Contributions through employment (from box 16 and box 17 on all T4 slips)	x 2 = −	9
Canada Pension Plan contributions payable on self-employment and other earnings: Line 8 minus line 9 (if negative, enter "0") Enter this amount on line 310 and on line 421 of your return.	=	10

Note: In some situations, we will prorate your CPP contributions. If this applies to you, we will calculate the correct amount and show it on your *Notice of Assessment*.

Appendix 7

T1A LOSS CARRY BACK FORM

Revenue Canada / Revenu Canada

REQUEST FOR LOSS CARRYBACK

- Use this form to claim a loss carryback under sections 111 and 41 of the *Income Tax Act*. Attach one completed copy of this form to your 1996 income tax return.
- Claim a loss carryforward on your income tax return for those years following the year of the loss within the limitations of sections 111, 41, and 80 of the *Income Tax Act*.
- Credits arising from the loss carryback adjustment(s) may be applied to outstanding taxes owing for any taxation year.
- Any late-filing penalty that applies to the return for the taxation year to which the loss is being applied will not be reduced by the loss carryback(s).
- Limited partnership losses cannot be carried back.
- The lines and guide items referred to in this form are found in the *General Income Tax Guide*.

Name in full (print)	Social insurance number
Address (print)	

Area I – Non-capital loss for carryback

Notes:
1. Enter the amounts below without brackets.
2. The following amounts will reduce the income or increase the loss (as appropriate) from the source(s) to which they relate: capital cost allowance relating to investment in Canadian motion picture films (see guide item 232); deductions allowed under subsections 20(11) and 20(12) of the *Income Tax Act*, and repayments of shareholder's loans.
3. If you have an amount on line 224 of your income tax return, deduct the amount against either your investment income or loss, or your partnership (limited or non active) income or loss, whichever applies. Do not deduct the amount twice.

	Income	Loss	
Employment income or loss (lines 101 and 104 of your income tax return **minus** lines 207, 212, and 229)			
Investment income or loss (lines 120 and 121 of your income tax return **minus** line 221)			
Partnership (limited or non active) income / loss (from line 122 of your income tax return)			
Rental income or loss (from line 126 of your income tax return)			
Business income or loss (from line 135 of your income tax return)			
Professional income or loss (from line 137 of your income tax return)			
Commission income or loss (from line 139 of your income tax return)			
Farming income or loss (from line 141 of your income tax return)			
Fishing income or loss (from line 143 of your income tax return)			
Taxable capital gains (from line 127 of your income tax return)		Nil	
Non-taxable income (from line 147 of your income tax return)		Nil	
Net capital losses of other years (from line 253 of your income tax return)	Nil		
Capital gains deduction (from line 254 of your income tax return)	Nil		
Allowable business investment loss (from line 217 of your income tax return)	Nil		
Employee home relocation loan deduction (from line 248 of your income tax return)	Nil		
Stock option and shares deductions (from line 249 of your income tax return)	Nil		
Other payments deduction (from line 250 of your income tax return)	Nil		
Income exempted by tax treaty (see guide item 256)	Nil		
Income from other sources (from lines 113, 114, 115, 119, 128, 129, and 130 of your income tax return)		Nil	
Subtotal	A		B
Subtract: Amounts on lines 208, 209, 214, 215, 219, 220, 232 and 235 (except amounts in Note 2 above)			C
Subtotal (if negative, enter "0")			D
Subtract: Line C from line B (if negative, enter "0")			E
Subtract: The lesser of line D and line J			F
Subtotal: (if negative, enter "0")			G
Subtract: Accumulated forward averaging amount withdrawal (from line 237 of your income tax return)			H
Total non-capital loss for the year available for carryback (if negative, enter "0")			
Subtract: Non-capital loss to be applied to 1993	753		
Non-capital loss to be applied to 1994	754		
Non-capital loss to be applied to 1995	755		
Subtotal			I
Balance of non-capital loss available for carryforward (line H **minus** line I - if negative, enter "0")			

T1A E (96)   (Ce formulaire existe aussi en français.)   0619

Canada

T1A, page 2

Area II – Farming or fishing loss for carryback

Loss from farming or fishing	
Subtract: Income from farming or fishing	
Subtotal (if negative, enter "0")	J

Enter the lesser of line D and line J	K
Enter amount from line G	
Subtract: Amount from line F	
Subtotal (if negative, enter "0")	L
Farming or fishing loss available for carryback (line K **minus** line L - if negative, enter "0")	M
Subtract: Farming or fishing loss to be applied to 1993	762
Farming or fishing loss to be applied to 1994	763
Farming or fishing loss to be applied to 1995	764
Subtotal	N
Balance of farming or fishing loss available for carryforward (line M minus line N - if negative, enter "0")	

Area III – Net capital loss for carryback

Notes: 1. Use this form for applying only 1996 net capital losses (refer to Chapter 5 of the income tax guide called *Capital Gains* for more information).

2. You can only apply 1996 net capital losses against taxable capital gains.

3. The amount of 1996 allowable capital losses which is more than 1996 taxable capital gains is the "1996 net capital loss available for carryback" (line O).

4. Applying a net capital loss carryback will result in a reduction of the capital gains deduction, if claimed, in the year(s) of the loss application. It may also reduce capital gains deductions you claimed in subsequent years.

5. The net capital loss you apply to preceding taxation years may affect the capital gains election you made on your 1994 income tax return.

Net capital loss for the year available for carryback (see note 3 above)	O
Subtract: Net capital loss to be applied to 1993	765
Net capital loss to be applied to 1994	766
Net capital loss to be applied to 1995	767
Subtotal	P
Balance of net capital loss available for carryforward (line O minus line P)	

Area IV – Listed personal property loss for carryback

Amount of listed personal property losses which is more than listed personal property gains for the year available for carryback (refer to Chapter 5 of the income tax guide called *Capital Gains*)	
Subtract: Listed personal property loss to be applied to 1993 listed personal property net gains	759
Listed personal property loss to be applied to 1994 listed personal property net gains	760
Listed personal property loss to be applied to 1995 listed personal property net gains	761
Subtotal	
Balance of listed personal property loss available for carryforward	

Area V – Restricted farm loss for carryback

Restricted farm loss for the year available for carryback (refer to Chapter 5 of the income tax guide called *Farming Income)*	
Subtract: Restricted farm loss to be applied to 1993	756
Restricted farm loss to be applied to 1994	757
Restricted farm loss to be applied to 1995	758
Subtotal	
Balance of restricted farm loss available for carryforward	

I hereby certify that the information given in this form is true, correct, and complete in every respect.	

(signature of individual or authorized representative)

Telephone number	Area code		Date	Year	Month	Day
			772			

Do you have a balance of tax unpaid from another taxation year? ☐ Yes ☐ No

Printed in Canada

Appendix 8

SCHEDULE 1 FEDERAL TAX CALCULATION, page 1

T1-1996   **Federal Tax Calculation**   **Schedule 1**

Part 1 — Taxable income

Enter your **taxable income** from line 260 of your return   _____ | 1

Part 2 — Complete ONE of the following sections

SECTION I — Complete this section if line 1 is **$29,590.00 or less**

Enter the amount from line 1   x 17% is   = _____ 2
                                                            Go to Part 3

SECTION II — Complete this section if line 1 is **more than $29,590.00, but not more than $59,180.00**

Enter the amount from line 1   3
Tax on the first   − $ 29,590 | 00   4   is $ 5,030 | 00   5
      Tax on the remaining (line 3 minus line 4) =   x 26% is   + _____ 6
                                   Add lines 5 and 6   = _____ 7
                                                   Go to Part 3

SECTION III — Complete this section if line 1 is **more than $59,180.00**

Enter the amount from line 1   8
Tax on the first   − $ 59,180 | 00   9   is $ 12,724 | 00   10
      Tax on the remaining (line 8 minus line 9) =   x 29% is   + _____ 11
                                   Add lines 10 and 11   = _____ 12
                                                   Go to Part 3

Part 3 — Instructions

Use Method A, **or** Method B, **but not both**, to complete the rest of this schedule.

Use Method A unless any of the following items apply to your situation, in which case, use Method B.

- tax adjustments (line 500 in the guide)
- federal dividend tax credit (line 502 in the guide)
- minimum tax carry-over (line 504 in the guide)
- overseas employment tax credit (included at line 506)
- foreign tax credit (lines 507, 508, and 511 in the guide)
- additional investment tax credit (line 518 in the guide)
- minimum tax (see page 34 in the guide)
- forward-averaging tax credit (Form T581)
- federal logging tax credit (see page 39 in the guide)

Method A (lines 13 through 18)
See the instructions above to find out if you can use this method.

Federal tax:
Enter the amount from line 2, 7, or 12 above, whichever applies   13
Total non-refundable tax credits: Enter the amount from line 350 of your return   − 14
              Federal tax: Line 13 minus line 14; if negative, enter "0"
                     Enter this amount on line 406 of your return.   = 15

Federal individual surtax:
Enter the amount from line 15   x 3% is   16
Minus: $12,500   − $ 12,500 | 00
      Result (if negative, enter "0") =   x 5% is   + 17
            Federal individual surtax: Add lines 16 and 17
                Enter this amount on line 419 of your return.   = 18

Use the pink form included in your income tax package to calculate your provincial or territorial tax.
See line 428 in the guide.

5006-S1

SCHEDULE 1, page 2

Method B (lines 19 through 40)

See the instructions on the other side to find out if you have to use this method.

Federal tax:

Enter the amount from line 2, 7, or 12, whichever applies		**19**
Tax adjustments (see line 500 in the guide) Specify:	500 +	● **20**
Add lines 19 and 20 =		**21**

Total non-refundable tax credits: Enter the amount from line 350 of your return		**22**	
Federal dividend tax credit: Calculate 13.33% of the amount on line 120 of your return	502 +	● **23**	
Minimum tax carry-over (see line 504 in the guide)	504 +	● **24**	
Add lines 22, 23, and 24 =		► —	**25**
Basic federal tax: Line 21 minus line 25. 506 =			**26**

Federal foreign tax credit: (see lines 507 and 508 in the guide)
Make a separate calculation for each foreign country.

Income tax or profits tax paid to a foreign country	507	● **27**

$$\frac{\text{Net foreign income}^*\ \boxed{508}}{\text{Net income}^{**}} \times \left(\begin{array}{c}\text{Basic federal}\\ \text{tax}^{***}\end{array}\right) = \underline{\hspace{3cm}} \quad \textbf{28}$$

* Reduce your net foreign income by any foreign income exempt under a tax treaty (included on line 256). If this amount is more than your **Net income****, enter your **(Basic federal tax*****) on line 28.

** Net income (line 236) (or if you filed a Form T581 election, use line 8 of that form; if negative, enter "0") minus any capital losses of other years allowed (line 253), employee home relocation loan deduction (line 248), stock option and shares deductions (line 249), other payments deduction (line 250), capital gains deduction (line 254), and any foreign income exempt under a tax treaty, and net employment income from a prescribed international organization (included on line 256).

*** Add to your Basic federal tax (line 506) any dividend tax credit (line 502) and subtract any refundable Quebec abatement (line 440), and any tax adjustments for CPP/QPP disability benefits for previous years (included on line 500).

Enter the amount from line 27 or line 28, whichever is **less** —		**29**
Federal tax: Line 26 minus line 29; if negative, enter "0"		**30**
Enter this amount on line 406 of your return. =		

Federal individual surtax:

Enter the amount from **line 26** above		**31**
Federal forward-averaging tax credit (attach a completed Form T581) —		**32**
Line 31 minus line 32; if negative, enter "0" =		**33**

Enter the amount from line 33	x 3% is		**34**
Minus: $12,500 — $ 12,500 00			
Result (if negative, enter "0") =	x 5% is	+	**35**
Add lines 34 and 35 =			**36**
Additional federal foreign tax credit from Part II of Form T2209	511 —		**37**
Line 36 minus line 37; if negative, enter "0" =			**38**
Additional investment tax credit from section II of Form T2038 (IND.)	518 —		**39**
Federal individual surtax: Line 38 minus line 39; if negative, enter "0"			**40**
Enter this amount on line 419 of your return. =			

> **Use the pink form included in your income tax package to calculate your provincial or territorial tax.**
> **See line 428 in the guide.**

Appendix 9

GST-370 GST REBATE FOR EMPLOYEES AND PARTNERS

I✦I Revenue   Revenu
Canada   Canada

EMPLOYEE AND PARTNER GOODS AND SERVICES TAX REBATE

This form is authorized for use pursuant to section 253 of the *Excise Tax Act*.
PLEASE COMPLETE AREAS A, B (if applicable), C and D ON THIS FORM AND ATTACH TO YOUR COMPLETED INCOME TAX RETURN.

- Instructions for completion of this form are outlined on the reverse side.
- The Employee and Partner Goods and Services Tax Rebate Guide contains information to help you complete this form.
- Please print or type.

AREA A — CLAIMANT IDENTIFICATION (To be completed by Claimant)

Claimant's Last Name

First Name and Initials

Taxation Year of Claim   **19** ____

Employer's/Partnership's
GST Registration No.

Social Insurance Number

Provision of the SIN is voluntary and if not provided, no right, benefit or privilege will be withheld and no penalty imposed.
The SIN will be used as an identifier to facilitate the matching of this application with your T-1 General income tax return.

AREA B — DECLARATION BY CLAIMANT'S EMPLOYER OR PARTNERSHIP   (Your employer or partnership must complete this section if you wish to claim a rebate for expenses for which you were paid an allowance which was included in your income for the

I hereby certify that for the Taxation Year stated above, the above-named claimant was paid the following allowance which at the time it was paid, I did not consider to be reasonable for the purposes of subparagraph 6(1) (b) (v), (vi), (vii), or (vii.1) of the *Income Tax Act* (e.g., which I may not include in determining an input tax credit pursuant to section 174 of the *Excise Tax Act*).

Amount Received $

Reason for Allowance(s)
(List Activities)

Name of Employer/Partnership

Signature of Employer
or Authorized Officer

Position of
Authorized Officer

Date   Y   M   D

AREA C — REBATE COMPUTATION (To be completed by Claimant)

Use the amounts reported on your income tax return for the Taxation Year stated above to complete the following.

I) Rebate on Expenses

Total expenses (all employee/partnership expenses other than Capital Cost Allowance [CCA])	Line 1	

Deduct:

Zero-rated and exempt purchases	Line 2	
Non-eligible expenses (Include all expenses for which you received an allowance from your employer or partnership except expenses that relate to the allowance reported in area B above)	Line 3	
Non-eligible expenses of a partner	Line 4	
Total deductions (Add lines 2 to 4 inclusive)	Line 5	▶
Net expenses (Subtract line 5 from line 1)	Line 6	
Personal use included in net expenses	Line 7	
Expenses eligible for rebate (Subtract line 7 from line 6)	Line 8	▶

II) Rebate on Capital Cost Allowance (CCA)

CCA on motor vehicles, musical instruments and aircraft (Do not include CCA with respect to which you received an allowance from your employer or partnership unless it	Line 9	
Personal use included in line 9	Line 10	
CCA eligible for rebate (Subtract line 10 from line 9)	Line 11	▶
Total for rebate calculation (Add lines 8 and 11)	Line 12	**051**

Multiply the amount on Line 12 by 7/107   X 7/107

GST rebate (Enter this amount on line 457 of your income tax return)	Line 13 ▶	

AREA D — CERTIFICATION (To be completed by Claimant)

I hereby certify that the information in this document is true and correct to the best of my knowledge and that I am eligible for the Employee and Partner Goods and Services Tax Rebate for the Taxation Year.

Signature

Date   Y   M   D

Personal information provided on this form is protected under the provisions of the *Privacy Act* and is maintained in Personal Information Bank RCT PPU 005.

GST 370 E (95/01) Cette formule est disponible en français(GST 370 F)

Canadä

GST-370, page 2

WHO QUALIFIES

You may qualify for a rebate of the GST paid on certain business-related expenses, such as travel, entertainment and professional dues that you deducted for income tax purposes if you were either:

- an employee who incurred expenses while your employer was a GST registrant (i.e., your employer has a GST registration number) and was not a listed financial institution (e.g., a bank, a trust company or a credit union); or
- an individual who incurred expenses while a member of a partnership that is a registrant for GST purposes.

COMPLETING THE REBATE APPLICATION

Complete Area A. If Area B is applicable, it must be completed by your employer or partnership before you complete Areas C and D.

AREA A - CLAIMANT IDENTIFICATION

Complete the identification area. The Taxation Year of the Claim should be the personal income tax return period for which you are calculating your rebate.

AREA B - DECLARATION BY CLAIMANT'S EMPLOYER OR PARTNERSHIP

If you were paid an allowance that was included in your income and you wish to include the expenses that relate to that allowance in your rebate computation, an authorized officer of your employer or partnership must complete and sign this area.

AREA C - REBATE COMPUTATION

Line-by-line instructions

To compute your rebate computation, use the amounts reported on your income tax return for the Taxation Year you recorded in Area A.

REBATE ON EXPENSES

Line 1 - Total expenses

If you were an employee, enter the total expenses you incurred while your employer was a GST registrant from the Statement of Employment Expenses (form T777E) filed with your income tax return or professional dues claimed on line 212 of your income tax return. Do not include deductions for Capital Cost Allowance.

If you were a member of a partnership, enter the total expenses you incurred while a member of the partnership but which were not included in your Partnership Net Income/Loss from one of the following schedules or equivalent filed with your income tax return:

- Statement of Income and Expenses from a Professional Practice (form T2032E)
- Statement of Income and Expenses from a Business (form T2124E)
- Statement of Farming Income and Expenses (form T2042E)
- Fishing Income and Expense Statement (form T2121E)
- Statement of Real Estate Rentals (form T776E)

Line 2 - Zero-rated and exempt purchases

Enter the total amount of expenses paid for zero-rated (e.g., basic groceries and prescription drugs) and exempt supplies (e.g., insurance premiums and interest). The Employee and Partner Rebate Guide contains information to help determine these amounts.

Line 3 - Non-eligible expenses

Enter the total amount of expenses paid for the following:

- all expenses that relate to any allowance(s) that were paid to you by your employer or partnership except for expenses that relate to the allowance that was reported in Area B of the application;
- expenses where no GST was paid or payable (e.g., most supplies acquired before 1991, or most supplies acquired outside Canada);
- supplies acquired from suppliers that are not GST registrants;
- expenses incurred when your employer or partnership was not a registrant for the GST; and
- lease payments that are grandfathered under subsections 340(3) and 340(6) of the *Excise Tax Act*.

Line 4 - Non-eligible expenses of a partner

If you are a member of a partnership which makes exempt supplies as well as taxable supplies, enter the amount of expenses relating to the making of these exempt supplies. This may be calculated on a percentage basis (e.g., by estimating the percentage of the expenses which relate to exempt supplies), or by identifying those expenses which relate specifically to exempt supplies made by the partnership.

Line 5 - Total deductions

Add lines 2 to 4. Enter the sum on line 5 and carry the sum over to the next column, as indicated by the arrow.

Line 6 - Net expenses

Subtract line 5 from line 1 and enter the result.

Line 7 - Personal use included in net expenses

Enter the amount of personal use included in the net expenses recorded on line 6.

Line 8 - Expenses eligible for rebate

Subtract line 7 from line 6. Enter the difference on line 8 and carry the difference over to the next column, as indicated by the arrow.

REBATE ON CAPITAL COST ALLOWANCE (CCA)

Line 9 - CCA on motor vehicles, musical instruments and aircraft

Enter only the amount(s) of Capital Cost Allowance (CCA) you claimed on motor vehicles, musical instruments and aircraft on which you paid GST. Do not include CCA that relates to any allowance(s) paid to you by your employer or partnership unless it relates to the allowance reported in Area B of the application.

If you are a member of a partnership which makes exempt supplies as well as taxable supplies, do not include CCA that relates to the making of these exempt supplies. To calculate this amount, refer to the guidelines for line 4 above.

Line 10 - Personal use included in line 9

Enter the amount of personal use included in the CCA amount recorded on line 9.

Line 11 - CCA eligible for rebate

Subtract line 10 from line 9. Enter the difference on line 11 and carry the difference over to the next column, as indicated by the arrow.

Line 12 - Total for rebate calculation

Add lines 8 and 11 and enter the sum on line 12.

Line 13 - GST rebate

Multiply the amount on line 12 by the rebate factor of 7/107 and enter the result on line 13. This amount is your total rebate claim. Enter this amount on line 457 of your income tax return.

AREA D - CERTIFICATION

Please ensure that you have signed the certification.

PLEASE SEND THE COMPLETED FORM ALONG WITH YOUR INCOME TAX RETURN.

NOTE: INCLUDING THE REBATE IN INCOME

Where an individual has received a GST rebate in respect of an expense, the rebate is included in computing the income of the individual for the taxation year in which the rebate is received. Where the rebate is in respect of capital property, the rebate reduces the capital cost of the property at the time the rebate is received.

Appendix 10

AUTO LOGS

SUMMARY OF AUTO TRAVEL AND EXPENSES
For tax purposes, prepare the following monthly summary from your Daily Auto Log (See next page.)

MONTH	KM BUSINESS	KM PERSONAL	KM TOTAL	GAS	PARK	WASH	M&R*	LEASE	INSURE	INTEREST	OTHER
JAN											
FEB											
MAR											
APR											
MAY											
JUNE											
JULY											
AUG											
SEP											
OCT											
NOV											
DEC											
TOTAL											

*Maintenance & Repairs

DAILY AUTOMOBILE DISTANCE AND EXPENSE LOG

Make, model, and year of car _____

Serial number _____

Acquisition date and price with all taxes _____

DATE	MEET WITH	WHERE	KM START	KM END	KM TOTAL	GAS & OIL	PARK	WASH	M&R	OTHER

Appendix 11

T2200 DECLARATION OF EMPLOYMENT CONDITIONS

◆✶ Revenue Revenu Canada Canada		**DECLARATION OF CONDITIONS OF EMPLOYMENT**

● For more information, see Interpretation Bulletins IT-352, *Employee's Expenses, Including Work Space in Home Expenses*, and IT-522, *Vehicle and Other Travelling Expenses - Employees*.

Employee information – To be completed by the employee

Family or last name | Usual first name | Social insurance number

Home address | Business address

If you used your motor vehicle for employment, indicate the:

● make and model of your vehicle _____

● number of days in the year you owned or leased the vehicle _____ ı total kilometres you drove in the year while you owned or leased the vehicle _____

● number of days in the year you used the vehicle for employment _____ ı total kilometres you drove for employment purposes in the year _____

Conditions of employment – To be completed by the employer

1. Indicate the period of employment during the year. From: _____ (Month) _____ (Year) To: _____ (Month) _____ (Year)

2. Area of travel

3. Did you normally require this employee to work away from your place of business or in different places? ☐ Yes ☐ No

4. Did this employee's contract require the employee to pay his or her own expenses? ☐ Yes ☐ No

5. Was this employee required to be away for at least 12 hours from the municipality and metropolitan area (if there is one) of your business where the employee normally reports for work? ☐ Yes ☐ No

6. a) Did you pay this employee wholly or partly by commissions or similar amounts according to the volume of sales made or contracts negotiated? ☐ Yes ☐ No
   b) If *yes*, indicate the: (1) amount paid $ _____
   (2) type of goods sold or contracts negotiated _____

7. a) Did this employee receive an allowance or a repayment of expenses he or she paid to earn employment income? ☐ Yes ☐ No
   b) If *yes*, indicate the:
   (1) amount received as a fixed allowance, such as a flat monthly allowance, for: | (3) amount received calculated according to a rate per kilometre:
   ● motor vehicle expenses $ _____ | ı rate used _____ /KM
   ● travel expenses $ _____ | ı kilometres driven _____
   ● other (specify) _____ $ _____ | ı total amount $ _____
   (2) amount received upon proof of payment of: | (4) amount charged to the employer, such as credit-card charges, for:
   ● motor vehicle expenses $ _____ | ı motor vehicle expenses $ _____
   ● travel expenses $ _____ | ı travel expenses $ _____
   ● other (specify) _____ $ _____ | ı other (specify) _____ $ _____

8. Indicate how much of the expenses and the amounts in 7b) above you included on this employee's T4 slip. _____

9. a) Did you require this employee to pay other expenses for which the employee did not receive any allowance or repayment? ☐ Yes ☐ No
   b) If *yes*, indicate the type(s) of expenses. _____

10. a) Did you require this employee under a contract of employment to:
    ● rent an office away from your place of business, or use a portion of his or her home? ☐ Yes ☐ No
    ● pay for a substitute or assistant? ☐ Yes ☐ No
    ● pay for supplies that the employee used directly in his or her work? ☐ Yes ☐ No
    b) Did you repay or will you repay this employee for any of the expenses in 10a) above? ☐ Yes ☐ No
    If *yes*, indicate which expenses the repayment is for, and whether the repayment is shown in 7b) above.

Employer declaration

I certify that the above conditions of employment for this employee are, to the best of my knowledge, true, correct, and complete.

Name of employer (please print) | Name of authorized person (please print)

Date | Telephone | Signature of employer or authorized person

T2200 (96)
Printed in Canada | (Français au verso) | 1090 | Canada

INDEX